Life-Altering

Life-Altering

Abortion Stories from the Midwest

Angie Leventis Lourgos

UNIVERSITY OF MISSOURI PRESS
Columbia

University of Missouri Press, Columbia, Missouri 65211
Printed and bound in the United States of America
 First printing, 2023.

Library of Congress Cataloging-in-Publication Data

Names: Lourgos, Angie Leventis, author.
Title: Life-altering : abortion stories from the Midwest / by Angie Leventis Lourgos.
Description: Columbia : University of Missouri Press, [2023]
Identifiers: LCCN 2023025647 (print) | LCCN 2023025648 (ebook) | ISBN 9780826222985 (hardcover) | ISBN 9780826274946 (ebook)
Subjects: LCSH: Abortion--Middle West.
Classification: LCC HQ767.5.U5 L687 2023 (print) | LCC HQ767.5.U5 (ebook) | DDC 362.1988/800977--dc23/eng/20230731
LC record available at https://lccn.loc.gov/2023025647
LC ebook record available at https://lccn.loc.gov/2023025648

∞™ This paper meets the requirements of the American National Standard for Permanence of Paper for Printed Library Materials, Z39.48, 1984.

Typefaces: Caslon and Bodoni

Permissions appear beginning on page 235

For Pete.

Thanks for always listening.

Contents

For Pete.

Thanks for always listening.

Acknowledgments

Life-Altering: Abortion Stories from the Midwest would not have been possible without the many women who had the courage and fortitude to share their abortion stories with me and *Chicago Tribune* readers. Some patients spent hours over the course of several interviews going over ultrasounds, medical records, old photos and journal entries to help me capture their emotions as well as critical details of their experiences. Others spoke with me at abortion clinics before and after their procedures, or during their medication abortions, often amid moments of intense anxiety. I'm extremely grateful for their time, patience and bravery.

I would like to thank the University of Missouri Press for publishing *Life-Altering*, particularly my editor, Mary Conley, whose thoughtful edits helped turn a series of news stories into a book.

I'm also in debt to many editors and colleagues at the *Chicago Tribune* who have been formative in my career as well as in the articles that shaped the pages of *Life-Altering*. Special thanks go to Mark Jacob, John Hector, Stacey Wescott, Tracy Van Moorlehem, Patrick Regan, Jane Hirt, Ted Gregory, Ray Long, Mary Schmich, Phil Jurik, Dan Mihalopoulos, John Keilman, Diana Wallace, Kori Rumore, Erin Hooley, Stacy St. Clair, E. Jason Wambsgans, Christy Gutowski, Susan Keaton, Kay Manning and Claudia Banks.

Most of all, I've been blessed to have the emotional support of my family, including Peter Lourgos, Olga Leventis, Angelo Leventis, James Leventis and Calli Leventis. I'm thankful for my kiddos, Constantine and Anna, who were encouraging despite their slight disappointment that the book wasn't a graphic novel involving superhero animals or a hypnotized, underwear-clad principal.

Life-Altering

Introduction

After the U.S. Supreme Court overturned *Roe v. Wade* on June 24, 2022, roughly half of all states moved to ban or significantly restrict abortion, sharply dividing the nation over what was once a constitutionally protected right. Abortion trigger bans in some states immediately outlawed terminating a pregnancy in all but the narrowest of circumstances, prompting many clinics to abruptly halt abortion appointments, leaving patients scrambling for care. For months after the ruling, lawmakers and courts tussled over the legality of century-old bans as well as new abortion prohibitions, spurring day-to-day uncertainty over whether terminating a pregnancy was still lawful.

While the level of confusion was unprecedented, this sense of precariousness surrounding abortion access wasn't entirely new in some parts of the country. In the Midwest in particular, many patients already faced mounting legal and logistical barriers to terminating pregnancy in the years leading up to the high court's reversal of a near half century of reproductive rights protections. Even when *Roe* guaranteed the right to end a pregnancy nationwide, abortion seekers in much of Middle America had to negotiate a complicated web of restrictions including early gestational limits, mandatory ultrasounds, waiting periods and additional requirements for minors, as well as strict regulations targeting clinics and medical providers.

Life-Altering: Abortion Stories from the Midwest shares the personal accounts of women who traversed this challenging reproductive rights landscape in order to terminate their pregnancies—experiences that have become even more salient after *Roe*'s demise. Based on a series of articles from the *Chicago Tribune*, the gripping and emotional accounts in this collection of stories illustrate how court cases and state legislation can shape the lives and choices of individuals. With the Midwest as its focal point, *Life-Altering* unravels the myriad of political, legal, religious and social factors these women encountered when making decisions about their reproductive care.

For years, the nation had been shifting toward the end of *Roe*, which was foreshadowed by a series of anti-abortion court rulings, conservative U.S. Supreme Court appointments and boldly strict state laws. These stepping-stones had a formative impact on the women featured in *Life-Altering*, from hampering their attempts at terminating their pregnancies to galvanizing the pro-choice nonprofits and new means of access that made their abortions possible. Their narratives offer intimate insights on some of the most nuanced and controversial aspects of abortion, including use of taxpayer funding to pay for the procedure, special regulations for patients under 18, limits on terminations later in pregnancy, proper disposition of fetal remains, and instances where the health of the fetus or life of the pregnant patient is in jeopardy. These issues and themes have only become more relevant—as well as controversial—in the absence of *Roe*.

A 17-year-old from Ohio traveled to Chicago to have an abortion without the consent or notification of her parents, who thought she was still in her hometown sleeping over at a friend's house. Her account analyzes abortion restrictions aimed specifically at minors and chronicles the often-complicated legal process a young person encounters when attempting to bypass laws that mandate parental involvement. An Iowa couple flew more than 800 miles to Colorado to terminate after an ultrasound revealed multiple severe fetal anomalies, raising questions about the ethics and implications of abortion restrictions later in pregnancy. A young mother's emergency abortion tackles the complexities of life-endangerment exemptions, showing how the threshold for what constitutes "life-threatening" can vary according to the perception and beliefs of different medical providers, lawmakers, and members of the clergy.

These stories and others in *Life-Altering* provide a glimpse at the spectrum of circumstances that can surround a decision to abort, as well as how laws and regulations can influence private choices and outcomes. The writing serves as a resource not only for academics but also for everyday folks who are tentative or unsure about how to discuss abortion in their daily lives. Ending a pregnancy is still a subject that's often very taboo in the United States, particularly in the Midwest. The abortion stories in *Life-Altering* offer rare personal context for the stunning reversal of *Roe* and the dramatic legal, political, and cultural fallout that ensued in the months after the landmark decision was overturned.

Even as some states outlawed or drastically curbed the ability to terminate a pregnancy post-*Roe*, states with strong reproductive rights laws encountered a surge in abortion seekers traveling there for care. While abortion providers had been preparing for the end of federal abortion rights for years, the influx of patients was still overwhelming, often leading to longer appointment wait times and expanded clinic hours.

In response, reproductive rights advocates crafted new and innovative avenues of abortion access to circumvent these bans and restrictions. A few weeks before *Roe* was overturned, a nascent Illinois-based nonprofit began flying patients across state lines to their abortion appointments aboard small passenger airplanes. An already-established network of Chicago volunteers hosted traveling patients in their homes, gave abortion seekers rides to clinics and provided meals before and after the procedure. Planned Parenthood announced plans to launch its first mobile abortion clinic in southern Illinois; the retrofitted recreational vehicle equipped with a standard lab and exam rooms was designed to travel along the state border, with the intent of cutting down patient travel times and distances.

Clinics began moving across state boundary lines to new brick-and-mortar locations in states where terminating a pregnancy remained legal. Abortion pill-by-mail and telehealth services in some cases eliminated the need to ever leave home to terminate a pregnancy. Abortion opponents in turn fought back, filing legal challenges targeting a popular abortion medication and pushing for local ordinances outlawing the mailing and shipping of abortifacients.

Rather than resolving the abortion debate, *Roe*'s absence caused the nation to grow increasingly polarized over reproductive rights, spurring extraordinary levels of violence. Abortion clinics and pro-life organizations reported more threats, harassment, vandalism, arson and other malicious acts than ever before.

Abortion won't cease in the post-*Roe* world. But the path to ending a pregnancy has become even more complicated and challenging in large sections of the nation—a burgeoning topography explored in *Life-Altering* through the voices of women who navigated similar obstacles across the Midwest in the years leading up to *Roe*'s historic fall.

1.
Crossing the Mississippi River

The young woman zipped her gray hoodie and grabbed a light backpack before boarding a bus alone just before midnight, anxious but determined as she began a 260-mile interstate journey to make the most pivotal decision of her 24 years.[1]

It was late winter 2017, warmer than usual for that time of year in the Midwest but still a little chilly without a coat. A thunderstorm whipped rain at her bus window as lightning illuminated in flashes the rugged plateau of the Ozarks of Missouri. Her family and most of her friends back in her small rural town didn't know where she was headed. Nor did they realize the fabric of her sweatshirt concealed a 12-week pregnancy, unplanned and undesired.

"I'm kind of in a panic mode, but I'm not panicking," recalled the young woman, who wanted to remain anonymous. "I knew what I wanted to do. I was just worried I wouldn't be able to do it."

Her bag held only a few items: A wallet with her identification. A pair of earbuds. Her cell phone. She had also packed an extra pair of underwear and some sanitary pads, but no other clothing.

The young woman in the gray sweatshirt remained awake throughout the night, peering through square-framed glasses as the forested landscape turned into a gently rolling countryside and then suburban sprawl. Before daybreak, the rain died down to a mist as the dense high-rises and historic row houses of St. Louis came into view, and she stepped off the bus.

But her final stop was just beyond St. Louis and its iconic Gateway Arch, the 630-foot steel monument famous for dividing the nation, separating East from West. She called an Uber to take her across a bridge over the Mississippi River, a roughly eight-mile drive into

Illinois. This last leg of her journey lasted only about 15 minutes, but that short span of distance and time meant the difference between a future she wanted and one that terrified her.

The driver tried to make conversation, the usual small talk and pleasantries of tourists. *Where are you headed? What brings you to the St. Louis area?* He kept cracking jokes, she recalled. From the back seat, she said as few words as possible, wishing the ride would end.

"I didn't want to tell him why I was up there," she said.

She had the car drop her off within walking distance of her destination: Hope Clinic for Women in Granite City.

The young woman knew her afternoon appointment at the 10,000-square-foot brown brick surgical center might be her only chance to end the pregnancy in secret. Even as she stood out front, hours before her scheduled procedure, she kept thinking something would go wrong, that clinic staff would turn her away or the doctor would somehow find her ineligible for the surgery or some other unexpected barrier would pop up and she'd be forced to carry to term.

There was no backup plan.

"I've seen what unplanned pregnancies do to people," the woman said. "I don't want to be put through that. I don't want to be forced into a marriage. I don't want to raise a child alone."

The landmark U.S. Supreme Court case *Roe v. Wade* was still the law of the land, guaranteeing the constitutional right to an abortion nationwide since 1973. But even then, lower courts and states legislatures repeatedly scuffled over the boundaries of those freedoms. The result was a mélange of state laws governing the procedure, often spurring contrasting protections and restrictions along state boundary lines.

Some states had strict gestational limits early in pregnancy; others had none. Some states mandated waiting periods, government-scripted counseling and ultrasounds before an abortion; others did not. The same abortion for the same patient could be legal in one zip code and illegal in an adjacent one, as was the case along the Missouri-Illinois border.

As the young woman in the sweatshirt faced the prospect of her unplanned pregnancy, the nation's tenor on reproductive rights was shifting rapidly.

During the contentious 2016 presidential campaign, Republican nominee Donald Trump vowed that if he were to be elected, *Roe* could be reversed "automatically, in my opinion, because I am putting pro-life justices on the court," sending the matter of abortion rights back to be determined by individual states.[2]

This was a brief comment during the final presidential debate against opponent Hillary Clinton, at a time when many pundits and pollsters naively thought Trump's November 8, 2016, win unfathomable. But the underdog candidate's words would prove remarkably prescient as the next few years unfolded, incrementally fulfilling Trump's prophecy.

In January 2017, President Trump nominated to the Supreme Court conservative judge Neil Gorsuch, who was confirmed in April that year.[3] He was the first of three conservative justices appointed by Trump—followed by Justice Brett Kavanaugh in 2018 and Justice Amy Coney Barrett in 2020—tipping the balance of the high court solidly to the right.[4]

"Many pro-lifers cared most about Trump's impact on the courts," law professor Mary Ziegler wrote in *Dollars for Life: The Anti-Abortion Movement and the Fall of the Republican Establishment*. "The Senate confirmed more than 220 of his nominees to the federal bench, including 54 to the circuit courts of appeal. Three Trump nominees ultimately sat on the U.S. Supreme Court. . . . When Trump left office, the Supreme Court had not yet said a word about *Roe*, but few expected that silence to last."[5]

Trump made history on January 24, 2020, as the first sitting president to attend the annual March for Life in Washington, D.C.[6] As he pledged to protect the unborn before a cheering crowd at the National Mall, he commended the turnout at the rally, especially the many high school and college students "who took long bus rides to be here."[7]

"All of us here today understand an eternal truth—every child is a precious and sacred gift from God," he said. "Together we must protect, cherish, and defend the dignity and the sanctity of every human life. When we see the image of a baby in the womb, we glimpse the majesty of God's creation. When we hold a newborn in our arms, we know the endless love that each child brings to a family. When we watch a child grow, we see the splendor that radiates from each human soul. One life changes the world. . . . And from the first day in office, I've taken historic action to support America's families and to protect the unborn."[8]

* * *

When the young woman in the gray sweatshirt arrived at Hope Clinic, abortion was technically still legal across the country. But even with the strong protections of *Roe*, her path wasn't easy or certain.

"There's definitely more than a few hurdles to getting this done," she said. "And there's definitely a time clock, a window of time after you get pregnant to have an abortion. And it's clicking down."

By the time she learned she was pregnant, she was already about 10 weeks along. She had hoped her missed period was due to stress or irregular menstrual cycles from birth control use. But the second pink line on the positive at-home pregnancy test relayed her worst fear.

"Maybe I have double vision," she thought.

She took another test, a digital one. The word "pregnant" appeared clearly on the screen.

"I still just didn't believe it," she said.

At her local health department, she took yet another pregnancy test, with an identical result. Sitting on a bench outside the health department building, she immediately began researching and calling the closest abortion clinics to her town. She had recently broken up with her boyfriend and was finally living on her own, just starting to save part of her paycheck from a retail job but not exactly thriving financially. Having a baby seemed unfair to both her and the prospective child, she thought.

"I'd want them to have a better life than I did," she said. "I don't think I could make a child feel valued because I don't know how to value myself. I'm learning right now. I'm taking care of myself. I'm finally getting there."

Her own childhood was a whirlwind of moves from town to town, most of them in various parts of the Bible Belt. She described her level of education as poor. As a little kid, she loved the freedom of playing outside amid nature—raising chickens, cows and occasionally turkeys. But the transient and often isolated lifestyle made it hard to form deep, lasting friendships with other children during her formative years, she said.

"We were all we knew for a long time," she said. "I wasn't prepared for life when I moved out at all. Because I was never part of the world at all."

As an adult, she settled with her family in a rural Missouri town with a few thousand people.

"Everyone knows everyone," she said. "It's the church crowd."

Abortion was widely reviled but rarely talked about in her conservative Christian community. The only time she could remember the word mentioned was when her parents found out they had conceived a fetus with a fatal anomaly. Physicians offered abortion as an option.

"They thought it was very wrong to do that," she said.

Her parents chose to deliver rather than terminate. She recalled holding her newborn sister briefly, before the baby died shortly after birth.

The young woman told no one in her family about the unplanned pregnancy or her plans to end it. At first, she only shared the news with a few friends she knew online but had never met in person because they lived hundreds of miles away. She said she felt no attachment to the pregnancy and had no desire to become a mother. Yet she was so unsure she would be able to access the procedure that she started selecting baby names, just in case: Caroline for a girl, Garrett for a boy.

There were few abortion options available, and all were geographically far and legally complicated. To the west, Kansas mandated a 24-hour waiting period before having an abortion, requiring one appointment for state-directed informed consent and then a second appointment to have the procedure.[9] Her home state of Missouri also required in-person, state-directed counseling and a 72-hour wait time before terminating a pregnancy, necessitating two trips to the clinic.[10] The young woman didn't think she could travel that far twice in secrecy, nor could she miss work for multiple days. At the time, around half of all states in the United States mandated a specific waiting period between counseling and having an abortion, many necessitating two trips to a clinic.[11]

There was only one abortion clinic in Missouri—a Planned Parenthood in St. Louis that was hundreds of miles from the young woman's home. The dearth of providers in her state was largely due to strict laws mandating that abortion facilities meet the standards of surgical centers as well as requirements that abortion providers have hospital admitting privileges.[12]

The legality of many of these abortion restrictions could at times feel like whiplash, with courts blocking enforcement at one moment only for the ruling to be overturned by a higher court later. About half of all states had these abortion clinic regulations or had attempted to enforce these measures; between 2011 and 2017, these requirements resulted in the closing of around half of all abortion clinics in the states of Arizona, Kentucky, Ohio and Texas, and five clinics in Virginia, according to a 2018 report by the Guttmacher Institute, a research group that supports reproductive rights.[13] After clinics shut down, they often don't return, even if the regulation that spurred their closure is ultimately blocked by the courts, the report said.

The young woman in the sweatshirt found the nonprofit NARAL Pro-Choice Missouri online. The organization advised her to go to Illinois, which had few restrictions and no mandatory waiting period, as Missouri and many surrounding states had.

The nonprofit's executive director at the time, Alison Dreith, said she often referred abortion patients to Illinois.

"Because I know what our laws are," she said. "It's devastating, especially for low-income women or women who don't live in the area. That's extra time off work where they're not getting paid. . . . It's an undue burden."

Dreith said she had her own abortion at Hope Clinic in 2016, even though she lived closer to the Planned Parenthood clinic in St. Louis at the time, because the waiting period and other regulations made terminating a pregnancy in Missouri so hard.

"I never even thought twice about making the decision to go to Illinois," she said.

While many states in the Midwest and South have grown increasingly restrictive in recent years, Illinois has served as a haven for reproductive rights, drawing more and more women seeking abortions. While the number of terminations by in-state patients has fluctuated over recent years, the number of out-of-state residents receiving abortions has risen annually since 2014.[14]

The woman in the gray hoodie was among roughly 5,500 patients who crossed state lines to have an abortion in Illinois in 2017.[15] By 2020, that number had risen to almost 10,000, roughly 21 percent of the 46,000 or so total abortions performed in Illinois that year.[16] More than 6,500 of those patients came from Missouri, accounting for over two-thirds of all out-of-state abortions.[17]

For reproductive rights activists, Illinois's status as an oasis for abortion care is a badge of honor.

"It's unfortunate that in some states politicians have felt they can restrict access, and that means women need to go out of state," said Brigid Leahy of Planned Parenthood of Illinois. "Your rights shouldn't depend on your zip code or the state you live in."

For abortion opponents in Illinois, the state's permissive laws have long been a source of deep shame.

"It is embarrassing, because we are so out of line with the rest of the Midwest when it comes to protecting women and the unborn," said Emily Troscinski, who served as the executive director of the nonprofit Illinois Right to Life in 2017.

Interstate travel for an abortion is common across the nation, according to a study on the frequency of people crossing state lines for abortion care that was published in *Lancet Regional Health-Americas* in March 2022.[18]

The study found that in 2017, an average of 8 percent of abortion patients nationwide left their home states to have the procedure or medication abortion; states with more restrictive abortion laws averaged 12 percent of patients leaving their state, while states with supportive laws averaged around 3 percent. In Missouri, 56 percent of patients terminating a pregnancy that year did so in another state, according to the study.[19]

Researchers also analyzed some of the negative impacts that can result from the need to travel to terminate a pregnancy.

"These include delays to care (and as care is delayed, patients face some increased risk of complication from their abortion) as well as increased cost," the study said. "Similarly, low facility density may result in longer wait times and facility congestion, where facilities may not be able to meet the demand of a relatively high number of patients. These burdens are particularly meaningful for those who have low incomes, are traveling further due to living in rural areas or abortion deserts, or experience other intersecting forms of structural oppression (for example related to race, gender, sexuality, or ability) that limit access to holistic reproductive healthcare."[20]

* * *

After spending so much time searching for clinics in other states, the young woman in the gray hoodie was a bit stunned to learn she could get the procedure done in one day at Hope Clinic in Illinois—and there was an appointment available the following week. There would be no mandatory waiting period, no requirement for two appointments on different days and no need to travel long distances on multiple occasions.

"It was this relief and I was kind of numb," she said. "The whole time it didn't feel real. The idea that it could be over already and not drawn out for weeks more was very surreal."

As she approached the clinic, anti-abortion protesters outside called her and other women who walked past murderers, she recalled.

The young woman in the hoodie felt vulnerable and a little exposed. She put on her earbuds to drown out the sounds of demonstrators with music.

"Everyone else who was waiting outside had someone with them," she said.

When the clinic opened, she went inside and filled out some paperwork. A clinician performed an ultrasound, which showed she was 12 weeks and four days along. The young woman said she never saw the image, and that was fine with her.

"I'm very confident in my decision," she said repeatedly, and it was a feeling that never wavered or waned throughout the day.

In the waiting room, she felt sorry for several other patients there whose circumstances seemed more difficult than hers. Some women already had children and couldn't care for more. Some women had health conditions that made it difficult to carry to term, she recalled. Others had pregnancies with medical problems.

One patient couldn't stop crying, saying, "God will forgive me for this."

"And I felt so bad for her," the young woman in the sweatshirt said. "Because you could tell she didn't want this. But she felt it was best."

Since she had to take the bus back home that night and had no one with her, she declined general anesthetic prior to the abortion. This meant she could avoid paying for a pricey hotel or other overnight lodging and she could get back to work as soon as possible.

Most of her time at the clinic was spent waiting. The procedure itself took only a few minutes, she recalled.

It was a weird sensation to have a vacuum inside her body, and her stomach kept dropping and clinching, similar to how it might feel while riding a roller coaster. While the surgery was uncomfortable, she said she tends to have a high pain threshold, so the sensation was not intolerable. She held the hand of a nurse but never felt the need to squeeze.

"Just like that, it was done," the young woman said, adding that she didn't mind going through the procedure by herself. "I've kind of been alone most of my life, in my own way. I'm very independent in that I don't need anyone. I didn't wish there was someone else with me."

Afterward, she was taken by wheelchair to the recovery room.

"I can walk," she insisted, trying to stand up on her own.

"No, everyone gets star treatment," she recalled the staff member insisting.

"OK, I'll let you push me around," she responded, lowering herself into the chair.

While she rested, she munched on a few graham crackers and sipped on a Sprite. Then she changed into her clothes, first inserting a surgical tampon and later using a pad as her body began to heal. Before leaving Hope Clinic and Illinois, she received a three-month hormonal birth control shot.

Back at the bus station, a little before midnight, she recharged her dying cell phone at a spare electrical outlet along the wall. She put her earbuds back on, covered her head with her gray hoodie and looped the straps of her backpack around her shoulders so no one could take it. Curled up on an open patch of floor, amid the traffic and bustle of the bus terminal, she briefly fell asleep.

"I felt relieved," she said. "It's the best decision for me. It was difficult to do. And it shouldn't be so difficult."

The whole trip took about 30 hours. She arrived at home early the next morning. Only the people at NARAL Pro-Choice and a handful of online friends knew what she had been through. Her only regret was that she felt she had to hide her abortion and couldn't talk about the experience with friends in her hometown or her family, especially her sister.

"It's a taboo thing, but it shouldn't be," she said. "I wish I didn't have to be anonymous. I wish my family wouldn't shut me out because of this. It should be something that is accepted and not hated upon. I really don't think this is the wrong choice for me."

* * *

Five years later, many of the young woman's friends from her church in Missouri were on social media, celebrating the biggest pro-life victory of the past half century: On June 24, 2022, the U.S. Supreme Court overturned *Roe*, a decision that ended federal abortion protections.

"They were very happy," she said. "They were very proud."

Their reactions were so disparate from her feelings of overwhelming frustration, as the court ruling revived memories of her long, anxiety-ridden journey to Illinois.

"Because I know how difficult it was for myself five years ago," she said. "It should become easier, but now it's harder."

A few years after terminating her pregnancy, she moved from Missouri to Arkansas, two states where abortion became illegal, with few exceptions, immediately after the fall of *Roe*.

By the time the Supreme Court decision came down, she had a girlfriend; they had been together for three years and lived with one another. Her girlfriend was one of the few people in her life who learned about her abortion. Fairly early in their relationship, she shared the story of traveling to Hope Clinic and terminating the pregnancy.

"If that's something you're not OK with, that's fine," she recalled saying. "But it's not something I'm going to hide. I want you to know me and what I've been through."

Her girlfriend didn't judge or reject her, which was a relief, the young woman said.

Each year on September 19, the anniversary of what would have been her due date, she contemplates what her life would have been like if she had chosen to carry the pregnancy to term. She still has the positive pregnancy test, bus ticket and clinic paperwork from her abortion of 2017, as well as her own handwritten notes with dates and times and confirmation numbers from that trip.

The gray hoodie is gone; she can't remember exactly what happened to it.

"I don't disregard the past or the possibility of what could have been," she said. "I think of how different my life could have been."

The young woman babysits very often. She adores her nieces and nephews, as well as the nieces and nephews of her girlfriend.

"But I know that my role will always be an aunt," she said. "I do not want children of my own."

She still expresses tremendous gratitude for her abortion.

"Something I felt I always struggled with on a personal level is being grateful for things," she said. "But I've always been grateful for that, that I was able to do that. I still feel like it was the right decision, for myself."

2.
A Doctor without a Name

Just after nightfall, 17-year-old Leta Dally climbed into the back seat of a car driven by a stranger headed for an undisclosed location on Chicago's South Side.[1] Her mother—who had also never met the male driver before that evening—sat beside her during the short but nerve-racking ride to their clandestine destination, where an unnamed doctor was awaiting their arrival.

It was a summer weekend in 1966. The teen, who had recently learned she was pregnant, had never been more certain about any decision than the one she was making that night. But the choice required much planning, stealth and secrecy at the time. It also meant she would have to break the law.

"I wanted to do anything to make this horrible situation stop," recalled Leta, who grew up on the North Side of Chicago. "I did not want my life to be ruined."

She had just graduated high school with honors. None of her teachers at school knew of her pregnancy. Had her secret been revealed, she believes, the scandal would have been horrendous and potentially life-changing.

"The smartest thing I had ever done was not confide . . . in any of the counselors or advisers at school that I was pregnant," she said. "I probably would not have been allowed to graduate with my class."

She recalled how another student had previously stopped coming to school one day and then reappeared months later, just as suddenly, without explanation. Everyone kept saying the classmate "went away for a while," Leta recalled. Some suspected the girl might have been pregnant and the baby was adopted, but the theory was never confirmed.

"Nobody talked about anything," she said. "Sex ed was sperm and egg and that was about it, and everyone pretty much got that part. But the mechanics of it were a whole lot different. Nobody talked about sex. Children were born by immaculate conception."

Her childhood spanned the 1950s and early 1960s, an era when it was rare to see a married couple on a television sitcom even share a bed. While oral contraceptives were approved by the U.S. Food and Drug Administration in 1960, birth control was never discussed in her home or at school.[2]

"It was just so different," she said. "Today mothers take their daughters. Back then, you weren't expected to have sex."

When Leta missed her period, there were no at-home pregnancy tests available; they would be approved a decade later by the FDA in 1976. She had to go to see a doctor, who she believes used an old-fashioned "rabbit test": A sample of a woman's urine used to be injected into a female rabbit, toad, rat or frog, and changes in the animal's ovaries indicated the presence of the pregnancy hormone HCG.[3] The phrase "the rabbit died" was once a common euphemism for pregnancy, though the expression wasn't really accurate since the animal used for the test was always killed so it could be dissected to examine the ovaries.[4]

To get the results, she called the doctor's office from a nearby public pay phone, shrouded in privacy by the telephone booth's doors and the phone line's unlisted number. She hung up the receiver in disbelief, devastated by the positive result. After she told her mother and father, they seemed more baffled at the thought of her having sex than angry or disappointed about the unplanned pregnancy, she recalled.

"I think my father was trying to figure out how I got pregnant," she said. "I remember the phrase 'how did he get her panty girdle off?' I think he just couldn't understand that I might want to."

Her body felt no different after the diagnosis. There was no morning sickness, no swollen belly, no fatigue. Except for the absent period, the pregnancy seemed to have no signs or symptoms.

"I didn't feel like I had changed any," she said.

Initially, Leta thought she and her high school boyfriend would have to get married because that was just what anyone would do in these circumstances. Marriage wasn't something she wanted, but she assumed there was only one possible course of action for both of them. One evening, she and her boyfriend gathered with both sets of parents in her family's living room, for what she called "the big meeting."

Leta went into the kitchen to get ice for drinks, as everyone in the other room began discussing what should be done.

"I remember how odd it was to sit in a room and have people talk about the situation and how it affected all of them, but not how it affected me," she said.

Then her boyfriend's words shocked her.

"I remember finding out that he had absolutely no intentions of altering his plans for college," she said. "His life was going to go on. Mine, on the other hand, was going to be blown up."

She began sobbing and couldn't seem to stop until her mother gave her a strong sedative to calm her down.

"I felt like I had no control," she said. "It was a feeling of not having any options, although I wouldn't have thought of it in those terms then."

It was her boyfriend's mother who later asked if she would have an abortion, offering to arrange and pay for the $600 procedure. The cost would be equivalent to several thousand dollars today, adjusting for inflation.

"Yes," Leta recalled saying, with no hesitation. "I said yes, no looking back."

* * *

In eighteenth- and early nineteenth-century America, abortion was generally considered legal under common law until "quickening," the point when fetal movements like flutters could first be detected by the pregnant woman, often around four months.

"Indeed, the term *abortion* referred only to the miscarriages of later pregnancies, after quickening," wrote history professor Leslie J. Reagan in the book *When Abortion Was a Crime*. "What we would now identify as an early induced abortion was not called an 'abortion' at all. If an early pregnancy ended, it had 'slipp(ed) away,' or the menses had been restored."[5]

Common law and the general understanding of abortion during this era were "grounded in the female experience of their own bodies," Reagan wrote.

"Because women believed themselves to be carrying inert nonbeings prior to quickening, a potential for life rather than life itself, and because the common law permitted them to attempt to rid themselves of suspected and unwanted pregnancies up to the point when the potential for life gave a sure sign that it was developing into something actually alive, some American women did practice abortion in the early decades of the nineteenth century," history professor James C. Mohr wrote in *Abortion in America: The Origins and Evolution of National Policy*.[6]

Mohr cited home medical manuals available during the time period that included information on abortifacients.

"One listed in explicit detail a number of procedures that might release 'obstructed menses,' and the other identified a number of specific things to be avoided in a suspected pregnancy because they were thought to bring on an abortion," Mohr wrote.

Abortifacients were also sold publicly through euphemistic newspaper advertisements. One in the *New York Herald* in 1840 offered "preventative powders for married ladies, whose health forbids too rapid increase of family."[7] Another, in the *New York Sun* in 1842, advertised advertised help to ladies who wanted to be treated for "obstruction of their monthly periods."[8] Illinois in 1827 was among the first states to pass any kind of abortion statute, and this was an anti-poisoning law that prohibited administering or taking a substance "with an intention to cause the death of such person, or to procure the miscarriage of any woman, then being with child."[9] The penalty was up to three years in prison and a maximum fine of a thousand dollars. In 1867, abortion was criminalized in Illinois "by means of any instrument(s)," with a punishment of imprisonment for two to 10 years.[10]

* * *

By the 1960s, the pages of Leta's hometown newspaper, the *Chicago Tribune*, were sprinkled with stories about physicians and abortion arrangers arrested during sting operations. A 40-year-old woman and 39-year-old man were arrested in May 1966 when a "policewoman posing as a 'girl in trouble'" arranged to have an abortion; police targeted the couple after "the vice control department received information that an abortion racket was being operated on the northwest side" of Chicago.[11] In September 1966, two doctors were arrested on the South Side of Chicago after a St. Paul woman identified them as the physicians who had terminated her pregnancy years earlier; police took the doctors into custody "after the woman aided them in setting a trap."[12] A 70-year-old retired nurse who was a "previously convicted abortionist" was "found guilty of abortion" in December 1966 after being caught by police in her home as she performed the procedure on an 18-year-old.[13]

A 1966 *Chicago Tribune* article written by the director of the American Medical Writers Association claimed that some 10,000 pregnancies were illegally terminated in Chicago annually back then.[14] The story ticked off a variety of methods a woman desperate to end a pregnancy might choose, each one progressively more horrifying and unsafe than the last.

"The woman may find a physician who disregards the law—he may feel a need to help such women; he may just want the money," the article said. "Or she may make connections with an abortion ring, secretly meeting someone on a street corner and suffering the degradation of an operation on a table set up in temporary, often unclean quarters that are moved every few days to elude police. Or she may be packed with irritating gauze, be given some pills, and rushed out after 15 minutes, to await pain, bleeding and expulsion of the fetus. Or she may go to a friend or stranger who tries to induce abortion with caustic soda solution . . . or who tries scraping the uterus with stiffened rubber tubing or crude instruments or even coat hangers, nails or knitting needles."[15]

In *Abortion and the Politics of Motherhood*, author Kristin Luker offers numerous first-person accounts from women who had illegal abortions prior to *Roe*; the stories show it can be hard to generalize about the experience.

"Depending on the era, the age of the woman involved, her social milieu, the experience of her friends and relatives, and simple chance, arranging an illegal abortion could be either quite difficult or relatively easy. . . . " Luker wrote. "The black market aspect of illegal abortion, combined with the fact that a pregnant woman seeking an abortion has only a very short period of time in which to find it, meant that it was hard to predict who would succeed in finding an abortion (and what kind)."[16]

One common thread Luker did cite was pain for the patient.

"Given the fact that illegal abortions constituted a black market and black markets have difficulty forcing out unscrupulous or unskilled practitioners, the illegal abortions reported by those we interviewed were painful in every sense of the word," she wrote.

For Leta, the procedure was safe and sanitary, though fraught with much anxiety. Her parents took her in the family's blue Ford across the city from their North Side home to a designated meeting spot on the South Side, where a male driver in another car was already parked.

The teen and her mother got inside the unfamiliar vehicle. The driver took them to a second location and parked again. The three exited the vehicle and by foot, the driver escorted the mother and daughter through an alleyway and in the back door of a nondescript, generic office building. No signs or advertising on the outside offered any clues as to what transpired inside. No one would know it served as a medical facility from the exterior, she recalled.

Neither Leta nor her mother ever knew the name of the doctor who terminated her pregnancy or the exact address of the site, an underground abortion clinic operating in the years before the procedure was legalized.

As the teenager stepped through the door, she felt this was her only avenue to preserve her future.

"My gut said this is my only option to not ruin my own life," she said. "My life would have been over."

There was no anesthetic available during the abortion. The teen winced in discomfort during the insertion of the cold metal speculum. A kind nurse by her side tried to chat with her about her charm bracelet on her wrist, to keep her mind off how much the inside of her body hurt. She said she was given a Valium beforehand to numb the pain, but the procedure was still agonizing.

"Horrible," she said. "It felt like someone is scraping inside your uterus."

She recalled the surgeon was a Black man but knew little else about him. After the procedure, the same driver who had guided them to the clinic drove her and her mother back to their parked car, and the family drove home. Her family doctor was aware of the terminated pregnancy and asked her how she was feeling afterward; she told him she felt fine and never ran a fever or had any complications.

"And it was all over with," she said.

Her parents never treated her differently or judged her for the pregnancy or abortion, she said. Most of her friends and relatives didn't know about either one.

"I had a relatively good experience," she said. "It wasn't a coat hanger. It was with a physician who wasn't a hack. . . . Most damaging to me, psychologically, was that I felt as though I was damaged goods."

While she never regretted terminating the pregnancy, for years she said she carried a certain inner shame.

"I was a 17-year-old girl who had already done the unspeakable," she said.

* * *

By the late 1960s, an underground abortion service often referred to as Jane had emerged on Chicago's South Side. Heather Booth, activist and founder of Jane, recalled the service started in the mid-1960s, when she was a University of Chicago student and arranged an abortion for the sister of a friend.[17] A few years later, other women took over the effort, she recalled. The grassroots movement started out referring patients to a medical provider, but the activists ultimately began performing the procedure themselves.[18]

"Some members of Jane, many of whom were college students, housewives and mothers, eventually learned how to perform abortions themselves—despite having no formal medical training—and did them in the bedrooms of various secret apartments around the city," the *Chicago Tribune* reported in 1999. "The idea was to decrease the cost and increase the availability and safety of the procedure for otherwise desperate women."[19]

Seven of the activists were arrested in 1972, but the charges were later dropped.[20]

"The thousands of women who came through Jane were so grateful for that procedure," Booth said. "They were grateful that we created a caring community. They were grateful that after the procedure they were no longer pregnant. But they were concerned because it wasn't legal."

Booth recalled that many of these abortions were performed by Dr. T.R.M. Howard, a noted Black surgeon and civil rights activist. While living in Mississippi, Howard had taken up the cause of Emmett Till, the 14-year-old Black boy from Chicago who was kidnapped, beaten and lynched for allegedly whistling at a white woman in Mississippi in 1955.[21] Howard gave speeches across the country denouncing the murder of Till, eventually fleeing violence and resettling his family in Chicago.

He went on to serve as the president of the National Medical Association, the highest office a Black physician could achieve in that era.[22] Howard was arrested in 1964 and 1965 for performing illegal abortions but never convicted.[23]

The *Chicago Tribune* recounted his second arrest in September 1965, when he was caught in a sting operation in his South Side office.[24] Authorities said a woman who was an undercover agent called Howard a few days prior, "reporting she had a 'problem,' and being told it would cost $500 to take care of her 'problem,'" the article said. The woman arrived at the clinic with an undercover sheriff's detective and gave Howard $500 in marked bills; the doctor and a 47-year-old female nurse took the undercover female agent to another room to prepare her for the procedure, when the detective entered the room and arrested Howard and the nurse on charges of attempted abortion and conspiracy to commit abortion.[25]

Leta has no way of knowing whether her abortion six decades ago was arranged through Jane or another entity. She doesn't know if the Black physician who terminated her pregnancy was Howard because she never learned his name or any other identifying information. The process had been too secretive, all the details intentionally kept so vague that she can't be certain if either of them made her abortion possible, against all odds of the time.

After that summer ended, she went on to Northwestern University, where she studied English literature and joined a sorority, milestones and opportunities she believes she would have missed out on had she carried the pregnancy to term.

During her years at college, the nation's political and cultural norms were evolving at a breakneck pace. Those years were marked by a proliferation of anti–Vietnam War protests and rallies on her campus and others around the country, reflecting the anti-government and anti-authority sentiment of the era. The Sexual Revolution hit its peak, liberalizing many perspectives on sex and morality.

Political and legal stances on abortion were also rapidly changing. In 1970, Hawaii became the first state to legalize abortion, rolling back its 100-year-old law prohibiting the procedure.[26] Soon after, that same year, the governor of New York signed abortion reform legislation permitting the procedure up to the 24th week of pregnancy.[27]

Then, on January 22, 1973, the U.S. Supreme Court voted 7 to 2 in favor of plaintiff "Jane Roe," a watershed decision establishing the constitutional right to an abortion. The next day, the headline on the front page of the *Chicago Tribune* declared, "Top court strikes down abortion laws: Supreme Court rules laws banning abortions are invalid."[28]

Leta was overjoyed, believing the nation had changed for the better.

"I was just happy that women could get an abortion," she said. "That it was legal. That they wouldn't have to go through what I did."

The director of Planned Parenthood Association in March 1973 predicted 20,000 surgical operations would be performed annually in the Chicago area.[29] That month, Howard began performing abortions as director of the Friendship Medical Clinic on the South Side, within two hours after receiving court approval.[30]

"I believe in the lunch hour abortion," he said at the time. "In the first three months of pregnancy abortions are easy and safe. There is no reason why a working woman can't have an abortion during her lunch break and then go back to work."[31]

Booth, the founder of Jane, recalled thinking of all the women who had come through the underground abortion service, seeking medical care in anonymity and from the shadows—and all the women who would no longer need to do so after the ruling.

"I was so relieved," Booth said. "I was relieved because so many women's lives would be better. The support would be greater. The threat of having a procedure would be less."

* * *

Throughout the years, Leta rarely spoke of her illegal abortion.

"I just wanted that to go away," she said.

In 1989, she traveled to Washington, D.C., to take part in a march in support of abortion rights. The Supreme Court was deciding *Webster v. Reproductive Health Services*, a case that ultimately upheld a series of Missouri restrictions on abortion.[32]

"Well, I actually had one," she recalled telling fellow marchers before a demonstration.

Even at a reproductive rights rally, she said everyone in the room seemed shocked by her admission.

"If you don't want to be a mother, you don't want to be a mother. Why should you be an incubator?" she said. "It helped make me who I am. I don't regret it and I don't regret who I am."

In 2019, Leta shared the story of her illegal abortion on the front page of the *Chicago Tribune*, motivated in part by a wave of boldly restrictive new state abortion laws.[33] The governor of Georgia on May 7, 2019, signed into law a ban on abortion once a fetal heartbeat can be detected, as early as six weeks' gestation and before many even realize they're pregnant.[34] About a week later, the governor of Alabama signed a measure that would make performing an abortion a felony in almost all circumstances, with no exceptions for rape or incest.[35]

"To the bill's many supporters, this legislation stands as a powerful testament to Alabamians' deeply held belief that every life is precious and that every life is a sacred gift from God," Alabama governor Kay Ivey said in a statement that day.[36]

Missouri governor Mike Parson signed legislation on May 24, 2019, that barred most abortions after eight weeks, with exceptions only in medical emergencies. Missouri Right to Life called it "groundbreaking legislation that will save lives and set the standard for pro-life legislation nationwide."[37]

As these state restrictions came down in rapid succession, Leta cautioned that large sections of the nation were reverting to the laws and customs of her childhood, stripping women of their hard-earned freedoms of the past five decades. Months later, all these state measures were temporarily blocked by the courts, citing *Roe*.[38]

But Leta predicted the federal protections *Roe* provided were fragile and wouldn't remain intact much longer.

"It doesn't take that long for people to forget," she said at the time. "If it becomes illegal, girls who are being born today aren't going to have options."

Three years later, her warnings proved prophetic: The U.S. Supreme Court voted 5 to 4 to overturn *Roe*, a historic decision reversing nearly half a century of abortion rights.[39]

"*Roe* was egregiously wrong from the start," the majority opinion stated. "Its reasoning was exceptionally weak, and the decision has had damaging consequences. . . . It is time to heed the Constitution and return the issue of abortion to the people's elected representatives."[40]

The case before the court, *Dobbs v. Jackson Women's Health Organization*, upheld the legality of a 2018 Mississippi law that barred abortion past 15 weeks of gestation, legislation designed in part to challenge *Roe*.[41]

Historians overwhelmingly disagreed with the overturning of *Roe*, based on decades of research on abortion history in the United States: In an amicus brief filed in *Dobbs v. Jackson*, the American Historical Association and the Organization of American Historians affirmed the correctness of Roe, asserting that the common-law approach to abortion was well-grounded in early American history and tradition.

"Even where states prohibited abortion, common-law reasoning resonated in public opinion, deeply affecting the practice of abortion," the amicus brief said. "These historical findings confirm that *Roe*'s central conclusion was correct: American history and traditions from the founding to the post–Civil War years included a woman's ability to make decisions regarding abortion, as far as allowed by the common law."[42]

The day the ruling came down, former president Trump credited the pro-life triumph to himself, citing his three crucial conservative Supreme Court picks, all of whom voted to dismantle long-standing federal abortion protections.

"Today's decision, which is the biggest WIN for LIFE in a generation, along with other decisions that have been announced recently, were only made possible because I delivered everything as promised, including nominating and getting three highly respected and strong Constitutionalists confirmed to the United States Supreme Court," he said in a written statement. "It was my great honor to do so! . . . These major Victories prove that even though the Radical Left is doing everything in their power to destroy our Country, your Rights are being protected, the Country is being defended, and there is still hope and time to Save America! I will never stop fighting for the Great People of our Nation!"[43]

In early May 2022, a leaked draft opinion obtained and reported by Politico had indicated the court's intent to overturn *Roe*, so the ruling wasn't entirely shocking or unanticipated.[44] Yet the implications of the decision still reverberated internationally, sparking protests and demonstrations across the United States as well as a spectrum of reactions from world leaders.

The government of Brazil put out a statement that day, saying the largest nation in South America "defends life from its conception and strengthens family ties."[45]

"May God continue to give strength and wisdom to those who protect the innocence and future of our children, in Brazil and in the world," tweeted President Jair Bolsonaro. "Good evening everyone!"[46]

But most heads of state of the developed world condemned the ruling, expressing fear for what the reversal of such a long-standing precedent might mean for Americans.

"Abortion is a fundamental right for all women," tweeted French president Emmanuel Macron. "It must be protected. I wish to express my solidarity with the women whose liberties are being undermined by the Supreme Court of the United States."[47]

Canadian prime minister Justin Trudeau called the news "horrific."

"My heart goes out to the millions of American women who are now set to lose their legal right to an abortion," he said on Twitter. "I can't imagine the fear and anger you are feeling right now."[48]

For Leta, the overturning of *Roe* evoked the memories and emotions of her illegal abortion more than 50 summers earlier.

"The hammer has come down, shattering a woman's right to control her own body," Leta said the day of the ruling. "A flood of memories washed over me and triggered in detail the fear and sadness I felt having my abortion. . . . Even though the decision to have the abortion was liberating it was not without its repercussions for me."[49]

Booth was outraged but not shocked, having watched as state laws and court cases in preceding years chipped away at both the legal right to an abortion as well as the practical ability to access the procedure. She predicted the high court's reversal would "mean there will be hardship, pain and even death for women."[50]

"It means the dismantling of an established freedom in this country and it means an attack on this most intimate decision of a person's life, about when or whether or with whom we have a child," she said.

Suddenly the matter of abortion rights fell to individual states. While many, such as Illinois, California and New York, had shored up abortion rights protections in anticipation of the demise of *Roe*, reproductive rights experts predicted roughly half of all states would ultimately either ban abortion or severely restrict it to only the narrowest of circumstances, such as incest, rape, the earliest weeks of pregnancy or when the life of the pregnant person is in jeopardy.

In some of those states, abortions ceased immediately after the ruling; some clinics even suspended all appointments for the procedure days before the official decision came down, in anticipation. In other states, court fights and tumultuous legislative sessions raged for months, ushering in an era of day-to-day confusion over whether terminating a pregnancy was legal or not.

Leta worried about women in those parts of the country where ending a pregnancy was no longer an option.

"I remember what it was like before and I remember my own experience," she said. "My heart goes out to them. Because if they are poor, I don't know how they are going to get to states that have abortion."

While the Supreme Court ruling angered and saddened her, she wasn't entirely surprised.

"For a long time, I had a feeling that for feminism and for women's rights, that we had won the battle, but we are losing the war," she said. "I don't believe I will live to see women's equality, and that makes me very sad."

3.
Taxpayer-Funded Abortion

The young woman arrived a little early for her appointment at a Chicago clinic one summer morning in 2018.[1] As she waited for her name to be called, she listed the various ways she had considered paying for the procedure that would begin in a matter of minutes.

Nearing the end of her first trimester, she knew she couldn't afford to continue carrying the pregnancy that she hadn't anticipated or prepared for. The 24-year-old with red highlights woven in a long, dark braid was barely getting by financially. Making rent and monthly bills was already a struggle. For the same reasons she couldn't financially support having the baby, she also didn't have the money on hand to pay for the $500 abortion, the option she deemed best given her tight finances and life circumstances. She had contemplated selling her only television or one of the few other items in her small one-bedroom apartment on Chicago's South Side, hoping the value offered would equal the bill.

"I don't have any help," said the woman, who asked to remain anonymous. "That's why I'm making the decision I am now."

Borrowing cash from family and friends was a possibility, but she cringed at the imposition, which would likely require an explanation delving into her privacy and personal life. Some of her loved ones might support her; some might try and dissuade her from a choice she had already firmly made.

She also couldn't be certain her relatives and friends would keep her abortion confidential, and gossip can spread so quickly.

At first, she had hoped she wasn't pregnant—that she'd wait a little longer and her period would come, ending the whole ordeal. Yet she couldn't ignore the growing tenderness in her breasts, the same unmistakable symptom that had signaled her daughter's conception a few years earlier.

Although the young woman was very nervous before the surgery, her face broke out in a smile as she mentioned her two-year-old. She took out her phone and scanned through dozens of photos of the little girl, whose eyes and cheekbone contours closely resembled those of her mother. The toddler was her joy. But the little girl also needed food, clothing, toys and a babysitter while the single mom searched for work. They shared their apartment's only bedroom and slept in adjacent beds. There was no room for anyone else, she said.

So the woman with the red braid had been surprised—and relieved—when the receptionist at the clinic informed her that the procedure would be free with her Medicaid card, the result of a controversial Illinois law that allows state taxpayer funding to cover abortions.[2] The measure had just gone into effect on January 1, 2018, about six months before her appointment.

Suddenly, the looming $500 bill that had kept her up at night had vanished, along with the prospect of selling her possessions or taking charity.

"I didn't know what I was going to do," she said. "I'm thankful I was able to use the medical card because I don't have the money right now."

* * *

Illinois governor Bruce Rauner signed House Bill 40 into law in September 2017, drawing sharp rebuke from others in his party as well as the Catholic church. Rauner, a moderate Republican who supported abortion rights, said he had to be "consistent with my values."[3] As a candidate three years earlier, he had expressed support for repealing restrictions on abortion coverage under state Medicaid plans and Illinois employee health insurance "because I believe it unfairly restricts access based on income," he wrote on a questionnaire for the abortion rights advocacy group Personal PAC in 2014, according to the *Chicago Tribune*.[4]

Conservative lawmakers accused Rauner of flip-flopping on the matter; some insinuated he had broken a promise to Cardinal Blase Cupich, the archbishop of Chicago, to veto the measure.

"He did break his word," Cupich said at the time. "He broke his word to the people, especially those who have continued to speak on behalf of the vulnerable child in the womb."[5]

A few months later, in the March 2018 primary, Rauner narrowly defeated challenger Jeanne Ives, a conservative state lawmaker whose frequently aired TV campaign ad featured a woman thanking the governor for "making all Illinois families pay for my abortions."[6]

Illinois has long been known as one of the most permissive states in the Midwest when it comes to abortion laws, with few legal barriers to the procedure. Yet debate over House Bill 40 bitterly divided the state, with foes arguing that taxpayers shouldn't be forced to pay for a procedure some consider immoral.

"The fact that the government is using taxpayer money to fund abortion is reprehensible to me," said Tim Moore, president of Springfield Right to Life. "I'm subsidizing the culture of death. The government, which is supposed to protect life, is willfully taking part in the slaughter of innocents."

The battle over House Bill 40 was just one front in a decades-long war over public funding for abortion that continues to rage nationwide.

The demise of *Roe* in 2022 cast a new spotlight on government subsidies for abortions, as liberal politicians rushed to shore up funding in states where the procedure would remain legal, in anticipation of a sudden crush of out-of-state patients. Chicago Mayor Lori Lightfoot in 2022 allocated $500,000 of city money to Planned Parenthood of Illinois and the Chicago Abortion Fund to help pay for transportation, lodging, follow-up services and other costs associated with travel to end a pregnancy.[7]

"The City of Chicago is committed to ensuring that no person will lose their rights to reproductive healthcare," she said in a statement. "No one deserves to be bullied, harassed or discriminated against for exercising their bodily autonomy. As Mayor of this city, I remain dedicated to protecting any person seeking reproductive care, safety and support—regardless of their zip code or which side of the state line they reside on."[8]

One week after *Roe* was overturned, during a virtual meeting on reproductive rights with President Joe Biden, some Democratic governors floated the idea of offering abortions on federal land, such as military bases and veterans affairs facilities, including in states that banned or significantly curbed abortion. Illinois governor J.B. Pritzker asked the president for more federal funds for medical transportation, upkeep of clinics and other costs that are permitted under federal law.[9]

Pro-life groups in Illinois decried the use of any public funding to assist abortion seekers.

"The majority of Americans do not support taxpayer funding for abortion," said Anna Kinskey, associate director of the annual March for Life Chicago, in a press release. "Yet, in the wake of the United States Supreme Court decision to uphold a state's right to restrict abortion, Governor Pritzker and Mayor Lightfoot continue to ignore the people they represent to push their extreme abortion agenda at taxpayer expense."

The U.S. Department of Veterans Affairs announced in September 2022 that the federal agency would provide abortion counseling—and, in some cases, abortions—to veterans and VA beneficiaries, regardless of state laws.[10] Those circumstances include instances where the life or health of the pregnant person is in jeopardy or when the pregnancy is the result of rape or incest. The determination of when life is at risk would be made on a case-by-case basis, the agency said.

"This is a patient safety decision," said Secretary of Veterans Affairs Denis McDonough in the press release on the VA announcement. "Pregnant Veterans and VA beneficiaries deserve to have access to world-class reproductive care when they need it most. That's what our nation owes them, and that's what we at VA will deliver."

Whether the initiative will be challenged and survive is uncertain as the 1992 Veterans Health Care Act prohibits the VA from offering abortion care.[11] Republican lawmakers tried to pass a resolution to reverse the policy, but the Senate narrowly voted against it in April 2023.[12] In a White House statement, President Biden had said he would have vetoed the resolution, adding that it "undermines patient safety and invites political interference into deeply personal decisions made by pregnant veterans and . . . beneficiaries in consultation with their health care providers, threatening their health and lives."[13]

* * *

Opposition to government subsidies for abortion has deep roots in Illinois, despite the state's reputation as a stronghold of reproductive rights protections.

After *Roe v. Wade* legalized terminating a pregnancy, Medicaid paid for an estimated 300,000 abortions for low-income women annually across the country, according to the nonprofit Center for Reproductive Rights.[14]

"Medicaid, a joint federal and state program that provided free or low-cost health care to low-income Americans, had transformed abortion in the United States after *Roe*," wrote law professor Mary Ziegler in *Roe: The History of a National Obsession*. "Before 1973, people of color had far fewer legal abortions than white patients but at least twice as many illegal terminations. Between 1972 and 1974, the percentage of legal abortions obtained by people of color rose nearly 7 percent. Between 1976 and 1977, the abortion rates for Medicaid recipients (61.5 per 1,000 women versus 20.7 per 1,000) and people of color (58 per 1,000 versus 19 per 1,0000) were higher than those for other women. For this reason, right-to-lifers in Congress believed that a national Medicaid ban would put a serious dent in the national abortion rate."[15]

But in 1976, Congress passed the Hyde Amendment, barring the use of federal funds to terminate a pregnancy. The provision, which isn't a permanent law but has been renewed in some form each year by lawmakers, was named after its sponsor, U.S. Representative Henry Hyde, then a relatively inconspicuous freshman congressman from the western suburbs of Chicago.

"For me, it's a matter of conscience," Hyde told the *Tribune* in 1989. "I have an open mind about what other people may think but I am convinced that abortion kills an innocent human life. And nothing political could make me vote to take that life away."[16]

The restriction first mainly curbed Medicaid funding but was later expanded to exclude abortion coverage under other federal programs, including Medicare, military benefits, the Peace Corps and federal employee health benefits; exemptions were made for cases of rape, incest and life endangerment.[17]

However, state governments can choose to expand the circumstances under which the state portion of Medicaid covers abortion care. By 2023, 32 states and Washington, D.C., followed the federal standard, according to the Guttmacher Institute; 17 states had Medicaid fund most or all medically necessary abortions.[18]

Nationwide, Medicaid covers roughly one-fifth of women of reproductive age, from 15 to 49 years old, according to a March 2021 report on the impacts of the Hyde Amendment by the nonprofit KFF (formerly the Kaiser Family Foundation). Half of women below the federal poverty level were insured by Medicaid in 2019, the report found.[19]

"Women of color are more likely than white women to be insured by Medicaid, and have higher rates of unintended pregnancy and abortion," the report said, adding that in 2014, three-quarters of abortion patients nationwide were low-income women and 53 percent were Black or Latina women.

"Young adults and teens, who are less likely to have a steady source of income, make up the majority (72 percent) of abortion patients," the report continued. "For women with medically complicated health situations or who need a second-trimester abortion, the costs could be prohibitive. In some cases, women find they have to delay their abortion while they take time to raise funds or in other cases, women are not able to obtain abortions because they cannot afford the costs of the procedure."

* * *

The young woman with the braided hair wasn't aware of the new Illinois law until she called to schedule the procedure a few days prior to the appointment. For her and other low-income patients in the crowded clinic waiting room, the expanded coverage meant access to an abortion despite their economic constraints.

The young woman chose to have her abortion at a Planned Parenthood on the North Side of Chicago. About a year earlier, she had faced another unplanned pregnancy and terminated the pregnancy at Stroger Hospital, a Cook County public facility on the West Side of Chicago, before the procedure was covered by Medicaid. The price was $75 at the time, she said.

Even at the reduced cost, she had had to borrow the money for that abortion.

"I had to go around asking for it," she said. "And when you borrow money, people want to know what it's for. . . . Then people look at you funny, like, 'Oh, why are you doing this?' You don't want to involve people because they're going to give their opinion and talk about you and spread it onto the next person."

The decision to terminate was difficult the first time, she recalled.

"I didn't believe in it," she said. "I was scared because people are so judgmental and have negative things to say and everything. People tell you, 'Oh, a baby's a good thing,' but nobody's actually going to help you. People will tell you, 'Oh, keep the baby, an abortion's not good.' But as soon as you don't do it and your baby's here, guess what, everybody disappeared. The baby's here and nobody's going to actually help you at all."

That was her experience after giving birth to her daughter. So she decided she wouldn't have another child until she was ready financially and emotionally, regardless of what others would think or say. This time, she said, she was less ambivalent about terminating.

"It wasn't a hard decision to make," she said. "Because I know what's important. I know what I'm capable of doing and what I'm not capable of doing. It'd be a bad idea to be really struggling more than I am right now. I'm making it happen right now, you know, I'm managing."

As she waited in the clinic, a few inches from her hand a wicker basket sat on an end table displaying samples of various birth control devices—a vaginal ring, an IUD, a birth control implant encased in plush material to simulate its texture under the flesh of an arm—near clinic pamphlets with information about each one. The young woman said she had been on a contraceptive patch but conceived between applications when she had trouble getting refills from her pharmacy.

She chose to go to the Planned Parenthood for her abortion because she wanted to be sedated during surgery, which was an option at their health centers but also increased the cost of the procedure. Patients terminating pregnancies at the county hospital were provided only a local anesthetic for pain but were not sedated during the outpatient procedure, according to county officials. This time an aunt—a relative who was compassionate and didn't cast judgment or spread gossip—accompanied her and would drive her home.

"I don't like pain," she said. "I need to be asleep. I don't want to feel it."

She had gone alone for her procedure at Stroger Hospital about a year earlier and said she kept flinching during the abortion, requiring the physician to stop and start again a few times.

"I was scared," she said, shuddering at the memory. "I had to be woke, and I felt all the pain. . . . It's very sharp. The pain is over quick, but you're still not going to forget that pain for those few minutes. . . . I can't be woke again because I made them start over because I was moving and everything. I couldn't take that pain."

* * *

Cook County has had its own turbulent history of taxpayer-subsidized abortions.

After *Roe*, about 18 first-trimester abortions were performed daily at Cook County Hospital, the former name of Stroger; physicians volunteered to perform the procedure.[20] Second-trimester abortions were added in early 1974 but were limited to 20 weeks' gestation; the number of terminated pregnancies at the public hospital peaked that year at 3,500.[21]

Then, in 1980, Cook County banned the procedure at the hospital except in life-saving cases.

Referring to the public hospital as an "abortion mill," George Dunne, then president of the Cook County Board, pointed to a shortage of nurses for other health care needs, as well as an Illinois law that had prohibited the use of public assistance to pay for abortions back then.[22]

The change was abrupt: The first day, 18 women who had already scheduled the procedure were turned away, the *Tribune* reported.[23]

"It's a matter of priorities," Dunne told the *Tribune* at the time. "A woman who wants to pay for her abortion should go to a private hospital or doctor, but we shouldn't be staffing [abortion procedures] when we're having to turn people away."[24]

Pro-life groups praised the move, but some health experts feared a resurgence of women coming to the hospital for treatment following botched abortions.

"I think one of the unanswered questions is that in the past, before abortions were a matter of choice, we used to have a complete ward filled with [patients who suffered] bungled abortions," one hospital official told the *Tribune* that year. "That is our greatest concern, that these indigent women will turn to something else, or that the money that would have gone to housing and food is going to go to abortions. The problem is still going to be there, and people are going to take care of the problem one way or another."[25]

Following protests and lawsuits, abortion services were restored 12 years later under a new county board president, Richard Phelan.[26] More than 500 women called the first day the hospital resumed appointments for the procedure in 1992, and many of them faced a long waiting list.[27]

"Every woman in this country has a legal right to an abortion," Phelan said at the time. "By denying poor women access, we deprive them of their constitutional rights just as surely as if we refused to allow them to vote. We must level the playing field and right the wrong."[28]

For the first year, hundreds of patients would call seeking one of 30 appointments rationed out each week, according to the *Tribune* in 1993.[29]

"Their telephone calls still jam the switchboard, a fact that remains astonishing even to those involved with family planning and reproductive services," the article said. "The women face long waiting lists."

* * *

As for the woman with the red braid at the Chicago clinic in 2018, she said the $500 she saved on the abortion would go toward paying her rent. The young woman has had jobs at restaurants and grocery stores. She's been searching for similar work but has no car or babysitter, which makes getting to job interviews challenging. She hopes to one day study culinary arts. She said she loves cooking and her dream is to become a chef.

After necessities, any extra money she has is spent on her daughter, she said.

"After I take care of my bills, I just give her things," she said. "I go without. She has everything she needs."

The mom boasted that her two-year-old was already potty trained and knew all her numbers and letters before starting preschool.

"She's very smart," she said. "She's going to go far in life. By her having a strong mother in me, myself, she's going to get far and make it in life and have me by her side to help her and push her further. She won't be alone. . . . I need to provide for her like I've been doing. Rather than bring somebody else until we're all the way stable."

4.
Last Clinic Standing

The couple donned sunglasses and baseball caps before entering Hope Clinic for Women on a spring weekday in 2019, to shield their identities from a throng of protesters outside.[1] Fearing for their safety, they also rented a car so their own license plate couldn't be traced.

The young woman's 21-week pregnancy was clearly visible to the small cluster of anti-abortion activists in front of the southern Illinois clinic. One of the strangers said she must be able to feel her baby moving and suggested adoption. Another mentioned to her partner that Father's Day was approaching.

Inside the clinic, the man and woman described their initial elation at the prospect of parenthood, eagerly preparing for their firstborn, whom they affectionately called Little One. They announced the pregnancy on social media with a photo of baby shoes. Then a 20-week ultrasound revealed the inconceivable: Large portions of the brain and skull were missing, a rare birth defect called anencephaly.

Their obstetrician in Missouri said the fetus wouldn't survive outside the womb.

"There was no top to the head, there was no top to the brain," said the man in the baseball cap, his sunglasses now clipped to his shirt and no longer concealing his eyes, which welled with tears. "The options were to either carry this child who had a death sentence. Or to terminate the pregnancy."

But they faced many barriers to the procedure in Missouri, including a three-day waiting period. The state of more than six million residents had only one abortion clinic—and the fate of that provider remained in limbo when the couple received the devastating diagnosis.

The pregnant patient's physician referred her to Hope Clinic, which performs abortions up to 24 weeks' gestation. The couple were confused and dismayed: They couldn't understand why they couldn't terminate the pregnancy in the same state where they received prenatal care. Although they lived nearby in southern Illinois, the young woman was treated throughout her pregnancy by doctors and nurses in Missouri and planned to deliver at a hospital there. In her time of grief, she said, it was difficult to understand why she had to find a new medical provider to terminate the pregnancy as they faced the worst possible outcome.

"I was in shock," said the young woman, who asked to remain anonymous to protect the couple's privacy.

Missouri lawmakers had just approved multiple abortion restrictions, including an eight-week gestational limit, a measure that would be blocked temporarily by the courts.[2]

"It's time to make Missouri the most Pro-Life state in the country!" Governor Mike Parson tweeted a month prior to the couple's appointment.[3]

At the time, Missouri was one of a half dozen states with only one abortion clinic: Kentucky, Mississippi, West Virginia, North Dakota and South Dakota were also down to a lone clinic providing abortions statewide.[4]

Then, in May 2019, Missouri health officials refused to renew the license of Missouri's last remaining clinic, a Planned Parenthood in St. Louis, a move that threatened to leave the state without a single dedicated abortion provider. The Missouri Department of Health and Senior Services in a statement alleged there were "failed surgical abortions" in which patients remained pregnant, as well as other health and safety problems at the clinic.[5]

The president and CEO of Planned Parenthood Federation of America accused Missouri officials of having "illegally weaponized the licensing process." A judge issued a temporary restraining order allowing the abortion provider to stay open as the case moved through the legal process.[6] But the clinic's unresolved future still impacted abortion access: Since the state had a three-day waiting period, many patients were afraid to book appointments there in case the clinic couldn't survive until their procedure date.

Missouri had 12 abortion facilities in 1992, but by 2014 the state was down to three providers, according to an American Civil Liberties Union report tracking clinic closures over several decades in six states.[7] The decline was largely due to regulations in numerous states requiring that abortion providers have hospital admitting privileges and that clinics meet the same standards as surgical centers. These types of mandates are often referred to as "targeted restrictions on abortion providers," or TRAP laws, by reproductive rights advocates, who argue the rules are medically unnecessary and designed to limit access to the procedure.[8]

"The TRAP requirements are difficult—in some cases impossible—to meet," the report said. "Many hospitals simply won't provide admitting privileges to doctors who perform abortions due to anti-abortion bias and stigma. Others require doctors to admit a certain number of patients at the hospital each year, but because abortion is such a safe procedure, abortion providers can't meet that threshold. Ambulatory surgical centers are far more complex and expensive than what is necessary to provide a safe abortion, and no other comparable medical procedure is subject to such requirements."[9]

The report found that more than two dozen states had these types of regulations on the books, though some measures were blocked by courts. In 2016, the U.S. Supreme Court struck down those regulations in Texas, and, shortly after, a federal district court enjoined the laws in Missouri as well.[10] But Missouri legislators swiftly approved new regulations that were strikingly similar to the old ones, and they survived legal challenges.[11] In 2018, the state was back down to one provider.[12]

"And with so few clinics in Missouri, a trip to the clinic could be 300 miles away," the ACLU report said. "That, in turn, requires additional time off of work and possibly extra childcare costs, given that the majority of women who have abortions are already mothers."

The same day the couple came to Hope Clinic, about a half dozen protesters gathered in the public right-of-way outside the Planned Parenthood in St. Louis, just past the property's black fencing. Many were praying for the facility to shut down.

One man walked up and down the sidewalk, fingering the small wooden beads of a rosary. He spoke of how children are the world's most precious gift and that gift must be preserved.

"I am praying for all those who need God's mercy," said Richard Tourville, who described himself as a devout Catholic. "I believe it's a terrible tragedy. . . . I just hope this finally comes to an end."

A woman praying nearby noted the St. Louis clinic's license was set to expire on May 31, a day of the year when many Christians commemorate the Visitation of the Blessed Virgin Mary, the moment the mother of Jesus first approached her cousin Elisabeth when both were with child.

The protester referenced scripture from the Gospel of Luke: "And it came to pass, that, when Elisabeth heard the salutation of Mary, the babe leaped in her womb; and Elisabeth was filled with the Holy Ghost: And she spake out with a loud voice, and said, Blessed art thou among women, and blessed is the fruit of thy womb."[13]

"We're just excited for when Missouri will no longer have abortion clinics," said the protester, who did not want to be named. "Our mothers will learn the joy of our Lord Jesus Christ."

* * *

Because the pregnancy was so far along, the abortion was a two-day procedure for the young woman at Hope Clinic. The first day her cervix was dilated. The following morning, she had a surgical abortion.

Afterward, she sobbed in a hospital bed, her limbs shaking beneath the blanket, a side effect of medication.

"It's over," she said. "The baby won't ever have to suffer."

In a private recovery room, the man in the baseball cap kissed her forehead and touched her left hand. The physician who performed the abortion held her right hand, telling her the procedure went well.

"We did the right thing," her partner said, weeping and repeatedly thanking the doctor.

"I feel like I did the best thing for the baby," the patient said, wiping her eyes. "And it won't ever hurt. It won't lay in a NICU or my arms and pass away."

As drivers cross into Illinois from Missouri on Interstate 55, a billboard greets them with the message "Welcome to Illinois, where you can have a safe, legal abortion." It was erected a few months before the couple's appointment by Hope Clinic.

The prospect of Missouri losing its last abortion clinic was daunting to the staff at Hope Clinic, which performed more than 3,700 abortions in 2018. Roughly 55 percent of patients that year came from Missouri, though the two-story brown brick medical facility also drew women from many other states in the Midwest and upper South as well as some foreign countries.

The clinic had already seen a 30 percent increase in patients since 2017 and had doubled the number of staff physicians in that time from two to four, said the clinic's deputy director, Alison Dreith, who had previously served as the executive director of NARAL Pro-Choice Missouri.

In the previous week or so, the abortion provider had hired several extra counselors and nurses as well as its first lawyer, Dreith said. More volunteers were also undergoing training, but it's difficult to plan for a potential influx of patients given the shifting legal and political landscape locally as well as across the country. While the St. Louis clinic was still seeing patients amid the battle over its license, more women from Missouri had been seeking appointments at Hope Clinic because of the uncertainty.

"Patients also know that there's a 72-hour waiting period, and the clinic's licensing issue is in the court," Dreith said. "So they're worried that clinic could close by the time they have their procedure or go in for their 72-hour consent."

A 2018 study published in the *Journal of Medical Internet Research* found a great disparity in the locations of abortion clinics across the country, with the Midwest having fewer abortion clinics than any other region, based on the population of women of child-bearing age.[14] The researchers highlighted 27 abortion deserts, cities primarily in the South and Midwest where the closest abortion facility was more than 100 miles away. The list included two cities in Missouri: One was Springfield and the other was Columbia.

"The lack of access to a common reproductive health service such as abortion is a public health concern in that more women in these cities could be forced to carry unwanted pregnancies to term if they are unable to travel long distances to obtain abortion care," the study said. "The six states that have only one abortion facility have combined populations of almost 4 million women of reproductive age who will be forced to travel out of their home state to access abortion care if those facilities close."

The study found 780 facilities across the country that provided abortions as of May 2017, roughly one for every 95,033 women of reproductive age. Yet there were tremendous differences across regions, with one clinic for every 55,662 women in the Northeast and one for every 67,883 women in the West. The Midwest had the lowest number of clinics per woman, with one for every 165,886 women, even lower than the ratio in the South, which had one clinic for every 145,645 women.[15] Illinois at the time had 25 clinics, roughly one for every 120,135 women of reproductive age, a much higher ratio compared to the rest of the Midwest, researchers found.

Faced with increasing hurdles in Missouri, Planned Parenthood of the St. Louis Region and Southwest Missouri in late 2019 opened an 18,000-square-foot health center in Fairview Heights, Illinois, near both St. Louis and Hope Clinic.[16] The location on the east side of the Mississippi River meant no extra regulations for the abortion provider and no mandatory waiting period for patients.

As the couple at Hope Clinic prepared to terminate their pregnancy, the national abortion debate roiled in headlines and on television newscasts. Multiple states had just passed some of the strictest abortion laws in the nation, with the intention of challenging *Roe*. In 2019, more than 50 abortion restrictions were enacted, and two dozen abortion bans were passed, primarily in midwestern and southern parts of the nation.[17]

"It's really unfortunate they're lumping all abortions into one category," said the young woman at Hope Clinic. "And that's not to say that I should get special treatment or be exempt, because everyone has a choice to do what is best for their body and baby, and no one else can make those decisions."

Four other women were resting on recliners in the Hope Clinic's main recovery room that day, either waiting to have a surgical abortion or recuperating after the procedure. That morning, three patients were from Illinois, one came from Missouri and another traveled from Tennessee.

"Everyone is here for a reason," she said, motioning to the other patients.

While abortion was still legal in every state at the time, clinic staff said looming abortion regulations in some parts of the country were stoking confusion and fear.

"The phones have definitely been ringing off the hook these days," said Aryn Hanebrink, the clinic's medical secretary. "A lot of people are scared, honestly. I've had girls call me and they're crying, because they're so thankful that we can still help them here."

In the clinic's changing room, three white binders labeled "patient journal" contain hundreds of handwritten notes chronicling the thoughts and emotions of women before or after their abortions.

"I am happy with my choice to make a better life for me and my family," one patient wrote, encircling the sentence in a heart.

"You cannot be judged by anyone who has breath in their lungs," another wrote. "They are not God, because he forgives. Dear Lord, I love you and have faith in you. I know you love me too and I know I will be forgiven."

"It's a choice—not a child," a third patient wrote.

In careful cursive, the patient from southern Illinois penned her parting words before leaving the clinic.

"Loving someone doesn't always mean you fight for them," she wrote. "Sometimes loving someone just means letting them go."

* * *

The Planned Parenthood clinic in St. Louis prevailed in May 2020, when a state administrative commission ruled that the abortion provider was entitled to renew its license and the Missouri Department of Health and Senior Services had failed to sufficiently justify its denial.

"Planned Parenthood has demonstrated that it provides safe and legal abortion care," the decision said. "In over 4,000 abortions provided since 2018, the Department has only identified two causes to deny its license. As such, we determine that Planned Parenthood has substantially complied with [the law]."

In the ruling, the commission acknowledged "the societal ethical dilemma abortion care entails," noting that all of the state health department's experts "hold openly pro-life viewpoints, and all of Planned Parenthood's experts hold openly pro-choice viewpoints."

One side believed physicians have a responsibility to advocate for access to safe abortion care for their patients, the other side considered the procedure "homicide," the ruling said.

For about two more years, Missouri would continue to be among the handful of states with only one abortion clinic. Another one was Mississippi, where the only abortion provider, Jackson Women's Health Organization, challenged a state ban on abortions past 15 weeks in 2018. The case sparked the most important reproductive rights ruling in almost 50 years: *Dobbs v. Jackson Women's Health Organization*, the lawsuit that prompted the U.S. Supreme Court to overturn *Roe*.

Jackson Women's Health Organization suspended abortion services in July 2022 after a Mississippi law banning abortion in almost all circumstances went into effect.[18] The clinic's website advised patients that "it's legal to travel out of state to get an abortion" and listed the phone numbers for three clinics. One was 600 miles away in Bristol, Virginia; another was 900 miles away in Richmond, Virginia; and the third clinic was more than a thousand miles away in Las Cruces, New Mexico.

"No woman can call herself free until and unless she decides when or whether to become a parent," Jackson Women's Health Organization stated on the clinic's website.

One month after the fall of *Roe*, seven states enacted abortion bans with few or no exceptions, and no longer had any clinics providing abortions.[19] Texas used to have 23. Alabama and Oklahoma each previously had five. Arkansas had two. South Dakota, Mississippi and Missouri had one abortion clinic at the time of the *Dobbs* ruling. In 2020, these seven states had provided 80,500 abortions. And in Wisconsin, uncertainty over the legality of the state's 1849 abortion ban led clinics to suspend terminating pregnancies the day of the Supreme Court decision.

As for that lone clinic in Missouri, Planned Parenthood officials notified the state health department "that we are ceasing abortion services in the state of Missouri" just after the Supreme Court reversed *Roe*.[20] After winning a lengthy and heated legal battle to remain licensed, the St. Louis clinic stopped providing abortions that day, as Missouri's trigger law effectively banned terminating a pregnancy in almost all circumstances.

Parson, the governor of Missouri, celebrated the ruling.

"Today, our efforts have produced what generations of Missourians have worked and prayed for: Today, we have won our fight to protect innocent life," he tweeted.[21]

Dr. Colleen McNicholas had been performing abortions for about 15 years, and most of her work had been in Missouri. While she had anticipated the ruling, it was still "a shock to the system," she said.[22]

"The vast majority of my abortion care career has been providing care where access has been difficult," said McNicholas, chief medical officer of Planned Parenthood of the St. Louis Region and Southwest Missouri. "Where our ability to have an abortion really depends on your zip code, where you live and how much money you make."

While the end of federal abortion rights was a blow, McNicholas added that "*Roe* was never enough."

She believes that one day, reproductive freedoms will be restored—and even strengthened—in the wake of *Roe*'s reversal.

"I'd like to think that I'm young enough where I will see a time when not just Missouri but the rest of the country will have rebuilt a system that is equitable and offers access to everybody, no matter where they live," she said. "We're going to continue to fight to bring access back to Missouri. We will be on the ground still fighting to rebuild that system."

In the meantime, Hope Clinic executive director Dr. Erin King said her clinic remained committed to ensuring "people from communities across the South and Midwest can still access the safe, quality health care they need and deserve."

"We are heartbroken by today's disastrous Supreme Court decision stripping away the basic right to abortion care in this country," she said in a written statement. "Today's decision has been preceded by years of extremist attacks on our fundamental human rights. The ruling will immediately affect every person in this country, but will disproportionately impact Black, Indigenous and people of color and other historically marginalized communities."

* * *

At first, the woman from Hope Clinic didn't think she ever wanted to try to have a child again.

"I was scared of the worst scenario," the woman said. "Having something really wrong in a pregnancy or having something that we really couldn't control or even getting surprised after another baby being born, if it was something fatal."

Yet, a few years later, they conceived again.

It was during her second trimester that the media leak revealed the Supreme Court planned to overturn *Roe*. Visibly pregnant, she attended a march in St. Louis protesting the looming end of federal abortion rights. She carried a sign reading "Pregnant and Still Pro-Choice."

"It was our choice to get pregnant again and have another baby," she said. "That was our choice. Fetal anomaly or not, being pregnant is a choice. I've always felt that way, and the anencephaly experience that we had, it just amplified my feelings about having the choice to have a baby or to continue a pregnancy."

At around six months pregnant, she awakened to news on social media that *Roe* had officially been reversed, and she began pacing. She went to take her dogs outside for a walk but collapsed in the grass, crying.

"It immediately took me back to the day I came home from my anatomy scan with a doomed baby in my stomach," she said. "All of a sudden I was taken back to that day and how horrible it felt to make that decision. But I had the ability to make that decision. And when *Roe v. Wade* was overturned, it just all came flooding back. And it was so anxiety inducing. Because someone somewhere was not able to make that decision and they were suffering. Emotionally. Physically. Like, all-around suffering."

If she had been denied an abortion and forced to carry the first pregnancy to term, she doesn't believe she would have gotten pregnant again. It would have been too traumatic, she said.

"I know if that was the reality, [if] I couldn't make the choice, in the end I probably never would have wanted to have another baby ever again," she said. "And I would have made sure that wouldn't have happened."

The second pregnancy was strikingly different from the first. Multiple ultrasounds and medical appointments indicated the fetus was healthy, and with each passing week their anxiety lightened just a little, though it never completely faded.

"I'm definitely a different person than I was before the anencephaly pregnancy," she said. "I remember wanting all of the baby stuff. I remember making the registry and planning the baby shower. It was intense. There was so much that I wanted and so much that I was looking forward to. I wanted all of the things."

Losing Little One completely altered her perspective on what their family needed. During the second pregnancy, she said she no longer desired all the traditional events and gifts and decorations, in part because she knew they could be ripped away at any moment with one piece of bad news. Their grave loss made her realize how little they truly required to be happy and raise a thriving child, she said.

Roughly three months after the fall of *Roe*, she delivered a healthy baby boy. Her partner recalled catching the newborn as he emerged from the womb, the first person to place hands on this new life entering the world.

"It was almost surreal," he said.

The mother touched and kissed the top of her baby's head, marveling at the perfectly formed ears and intact skull.

"I will never forget when it hit me," she said. "He's here. . . . He had his whole head and his whole brain. He had everything he needed to be healthy."

5.
Abortion by iPad, Phone or Mail

The college student was a little nervous yet firm in her decision as she spoke to a physician on an iPad framed by her fingertips one morning in winter 2017.[1]

"Any questions?" the doctor asked, his voice and image clear on the screen near her lap, just a few inches from the seven-week pregnancy that hadn't begun to show yet.

"No, everything has been explained very well here," responded the patient, from an examination room in a central Illinois clinic.

A nurse placed in the patient's outstretched palm a small white pill, which would stop the fetus from growing. With a few sips of water, the young woman swallowed the tablet. The doctor on the iPad screen observed from an out-of-state office hundreds of miles away.

A day or two later, the young woman would take a second medication on her own at home, ending the pregnancy.

At least twice a week, abortions at Whole Woman's Health of Peoria were performed via telemedicine, an intersection of technology and health care at the forefront of the reproductive rights debate. The clinic about 160 miles southwest of Chicago became a pioneer in remote abortion during a time when few providers in the United States offered this kind of service. About a year prior to the college student's visit, the small, one-story health center began performing telehealth medication abortions to help improve access to reproductive health care amid expanding restrictions on terminating pregnancies in the Midwest and across the nation.

For the college student, the iPad interaction came as a surprise. Telehealth medicine was still relatively rare at the time, particularly for abortion care, and she hadn't known the doctor would be off-site before her arrival at the clinic. But she said her interaction with the physician came across as very natural and the technology felt familiar. The conversation with the doctor took less than five minutes, about the same time frame as a typical first-trimester surgical abortion.

She seemed calmer, her speech less strained, after she took the pill.

"I feel so much better, I'm so glad I found this place," said the young woman, who asked not to be named. "This has been much, much simpler than I thought it would be."

Abortion pills are generally used in early pregnancy, up to 70 days' gestation, and often consist of a two-drug regimen: First the patient takes mifepristone, also known as Mifeprex, to block the hormone progesterone and stop the pregnancy from growing; that medication also causes the embryo or fetus to detach from the uterine wall.[2] The patient then takes a second pill, misoprostol, 24 to 48 hours later on her own, to make the cervix open slightly and the uterus contract, expelling the pregnancy.

Medication abortions have been available in the United States since 2000, when the U.S. Food and Drug Administration approved use of mifepristone after a long and bitter fight.[3] The two presidential candidates during this period were fiercely divided on the matter.[4] Democrat Al Gore supported the FDA's decision.[5] Republican George W. Bush—then the governor of Texas, who would go on to win the 2000 election—called the agency's actions "wrong."[6] His father, President George Bush, had banned the import of mifepristone for personal use in 1989.[7]

"I fear that making this abortion pill widespread will make abortions more and more common, rather than more and more rare," the younger Bush had said in a statement in 2000.[8]

* * *

At the Peoria clinic, the college student explained that so much of her life was in flux when she learned of her unplanned pregnancy, which she said came as a shock because she had always used condoms. The young woman still had to finish her education degree at her Illinois college, land a student teaching position and then find a permanent job.

She chose to have a medication abortion, which the Peoria clinic offered to patients who were up to 10 weeks pregnant.

"I feel like it's a less invasive process," she said. "It's more relatable, especially being a woman and having a period. . . . It just makes more sense to me, personally."

While she wasn't expecting the telehealth format—a less-prevalent form of health care then—she said she felt comfortable with the experience.

At the time, abortion via telemedicine was prohibited in 19 states, which had passed laws requiring the provider to be in the physical presence of a patient when administering the abortion pill, according to the Guttmacher Institute.[9]

Ann Scheidler of the Pro-Life Action League said she considers telehealth abortions particularly troubling.

"It's probably not ever a great idea to have a medical procedure without actually seeing the doctor," she said. "We of course would like to see all abortion outlawed. So finding other ways to get women access to an abortion is something we would never support, because it's not good health care for women and it's lethal to the unborn child."

But Whole Woman's Health president and CEO Amy Hagstrom Miller said telemedicine provides the same level of care, with precedents in other medical fields. A seven-year study of telemedicine abortions in Iowa found the method to be as safe as medical abortions where the provider is in the room with the patient, according to the findings published in the medical journal *Obstetrics and Gynecology* in 2017.[10]

"You've got abortion that is sort of legal on paper for all of us in the United States, but people's ability to access it in the first place—and access high-quality care—is so different depending on where you live," Miller said. "You shouldn't have to travel hundreds of miles to a big city to get a procedure that takes five or ten minutes."

The college student had traveled to the Peoria clinic from her home state of Missouri, which required a 72-hour waiting period prior to an abortion. There were few clinic options in Missouri, largely due to its laws mandating that abortion providers have hospital admitting privileges and that clinics meet the same standards as ambulatory surgery centers.

Whole Woman's Health—which operates clinics across the country—fought similar clinic constraints in Texas, leading to a 2016 U.S. Supreme Court ruling that declared these types of laws unconstitutional and an "undue burden."[11] The case *Whole Woman's Health v. Hellerstedt* had set the legal stage for clinics in Texas and many other states to stay open, reopen or expand to include abortion services.

The college student said she couldn't get an appointment for a surgical abortion in Missouri for a few weeks. Since she didn't want to wait any longer, she turned to neighboring Illinois. The young woman first had an ultrasound, lab work and a counseling session with clinicians on-site. Then, under observation of the off-site doctor, she took the first pill, mifepristone.

Before leaving, she was instructed to take four tablets of the second medication, misoprostol, a day or two later on her own. Mild to intense cramping and heavy bleeding typically follow. Two weeks after the abortion, patients are scheduled to come back for a follow-up with a nurse.

"I feel content," the college student said before exiting the clinic, holding a paper bag containing misoprostol and the number of an on-call nurse, as well as several pages of information specific to medication abortions and at-home care.

"Many people know and love a woman who has had an abortion," the first paragraph read. "You are not alone."

* * *

Another young woman came to the Peoria clinic later that day from Texas, bundled up against the unfamiliar Illinois winter cold in two coats, two shirts, a scarf and hat.

The decision to terminate wasn't easy, she said.

"I think you always make the decision instantly," said the woman, who also wanted to remain anonymous. "But deep down inside you're never, I don't think anyone's ever, sure that they're doing the right thing."

She found comfort after talking to a few close friends, who revealed that they had also had an abortion.

"It's not until you open up to them that you find out that they've also gone through the same experience," she said. "It's like you never know your friends go through it, because it's something no one wants to talk about."

As it happened, the young woman already had plans to travel to the Chicago area when she learned of her unplanned pregnancy. She found Whole Woman's Health online. She said she didn't come seeking a medication abortion; that just happened to be the service available the day she could make the appointment.

Other days of the week, doctors on-site perform surgical abortions. The room where telemedicine patients talk with the doctor on the iPad is typically a recovery room on surgical days, with women resting after the procedure in recliners draped with purple blankets under low lighting, some sipping herbal tea.

The Texas woman had first called another clinic in her home state but was told there was a two-week wait for the first appointment. Texas law required a 24-hour waiting period between the ultrasound and abortion, necessitating two trips.[12] When she inquired about scheduling the second appointment at the clinic, she recalled the response over the phone was "not sure."

She also worried about facing anti-abortion protesters, who were known to have a large presence at Texas clinics when abortion was still legal there, some encouraging patients to enter vans outside offering free sonograms.

"That's intimidating," she said. "It's scary. It makes you angry."

While the small clinic in Peoria also sometimes attracts protesters, none had ventured out that frigid winter day. The main entrance to the building had been reconfigured so patients could enter and exit from a back door leading to a parking lot shielded from public view.

By the time of the Texas woman's appointment, the Peoria clinic had performed roughly 630 abortions via telemedicine since it began offering this service in September 2016; about 25 percent of those patients were from out of state. At the time, telemedicine abortions were uncommon: Remote services weren't offered by any Planned Parenthood clinics in Illinois, or by most providers across the country.

One early telehealth abortion provider was Planned Parenthood of the Heartland in neighboring Iowa, which launched its program in 2008. In 2013, that state's board of medicine passed a rule barring abortion via telemedicine, but the Iowa Supreme Court later struck down the provision, declaring it unconstitutional.[13]

Then, in May 2017, Planned Parenthood announced that four Iowa clinics would close because of recent state funding cuts designed to target abortion providers.[14] One, in the Quad Cities—on the Illinois border—provided telemedicine abortions until it closed in December 2017.

"This is a case of extreme Iowa politicians deciding they know what's better for a woman's health than the women actually seeking care, with devastating consequences," Suzanna de Baca, president and CEO of Planned Parenthood of the Heartland, said in a statement. "We will do everything we can to continue to care for as many patients as we can. However, the harsh reality is that, despite all our efforts, there will be women who fall through the cracks and lose access to health care because of this dangerous legislation."

A little after noon, as the woman from Texas was in the middle of her appointment, snow began to drift outside the Peoria clinic, covering surrounding roads in an icy slush. Two patients—one traveling from Tennessee, the other in state but from hundreds of miles away—called to say they couldn't make their appointments.

"Women all the time face different barriers, whether it's transportation or funding," said Fatimah Gifford, spokeswoman for Whole Woman's Health. "The barrier that day was the weather."

The young woman from Texas put both her coats back on and wrapped her scarf tightly around her neck before leaving the clinic.

"I'm pretty sure I'll feel better once I've gone through the whole process," she said as she left. "I know when I go home, I can focus on work. On school. On life."

A few weeks later, she said she still believed she made the right choice, though it was a choice she continued to struggle with emotionally.

"You really sit down and you ask yourself, did you do the right thing?" she said. "Seeing baby clothes or anything related to babies, it reminds you of the decision you made. But it also motivates me to put effort into all of those reasons—school, work. I do want to build a better life for it when I do have a baby. To give it a better life."

* * *

The Peoria clinic closed in 2019, shortly before a revolution in remote health care took off, turning telemedicine into standard practice for abortion care as well as many other medical services, ignited largely by the COVID-19 pandemic.

In March 2020, outbreaks of the new coronavirus spurred lockdowns and stay-at-home orders across the country, disrupting all aspects of life, including abortion care. Various states, such as Iowa, Alabama, Ohio, Oklahoma, Texas, Louisiana, Arkansas and Tennessee, suspended most abortions.[15] Their elected leaders argued the procedure was a non-essential service so clinics' health care resources and protective equipment had to be conserved to battle the spread of the virus.

"This prohibition applies throughout the State and to all surgeries and procedures that are not immediately medically necessary, including routine dermatological, ophthalmological, and dental procedures, as well as most scheduled healthcare procedures that are not immediately medically necessary such as orthopedic surgeries or any type of abortion that is not medically necessary to preserve the life or health of the mother," Texas's attorney general, Ken Paxton, said in a March 2020 written statement. "The COVID-19 pandemic has increased demands for hospital beds and has created a shortage of personal protective equipment needed to protect healthcare professionals and stop transmission of the virus. Postponing surgeries and procedures that are not immediately medically necessary will ensure that hospital beds are available for those suffering from COVID-19 and that [personal protective equipment is] available for healthcare professionals."[16]

The Center for Reproductive Rights and other organizations fought back in March and April 2020, filing sweeping lawsuits across the South and Midwest demanding abortion services resume immediately. They accused these states' officials of using the coronavirus outbreak as an excuse to limit abortion access.

"These emergency abortion bans are an abuse of power and part of an ongoing effort to use sham justifications to shut down clinics and make an end run around *Roe v. Wade*," said Nancy Northrup, president and CEO of the Center for Reproductive Rights, in a written statement. "These are the same states that have tried to ban abortion access for years; no one should be fooled that this is warranted by the current crisis. We will use every legal means to ensure that abortion remains available during this critical time."[17]

By May 2020, abortions were permitted to resume in these states.[18]

Also prompted by the pandemic, the American College of Obstetricians and Gynecologists and other groups in late May 2020 filed a lawsuit challenging the FDA's mandate that mifepristone be dispensed at a hospital, clinic, or medical office.[19] The lawsuit argued that these requirements created unnecessary travel and exposure to COVID-19 at a time when the Centers for Disease Control and Prevention (CDC) was encouraging medical providers to use telehealth services when possible to decrease potential transmission of the virus.[20]

"Changes in the way that health care is delivered during this pandemic are needed to reduce staff exposure to ill persons, preserve personal protective equipment (PPE), and minimize the impact of patient surges on facilities," the CDC said on its website in June 2020. "Healthcare systems have had to adjust the way they triage, evaluate, and care for patients using methods that do not rely on in-person services. Telehealth services help provide necessary care to patients while minimizing the transmission risk of . . . the virus that causes COVID-19, to healthcare personnel (HCP) and patients."[21]

Medication abortions comprised 54 percent of all abortions in the United States in 2020, a large climb from 39 percent just a few years earlier in 2017, according to the Guttmacher Institute.[22]

If a patient could receive the medication by mail, the lawsuit argued, this could expand abortion access while limiting exposure to the virus.

"Of the more than 20,000 drugs regulated by the FDA, mifepristone is the only one that patients must receive in person at a hospital, clinic, or medical office, yet may self-administer, unsupervised, at a location of their choosing," the lawsuit said. "If not for this restriction, patients seeking abortion or miscarriage care who have obtained a prescription for mifepristone based on a telemedicine consultation or prior in-person visit could obtain the medication safely by mail without facing needless [COVID-19] exposure."

The FDA was court ordered to temporarily lift mifepristone's dispensing requirements in July 2020, but the Trump administration challenged the change and the Supreme Court reinstated the regulations in January 2021.[23] The most conservative lawmakers waged battle against the drug. Senator Ted Cruz of Texas and a group of other Republican senators in a September 2020 letter urged the FDA to classify mifepristone as an "imminent hazard to the public health," a change that would mean the removal of the pill from the market.[24]

"As you are surely aware, pregnancy is not a life-threatening illness, and the abortion pill does not cure or prevent any disease," said the letter. "Nevertheless, this pill that is specifically designed and intended to kill preborn children was raced to the market, with devastating consequences."

Then, in April 2021, under the Biden administration, the FDA announced that it would temporarily stop enforcement of the dispensing restrictions during the pandemic.[25] This allowed mifepristone to be mailed directly to patients in states with laws that permit the practice. The move was a game-changer for reproductive health care: In some cases, patients would be able to end their pregnancies without ever leaving their homes.

"We are pleased to see mifepristone regulated on the basis of the scientific evidence during the pandemic, rather than political bias against comprehensive reproductive health care, and we look forward to working with policy makers to ensure this principle governs post-pandemic care," the American College of Obstetricians and Gynecologists said in a statement.[26]

One of the providers in southern Illinois began offering telehealth and mail-order medication abortions a few months later.[27] Planned Parenthood of the St. Louis Region and Southwest Missouri had launched the program for Illinois residents in July 2020 to try and break down some of the barriers to traditional abortion care, such as long travel distances to get to a clinic, transportation challenges and difficulty securing childcare.

Some Illinois patients opted to have abortion pills shipped to their addresses overnight, via FedEx; the rest picked up their medication at the Planned Parenthood Fairview Heights (Illinois) Health Center, near St. Louis.

The service had to be suspended amid the court battle but was reinstated once the FDA temporarily ceased enforcement.

"We really strongly feel folks should have the abortion experience that they want, and that can mean a number of different things," said Dr. Colleen McNicholas, chief medical officer for Planned Parenthood of the St. Louis Region and Southwest Missouri.

Now patients can have their abortion appointments at work, during a lunch break. Women with kids might choose telemedicine over traditional in-person appointments to avoid the need for childcare. In rural areas, telehealth abortions can preclude hours of travel, overnight lodging and expensive transportation.

Some women also choose at-home access due to the stigma surrounding abortion. Telehealth visits and mail-order pills allow patients to bypass throngs of protesters that often gather at abortion clinics, McNicholas said.

"There is some real psychological harm that's done to folks as they have to navigate that experience," she said.

* * *

In a historic shift, the FDA in December 2021 permanently rolled back the long-standing restrictions on mifepristone, allowing abortion by mail in less restrictive states just a few months before the Supreme Court's reversal of *Roe*.[28]

The American College of Obstetricians and Gynecologists applauded the end to these regulations, reiterating that the professional organization considers medication abortions safe and effective.[29]

"Decades of evidence and the consensus of the medical community underscore that mifepristone is a safe medication, the FDA requirements do not benefit patients, and the FDA requirements disproportionately burden communities already facing structural barriers to care, including people of color and those living long distances from a healthcare professional," the organization said in a written statement.[30]

While reproductive rights advocates considered the rollback a victory, the change was decried by abortion opponents, who argued in part that the decision would compromise the safety of pregnant patients.

"Every life is sacred: the lives of mothers and the lives of the unborn," said Archbishop William Lori of Baltimore, chairman of the U.S. Conference of Catholic Bishops' Committee on Pro-Life Activities, in a statement. "Not only does this decision further the tragic taking of unborn lives but it does little to care for the well-being of women in need. Far from the accompaniment that women in crisis pregnancies deserve, this decision would leave women alone in the midst of trauma, often without any medical attention or follow up care."[31]

This backlash resulted in a slew of new regulations and prohibitions targeted specifically at abortion pills, which would become a prime battlefront of reproductive rights post-*Roe*.

"Medication abortion has become a primary target of anti-abortion politicians and activists seeking to restrict care in and out of clinical settings," a 2022 Guttmacher Institute report said. "Anti-abortion state policymakers have shown they are focused on further restricting access to medication abortion this year."[32]

In 2022, more than 100 restrictions were introduced in 22 states, including seven provisions that would entirely ban medication abortion, according to the Guttmacher report. Some of the other measures would specifically prohibit mailing abortion pills or would require physicians to provide medication abortions, as opposed to allowing other clinicians, such as advanced practice nurses or physician assistants, to do so.[33]

Yet it's unclear how states will enforce these regulations since numerous websites as well as providers in other countries offer the medications online, often without a prescription or medical information.

A 2017 study published in the journal *Contraception* found that abortion pills could easily be obtained from pharmaceutical websites without submitting a script.[34] Five researchers in Texas, Washington, California and New York were able to buy 18 mifepristone-misoprostol combination packs from more than a dozen websites. None of the packages included instructions, and some of the blister packaging containing the pills was damaged.

But laboratory testing found that most of the products contained the correct ingredients in sufficient amounts to cause an early abortion, according to the study, which was conducted by public health care organizations Gynuity Health Projects and Plan C.[35]

"Our study found no evidence that, at the time of the study, mifepristone and misoprostol products sold online were dangerous or ineffective," the study said. "We encourage reproductive health providers, advocates and policy makers to think creatively about how the internet might be useful for enhancing access to safe and effective abortion in the United States and other similarly disadvantaged settings."[36]

* * *

After the end of *Roe,* abortion pills became a new frontier in reproductive and sexual health care. As abortion bans and new restrictions emerged, medication abortions grew increasingly accessible to more patients.

Students at the University of California and California State University were able to access medication abortions more easily after January 1, 2023, when a state law went into effect requiring that public university campus health centers provide abortion pills. The statute estimated that more than 400,000 women attend California's state university campuses and noted that it's "central to the mission of California's public university student health centers to minimize the negative impact of health concerns on students' studies and to facilitate retention and graduation."

"Students seeking early pregnancy termination, especially those enrolled at institutions outside of major urban centers, face prohibitively expensive travel, often without reliable means of transportation, to a clinic that may require hours of travel from their campus, out of their city, county, or even geographic region," the law stated. "These financial and time burdens negatively impact academic performance and mental health."[37]

Abortion pills by mail became available to residents throughout Illinois a few weeks before *Roe* was struck down. Planned Parenthood of Illinois began offering the service in April 2022, eliminating the need for many abortion patients to ever visit a brick-and-mortar health care facility.[38] The agency—which covers most of Illinois except the southernmost portion—had been prescribing medication abortions through telehealth visits since 2021. But patients still had to visit a clinic to pick up the pills, under the FDA's old regulations.

Once the rules were revised, patients across Illinois could have the pills mailed to an in-state address. The agency said the new program would also free up clinic space for patients who need in-person services as well as those traveling from other states. The pill-by-mail service was only available to in-state residents: Patients from other states could still access medication abortions but had to first physically go to Illinois to have a telehealth or in-person visit with a clinician and then pick up the medication at an in-state health center.[39]

"Now more than ever it's crucial that our patients can access the care they need, when and where they need it," said Dr. Amy Whitaker, Planned Parenthood of Illinois chief medical officer. "There are over 20 years of data demonstrating the safety and effectiveness of medication abortion using mifepristone. Not only is this a safe method but it also increases access to care, especially for people of color, people living in rural areas and people with low incomes who already face barriers to care."[40]

Then, a few months after *Roe*'s end, an online clinic began offering abortion pills to patients who aren't even pregnant so the medications can be kept on hand.[41] The novel approach allowed those who haven't even conceived yet to stock mifepristone and misoprostol for future use. Choix, a sexual and reproductive health start-up, launched the service called "advance provision" in September 2022.[42]

"Everyone should be able to access supportive, nonjudgmental and trusted abortion," Choix CEO and nurse practitioner Cindy Adam said in a news release. "Unfortunately, we know that isn't the case for the countless people who increasingly face barriers to accessing abortion care in the U.S."[43]

The company promotes the ease and simplicity of the process: Patients fill out a questionnaire online, which includes questions about their medical history. Questionnaires are reviewed within 48 hours by the clinic's health care practitioners; a medical provider then text messages the patient to confirm information and send consent forms, the website says.

If a patient becomes pregnant in the future and decides to use the abortion pills, "we ask that they return to Choix for medical support and guidance throughout their abortion process," Adam said. Once the patient returns and completes a new medical intake, a clinician will evaluate the patient's information to ensure it's still safe to take the medications, she said.[44]

She added that health care providers review medical information such as the patient's last menstrual period or any bleeding or other irregular symptoms, as well as indications that an ultrasound might be needed.

"Telehealth in general is built on mutual trust within the patient-provider relationship, and it's core to our approach to care at Choix," Adam said. "We trust that our patients know their bodies and health histories and want the best outcomes for themselves."

Eric Scheidler, executive director of the Pro-Life Action League, called the service "a cynical marketing ploy to get women to effectively choose abortion before they're even pregnant."

"The American medical community is so drunk on abortion that now they want to sell abortion pills to women who aren't even pregnant, without regard for the risks involved in providing a treatment without any in-person consultation, and without regard to changes in medical history between the time of dispensing and use," he said. "Moreover, this proposal betrays blood-chilling hostility to unborn children—as if pregnancy itself were a deadly medical condition."

He lamented the FDA's scaled-back regulations, calling the policy change "tragic, because it leads to more abortion."

"Medication abortions seem to be more palatable to women, less obviously an act of violence against an innocent unborn child than surgical abortion," Scheidler said. "But this policy also makes it easy for abortion pills to be diverted—to other states, to sex traffickers, to boyfriends unhappy with a girlfriend's pregnancy, to minors seeking to skirt parental involvement laws."

Scheidler predicted abortion pills—both legally prescribed and unregulated—would become ubiquitous in Illinois and beyond.

"Illinois has embraced a new identity as the abortion capital of the Midwest, especially as the landscape is changing in other states," he said. "I expect to see Illinois become a major source for abortion pills for the entire region, both legally and clandestinely. Unfortunately, neither the public nor policymakers will be able to say with any confidence where those abortion pills really wind up."

* * *

Then, in April 2023, the decision of one Trump-appointed judge in Texas threatened to grind the post-*Roe* abortion pill revolution to a halt. In an unprecedented case, Judge Matthew Kacsmaryk of the Northern District of Texas ordered a hold on the FDA's approval of mifepristone, determining that the agency "acquiesced on its legitimate safety concerns—in violation of its statutory duty—based on plainly unsound reasoning and studies that did not support its conclusions," according to the ruling.[45] Although mifepristone had been used by millions of patients over the past two decades, the future of the abortifacient was suddenly in jeopardy.

The judge also raised questions about the legality of abortion pill-by-mail services. Kacsmaryk's ruling appeared to side with plaintiffs in the case—which was filed by the conservative Christian organization Alliance Defending Freedom on behalf of health care practitioners—who argued the mailing of abortion pills violates the 1873 Comstock Act. That 150-year-old law bars transporting by mail any "article, instrument, substance, drug, medicine, or thing which is advertised or described in a manner calculated to lead another to use or apply it for producing abortion."[46]

Named after Anthony Comstock, the head of the New York Society for the Suppression of Vice, the act "was the closest the federal government ever came to entering the abortion crusade," James Mohr wrote in *Abortion in America*.[47]

"Under this law of 1873 Comstock himself became a special agent of the national government empowered to enforce the act's provisions," Mohr wrote. "In this capacity Comstock became the country's best-known pursuer of abortionists for the remainder of the 1870s. In each of the years from 1873 through 1877 he probably prosecuted more abortionists, usually through their advertisements, than any other person in the United States. Indeed, in the wake of Comstock's first five years of federal activity, abortion-related advertising declined precipitously throughout the nation. Abortionists turned more and more frequently to the use of private cards and handbills by the middle of the 1870s, and those advertisements that remained in openly circulated publications were far more veiled than they had earlier been."

But the Comstock Act had rarely been applied when abortion rights were guaranteed under *Roe*.

The fate of the popular abortion drug seemed to be up in the air as battling court orders came down simultaneously. The same day the Texas judge ruled, an Obama-appointed district judge in the state of Washington handed down an order that appeared to be in direct conflict. Seventeen states—including Illinois—and the District of Columbia had proactively filed a lawsuit to protect access to mifepristone, and Judge Thomas Rice prohibited U.S. officials from making any changes that would restrict the use of the drug, at least in those states that had sued.[48]

With the fate of mifepristone uncertain, some Illinois clinics had a backup plan to continue offering medication abortions even in the drug's absence. Planned Parenthood of Illinois officials said their health centers would use multiple doses of misoprostol—a medication used to treat a number of medical conditions—as an alternative to the mifepristone-misoprostol regimen.[49]

But misoprostol alone is less effective than when used in combination with mifepristone, experts say. Using only the first drug can also be more burdensome on patients, particularly those traveling for care, because a dose of the medication is required every three hours or so, for three to four rounds of doses, depending on the gestation length of the pregnancy, Planned Parenthood of Illinois officials said.

"We also acknowledge that it will cause hardships for our patients," said Jennifer Welch, president and CEO of Planned Parenthood of Illinois. "It might mean that they have to stay longer or spend more time in Illinois. So it would be more difficult and more costly, so we're trying to prepare for all of that."

The American College of Obstetricians and Gynecologists says the use of mifepristone for medication abortions is safe and effective.

"It is one of the safest drugs on the market," said Molly Meegan, chief legal officer and general counsel with the professional membership organization. "It has been used for decades."

The organization's clinical guidelines recommend a combination of mifepristone and misoprostol as "the preferred therapy for medication abortion because they are significantly more effective than misoprostol-only regimens."[50]

"If a combined mifepristone-misoprostol regimen is not available, a misoprostol-only regimen is the recommended alternative," the guidelines say.

"It's not as effective, but it's still very effective," Meegan added. "And it's very safe."

In the wake of the court challenges, several Democrat-led states also began stockpiling abortion drugs. California governor Gavin

Newsom announced that his state had "secured an emergency stockpile of up to 2 million pills of misoprostol, a safe and effective medication abortion drug, in the wake of an extremist judge seeking to block mifepristone, a critical abortion pill."[51]

Maura Healey, governor of Massachusetts, posted on Twitter that the University of Massachusetts and health care providers had begun stockpiling mifepristone, at her request.

"Mifepristone is safe and effective. It's been the gold standard for over two decades," she tweeted. "We're keeping it available in Massachusetts—no matter what some extremist, Trump-appointed judge in Texas says."[52]

Then, in late April 2023, the U.S. Supreme Court preserved access to mifepristone for the time being, as the case continued to move through the lower courts.[53]

"While this is a temporary win for abortion rights, the battle is far from over," Planned Parenthood of Illinois said in a written statement.[54] "We will continue to fight and advocate for equitable access to all reproductive and sexual health care services because everyone should have the ability to make a decision that is best for their bodies, their lives, and their futures."

* * *

The more-than-a-century-old Comstock Act began inspiring communities to pass ordinances targeting abortion pills, often as a backlash against new abortion clinics settling in pro–reproductive rights states.

One of them was the city of Danville in central Illinois, about three hours south of downtown Chicago. After a heated meeting in May 2023, the city council there narrowly approved an ordinance that banned the shipping and mailing of abortion medications, which invoked the Comstock Act.[55] The measure followed recent news that an Indiana abortion provider had purchased property in Danville, just a few minutes from the Indiana border. At a protest at the site of the future clinic, Mary Kate Zander, executive director of Illinois Right to Life, argued the abortion provider was unwelcomed by residents.[56]

"This is a conservative community," Zander said. "It's a conservative, pro-life community that wants to support women, that wants to support women who are experiencing crisis pregnancies—that is not interested in killing babies."

Illinois leaders and the American Civil Liberties Union of Illinois had warned Danville leaders that the measure was illegal and would only risk litigation. Prior to passing the ordinance, the council amended it so it could not go into effect until the city "obtains a declaratory judgment from a court" that the ordinance could be enacted and enforced, and all court appeals would have to be exhausted. Some city leaders seemed to believe the language would protect them from lawsuits.

Illinois attorney general Kwame Raoul said the last-minute amendment meant the ordinance was not in effect and he added that it "will not take effect."

"Even if the city's ordinance is merely symbolic, I do not want it to instill fear and confusion," he said in a statement. "Let me be clear: All residents of Illinois continue to enjoy the fundamental rights guaranteed to them under state law, and my office will continue to ensure that all localities in the state understand that access to reproductive health care is a fundamental right in Illinois."[57]

Several communities in New Mexico—another state with strong reproductive rights protections—had recently passed similar ordinances citing the Comstock Act, though the New Mexico Supreme Court blocked them from being enforced amid challenges.[58]

The Danville ordinance drew hundreds of demonstrators—both for and against abortion access—to the city council meeting, where they packed the meeting room and spilled outside. For more than three hours, members of the public offered passionate and emotional perspectives on moral issues as weighty as bodily autonomy and when life begins.

One speaker during the public comment session recounted the pain following her own abortion.

"It is trauma and it affects you for the rest of your life, if you do not find a way to heal through that," she told the council.

Another speaker said the ordinance was critical to protect the sanctity of life.

"My perspective is pretty simple: Life begins at conception," the man said. "The rights of any human to end or terminate another life, that's where their rights end. . . . It's not about religious right. It is about preserving life."

Others supported the prospect of an abortion clinic settling in the community.

"Danville rests in the great state of Illinois," one woman told the council. "Our state laws protect women and their personal health choices."

Another woman implored the council to vote against the ordinance, arguing it would jeopardize the health and safety of women.

"With this ordinance, we're actively trying to prevent a women's healthcare clinic from opening," she said. "This clinic can provide necessary and safe services to women in our community. It's more than just abortion. This is vital. Passing this ordinance will not stop women from seeking out abortion services. It will, however, encourage women to seek unhealthy means to terminate their pregnancies, isolate themselves from those around them due to fear of getting in trouble or paying heavy fines that most people are unable to afford."

6.
Tiny Footprints

Their family was about to be complete.

Cyndi Portteus of the Indianapolis area recalled that her belly was already quite swollen during the ultrasound at 22 weeks, when she and her husband learned they were having a boy in August 2013.[1] They both loved the name William.

Her second pregnancy felt no different from her first, when she had carried her healthy, thriving daughter about two years earlier. It was her husband who noticed the ultrasound technician seemed to linger around the heart more than the rest of the image on the screen, the first subtle sign something wasn't quite right.

Then there was an unusually long span of time between the technician's exiting the examination room and the obstetrician's arrival. Later Cyndi would learn her physician had spent that time on the phone making emergency appointments with specialists.

"We were just looking forward to seeing our baby," Cyndi said. "I was blissfully ignorant during the ultrasound. I was just happy we were having another baby. We were very happy to have our boy."

A fetal echocardiogram shortly after revealed the rare birth defect: hypoplastic left heart syndrome, which afflicts approximately 960 babies born in the United States each year, according to the Indiana Department of Health.[2] The left side of the heart, which is responsible for pumping oxygenated blood throughout the body, was too small and underdeveloped to perform this critical function.

The expectant mother wished there was a way to keep the son she longed for in her womb forever. Her child was safe in utero, nourished by her oxygen-rich blood.

"But once they've been birthed and they're not in their mom, that's when they're really in danger," she said.

There was very little time to determine the fate of the pregnancy because it was so far along. Specialists went over the options. One was a series of three open-heart surgeries, the initial one shortly after birth, likely followed by lifelong medical care. While statistics online varied, Cyndi said her baby was given a 50 percent chance of survival to age five. Another alternative was delivery followed by hospice care, keeping the baby comfortable until his natural death.

The third choice was termination for medical reasons.

At the time, Indiana law prohibited abortion past 20 weeks post-fertilization—or 22 weeks into pregnancy as calculated by physicians—unless the pregnant patient's life or physical health was endangered.[3] Nationwide, nine states had banned abortion at about 20 weeks post-fertilization as of October 2022, according to the Guttmacher Institute.[4]

Ending a pregnancy that's this far along is extremely uncommon: Most abortions take place in early pregnancy, with almost 93 percent of terminations nationwide performed before 13 weeks' gestation, according to CDC abortion data from 2019.[5] A little over 6 percent occurred between 14 and 20 weeks, and less than 1 percent of pregnancies were terminated at or after 21 weeks.

"Nearly 99 percent of abortions occur before 21 weeks, but when they are needed later in pregnancy, it's often in very complex circumstances," according to the website of Planned Parenthood Action Fund, the agency's advocacy group, in a criticism of early gestational abortion bans. "For example, severe fetal anomalies and serious risks to the pregnant person's health—the kind of situations where patients and their doctors need every medical option available."[6]

Gestational limits often hit before or right around the time when a 20-week ultrasound scan, sometimes referred to as an autonomy scan, is often performed to check fetal development; it's the time when a host of congenital conditions can be detected, including heart abnormalities, missing kidneys, a hole in the diaphragm, bone problems,

Down syndrome, spina bifida and anencephaly, where the fetal brain, skull and scalp don't develop in utero.[7]

One physician suggested Cyndi could try appealing to an in-state hospital's medical ethics board after 22 weeks, given the dire health of the fetus. This would have given the family more time to seek out other experts and consider their choices, with termination still a possibility. But that doctor also warned that a ruling might not be favorable with post-delivery surgery still an option, even though the prognosis was poor.

This process would also take time, potentially threatening the backup plan: traveling a few hours across the border to neighboring Illinois, which permitted abortion until fetal viability, generally considered to be around 24 to 26 weeks into pregnancy.

"What these 20-week bans force people into is making faster decisions than they want to," Cyndi said.

* * *

While Cyndi was growing up in a conservative Catholic family in rural Indiana, her views on abortion were generally ambivalent. In her early twenties, while getting a master's degree in Indianapolis, she shifted to staunchly pro-choice. While it was not a right she would ever need, she reasoned at the time, it was not a choice she could make for anyone else.

Looking back, she considered her younger self to be a bit naive.

When she and her husband weighed their alternatives, the rounds of surgery seemed so intense and the chance of success so small. The prospect of delivering a baby into certain death also didn't feel right, she said.

One week after that first troubling ultrasound, she was at a Chicago hospital getting the opinion of a final physician before ending the pregnancy.

The night before the procedure was agonizing, she recalled.

"We'd made our decision at that point, but he's still kicking, he's still getting good oxygenated blood," she said. "We had seen my son's heart in 3D. They can turn on colors that show you the blood flow through the heart. We had seen my son's heart through nine million angles."

She was grateful she was able to terminate the pregnancy at a hospital and didn't have to traverse a line of protests at an abortion clinic. Yet she was still astounded that she had to travel out of state for treatment.

"The fact that we had to leave the state to seek medical care is just mind-blowing," she said.

Afterward, empty and numb, she went through the motions of life as if in a fog for the rest of that painful month of August.

The hospital was able to get prints of her son's tiny feet on the kind of card often given to the parents of newborns. Lines reserved for a baby's name, birth date and size remained conspicuously blank. She fingered that ink-stained paper while sitting at her kitchen table on a recent weekday afternoon.

It was the right choice, she said, but one made with no good alternatives.

"Suddenly you're not pregnant, and you don't have a baby," she said. "It's awful."

In 2016, when Mike Pence was governor of Indiana, he signed a bill that included a ban on abortions based on the race, sex or disability of the fetus.[8]

"I believe that a society can be judged by how it deals with its most vulnerable—the aged, the infirm, the disabled and the unborn," Pence tweeted.[9]

This provision was blocked by a federal judge and argued up to the U.S. Supreme Court, which in 2019 declined to hear the case challenging that portion of the law in *Box v. Planned Parenthood of Indiana and Kentucky*.[10] Even though the high court didn't take up the matter, Justice Clarence Thomas addressed the issue, likening terminations on the basis of sex, race or disability to modern-day eugenics.

"Enshrining a constitutional right to an abortion based solely on the race, sex, or disability of an unborn child, as Planned Parenthood advocates, would constitutionalize the views of the 20th-century eugenics movement," he said in his opinion. "In other contexts, the Court has been zealous in vindicating the rights of people even potentially subjected to race, sex, and disability discrimination. . . . Although the Court declines to wade into these issues today, we cannot avoid them forever."[11]

The Guttmacher Institute in a 2020 report countered that "U.S. bans on sex- and race-selective abortions send the message that women, and especially women of color, cannot be trusted to make their own medical decisions."[12]

As for bans on abortion in cases of genetic fetal anomaly, the Guttmacher Institute said these measures "restrict individuals' ability to make decisions that are best for themselves and their families."

To Cyndi, these laws seem "horribly inhuman," particularly for prospective parents who might have undergone years of fertility treatments before learning of a potentially life-threatening defect.

Cyndi had expected to give birth on December 13, 2013. That night, she conceived once again. About nine months later, after another pregnancy laced with fear and anxiety and many nerve-racking ultrasounds, she gave birth to a son with a healthy heart.

"It was healing," she said.

His name is August William. The baby grew into an impish little boy who loved to follow his big sister everywhere, completing their family.

* * *

The demise of *Roe* had major implications for prenatal screening in large sections of the country where abortion was suddenly banned entirely or severely restricted.

The American College of Obstetricians and Gynecologists recommends noninvasive genetic screening be discussed with and offered to all patients, regardless of maternal age or risk of chromosomal abnormalities. Patients should also be offered a second-trimester fetal anatomy ultrasound to check for structural defects, and "ideally this procedure is performed between 18 and 22 weeks of gestation," according to the professional organization.[13]

While the end of federal abortion rights didn't immediately alter access to prenatal testing, it did severely compromise the option to terminate for many patients when testing reveals anomalies or defects. By December 2022, about a dozen states were enforcing total abortion bans, some with exceptions for rape, incest and threat to maternal life; a few had exceptions for "lethal fetal anomalies."[14] But some experts say lethal fetal anomalies can be hard to define in practice.

"Bans in several states contain exceptions for lethal fetal anomalies, usually limited to those anomalies that would result in the death of the baby at birth or soon after," a May 2023 report by KFF stated.[15] "As with health exceptions, lethal fetal anomaly exceptions are poorly defined and limited in statute."

At the time, 14 states had abortion restrictions where "no diagnostic testing could be completed in time for a patient to terminate the pregnancy legally," according to a March 2023 article in *Obstetrics and Gynecology*.[16] Several states specifically prohibited termination based on fetal abnormality; roughly a half dozen states had gestational limits on abortion before many forms of genetic screening and diagnostic testing could be performed, from 6 to 20 weeks' gestation.

"Providing timely genetic testing results is essential to improve the equity of reproductive options for pregnant individuals throughout the United States," the article stated. "Choosing whether to terminate a pregnancy after receiving an abnormal genetic test result is a nuanced and personal decision."[17]

The National Society for Genetic Counselors, the American Society of Human Genetics and the American College of Medical Genetics have all opposed the overturning of *Roe*, calling the decision "unprecedented and deeply alarming."[18]

"As genetics and genomics medical and research organizations, we affirm our belief that all pregnant people deserve care, including access to abortion, based on scientific and clinical evidence and their personal choices," the organizations said in a joint statement. "Board-certified professionals provide accurate, evidence-based and unbiased information that allows patients to make informed reproductive choices. Legislation restricting access to abortion denies our patients the ability to make informed decisions about their healthcare based on prenatal imaging or diagnosis."

* * *

Nancy Kreuzer keeps a sonogram picture on her bedroom dresser, next to photos of her adult daughter and son.[19] The grainy black-and-white image is a tangible remnant of her other child, the one who was never born.

At 22 weeks' gestation, the daughter she very much wanted was diagnosed with hydrocephalus and Down syndrome, recalled Nancy, who lives in suburban Chicago. There was an abnormal buildup of fluid in the brain and neck of the fetus. Due to the fetal anomaly, Nancy said her doctor advised terminating the pregnancy.

"There were so many signs that the scars from that abortion existed, and they went on for years and years and years," Nancy said. "There's just this huge emptiness. It wasn't until years later . . . in a flashback I recalled sitting there and remembering the movement of my child in my womb. And then you leave, and there's no movement."

There were lilacs blooming outside her bedroom window at the time when she had her abortion. Years after the procedure, the scent of lilacs still nauseated her. Although she tried to keep her feelings buried, emotions would emerge violently and unexpectedly at times. Once, at the Museum of Science and Industry in Chicago, she passed by an exhibit on prenatal development, a collection of 24 human embryos and fetuses, ranging from 28 days to 38 weeks of gestation. At the sight of the five-month-old fetus on display, she broke down and was inconsolable.

She said she named her daughter Melanie. If given a chance to go back, she said, she would have carried the pregnancy to term. The baby was sick, Nancy said, but that didn't make her any less human or worthy of life.

"I thought, had she lived, what a not-so-perfect baby would have meant," she said. "I thought of some of the Down syndrome children that I do know and what their contribution is to us as a society. It's huge. And I think we're losing that."

News reports around the globe in the mid- to late 2010s noted plummeting rates of Down syndrome in some European nations, primarily due to advances in prenatal testing and abortion.[20]

One of the most striking examples was Iceland, where Down syndrome has all but disappeared in the Nordic country of about 366,000 people. On average, only about two or three babies with Down syndrome had been born there each year over the previous decade, according to the Icelandic Ministry of Welfare in 2018.[21] About 6,000 babies are born with the chromosomal condition in the United States annually, about 1 in every 700 births, according to CDC statistics.[22]

CBS News reported on Iceland's steep decline in Down syndrome births in 2017, and a tweet promoting the story drew a firestorm: "Iceland is on pace to virtually eliminate Down syndrome through abortion."[23]

Abortion opponents were incensed.

"Truly sad," Senator Ted Cruz, a Republican from Texas, tweeted. "Downs children should be cherished, not ended."[24]

Also outraged was actor Patricia Heaton, famous for her portrayal of sitcom moms on the shows *Everyone Loves Raymond* and *The Middle.*

"Iceland isn't actually eliminating Down syndrome," she tweeted. "They're just killing everybody that has it. Big difference."[25]

Former vice presidential candidate Sarah Palin, whose son Trig was born with Down syndrome in 2008, said during a Fox News interview that she couldn't get through the entire CBS report "without my heart just absolutely breaking."

"Because this intolerance for people who may not look like you, it's just so—so wrong," she said. "It's so evil."[26]

The Icelandic Ministry of Welfare issued a press release clarifying "misleading information" about the birth of children with Down syndrome there.[27]

"Among the misconceptions which have been promoted is the claim that the policy has been adopted by the Icelandic authorities of preventing mothers from giving birth to children with Down's syndrome," the government agency said, adding that all pregnant women in Iceland are offered prenatal care, including screening for chromosomal disorders.

The choice to accept or decline screening is the decision of the prospective mother, the statement said, and on average 15 to 20 percent of pregnant people choose not to undergo a screening of the fetus.

"Screening only reveals whether there is an increased probability of the fetus having Down's syndrome, and further tests are needed to confirm this," the agency said. "Some 15 to 20 percent of women who are informed of the increased probability of Down's syndrome following screening elect to continue the pregnancy and decline further testing in this regard."

The agency added in the statement that the government of Iceland respects diversity and the rights of the disabled.

Since 2016, numerous states, including Ohio, Arkansas, Kentucky, Missouri, Utah and Tennessee, have tried to prohibit abortion in cases of a potential fetal anomaly or bar medical providers from offering information to patients about abortion after an anomaly is detected.[28] Many of those state statutes, however, were blocked by the courts when *Roe* was intact.

The ACLU in a 2019 opinion piece published in *The Hill* called this type of abortion ban "offensive" and accused its supporters of hypocrisy.[29] Citing an Ohio measure, the ACLU noted that the law didn't include any resources to help parents raise children, nor expand services or protections for people with disabilities.

As for Nancy, she said she hopes the undoing of *Roe* will help heal some of the divisiveness in the nation.

"I felt a lot of hope *Roe* might be overturned, not just because of how I personally feel about the travesty of abortion but also hope that in the long run the divisions in our country might dissipate," she said. "I realize that could take some time. But perhaps it could give way to a more peaceful future for us all."

The matter of abortion rights should have always been a state matter, she said.

"Kicking it back to the states, and to those who the states elect, would give the people of that state more of a voice in deciding how they want to proceed with the subject of abortion," she said.

She often protests at abortion clinics, holding a sign that reads "I regret my abortion." Sometimes people ask if she wants terminating a pregnancy to be illegal.

"I think what I really want is for abortion to never have to be considered," she said. "Because I don't want another woman to ever have to go through what I did. And I certainly don't want her pre-born baby to have to go through it."

7.
Funerals for Fetal Remains

Although 40 years had passed since her abortion, the woman at the cemetery still felt a sense of loss and sorrow that transcended time. Someone will always be missing, was how Jennifer Shea described the pain following her decision at 19 to terminate an unplanned pregnancy in 1979. The memory of the child who was never born will be with her forever.[1]

Yet she finds some comfort and peace while praying at the site of a small tombstone inscribed with the epitaph *Holy Innocents Preborn Children of God.* The slate slab marks the grave of hundreds of fetal remains, which were salvaged by anti-abortion activists from an old clinic in downtown Chicago and later buried at St. Mary Catholic Cemetery in the southwest suburb of Evergreen Park.

Each year, opponents of abortion gather at this burial place for an event called the National Day of Remembrance for Aborted Children. The prayer vigil is one of about 200 similar memorials held simultaneously at cemeteries scattered across the country, many containing other burial grounds dedicated to fetal remains. Jennifer was a featured speaker at the event at St. Mary on September 14, 2019.

"It's the least I can do to honor my own lost child, to honor each of those here and to honor God for the mercy and forgiveness he has shown me," she told the crowd of about 80 who also came to commemorate the unborn.

Usually these fetal tissues are considered medical waste, often disposed of in landfills or incinerated alongside the byproducts of other medical treatments or surgeries. Yet abortion opponents have long held that fetal remains deserve a dignified end, with the same rites and rituals afforded any human death. Increasingly, court rulings and state legislation have been favoring this position, sparking emotional debates about what fetal remains signify and how they should be treated in their final disposition.

The U.S. Supreme Court in 2019 upheld a provision of an Indiana law that required cremation or burial following an abortion or miscarriage that takes place at a medical facility, mandating fetal remains be separated from other surgical tissue.[2] The legislation had been signed by Governor Mike Pence, who tweeted he was proud to have signed a law that "requires remains of aborted babies be treated with dignity and respect" and called the court's decision "a victory for life."[3]

While the outcome of the case, *Box v. Planned Parenthood*, didn't restrict patients from accessing abortions, pro-choice advocates saw the ruling as a harbinger of the high court's newfound—and extremely conservative—stance on reproductive freedoms. The language of the majority opinion, sprinkled with phrases like "aborted children," was particularly telling.[4]

"Indiana law prohibits abortion providers from treating the bodies of aborted children as 'infectious waste' and incinerating them alongside used needles, laboratory animal carcasses, and surgical byproducts," Justice Clarence Thomas wrote. "I would have thought it could go without saying that nothing in the Constitution or any decision of this Court prevents a State from requiring abortion facilities to provide for the respectful treatment of human remains."

Planned Parenthood officials accused Indiana officials of trying to "shame and stigmatize women and families," adding that these requirements for fetal remains had "nothing to do with medical care."

After Indiana's win, other states followed. The governor of Ohio signed a law requiring that aborted fetuses be disposed of "in a humane manner" in December 2020, but the law was blocked by the courts in 2022.[5] Texas in September 2019 tried to revive its burial-of-fetal-remains law, which was previously blocked by a federal judge.[6]

In September 2022, a federal judge in Indiana temporarily blocked the state from enforcing its fetal-remains-disposition law. A new lawsuit had been filed in 2020 on behalf of Indianapolis abortion clinic

Women's Med Group, which included three anonymous women, each listed as "Jane Doe," and several of its employees. The judge ruled that the measure violated the free speech and religious freedoms of individuals who don't believe fetuses must be buried or cremated.[7]

Plaintiffs Jane Doe 1 and Jane Doe 3 both had had aspiration abortions at Women's Med Group and the clinic had stored tissue from those procedures awaiting the outcome of the legal proceedings because both patients "believe that treating fetal tissue as anything other than medical waste violates their moral and religious beliefs," according to court documents.

Jane Doe 3 explained to the court that, based on her Baptist faith, she understands the Bible to indicate that "life begins at the first breath, following birth" as opposed to in the womb, court documents stated. Doe 3 felt that "burial and cremation are religious rituals reserved for people and animals with souls."[8] Jane Doe 1 said she had a moral rather than religious belief that fetal tissue isn't the remains of a person and sued so the clinic could dispose of the remains "using standard medical means."[9]

"Both Doe Plaintiffs believe that burying or cremating the tissue signified that the fetal tissue was a person," court documents said. "They further believe that treating the tissue as standard medical waste signifies that the fetal tissue is not a person."

But in May 2023, the U.S. Supreme Court declined the chance to review the case, once again allowing the Indiana fetal remains law to stand.[10]

New debates have also emerged about ethical use of fetal tissues in science and medicine. The Trump administration in 2019 announced that it would deviate from standard practice by barring government scientists from using human fetal tissue in medical research.[11]

This was long a priority of the president's pro-life supporters but was generally denounced by the scientific community.

"This research is critical for the development of new treatments for a wide range of serious diseases," states a July 2019 letter to the secretary of the U.S. Department of Health and Human Services signed by dozens of science and medical organizations. "Decades of thoughtful deliberation on fetal tissue research has provided an ethical and regulatory framework for valuable medical research to progress, enabling the discovery of therapies that would not otherwise have been possible."[12]

Contentions flared again in 2020 during the COVID-19 pandemic. Scientists and physicians appealed to the White House to reverse the prohibition, arguing the ban hindered the potential to uncover preventions and treatments for the new coronavirus,[13] which would be the cause of death for more than six million people worldwide over more than two years. The Biden administration rolled back these restrictions in April 2021.[14]

Abortion opponents decried the reversal, including Archbishop Joseph F. Naumann of Kansas City, Kansas, chairman of the U.S. Conference of Catholic Bishops' Committee on Pro-Life Activities.[15]

"Our government has no right to treat innocent abortion victims as a commodity that can be scavenged for body parts to be used in research," he said in a written statement. "It is unethical to promote and subsidize research that can lead to legitimizing the violence of abortion. Researchers have demonstrated that we can do effective scientific research and develop efficacious clinical treatments without harvesting tissue from aborted babies. It is also deeply offensive to millions of Americans for our tax dollars to be used for research that collaborates with an industry built on the taking of innocent lives."

* * *

Decades ago, a group of about a half dozen anti-abortion activists used to head out after dark on a series of missions to retrieve boxes of fetal remains they had discovered were being placed in the garbage behind a Chicago abortion clinic. They made multiple trips there over a two-month period in 1987, ultimately recovering hundreds of aborted fetuses.

One of the activists, Monica Migliorino Miller, recounted these nights in her book *Abandoned: The Untold Story of the Abortion Wars*.

"I was living an unusual life, digging through trash dumpsters on a Chicago loading dock and picking the bodies of human beings out of the trash," she said in the book. "I kept boxes of aborted children, draped with a rosary, in my closet. . . . My mind became forever etched with the memory of hundreds of dismembered, broken bodies—their blood, intestines and torn skin."[16]

Before these remains were buried at St. Mary cemetery, she and her fellow activists displayed some of the fetuses outside the abortion clinic on Michigan Avenue in downtown Chicago in May 1987.[17] The demonstration was intended to highlight "the abortion holocaust that is going on all over America today," Joseph Scheidler, founder of the Chicago-based Pro-Life Action League, told the *Chicago Tribune* at the time.[18]

Scheidler—whose son, Eric Scheidler, serves as executive director of the organization—was widely known across the country as "the godfather of pro-life activism"; his wife, Ann Scheidler, recalled a time when boxes of aborted fetuses were stored in the garage of their home.[19]

"Each little tiny baby was in its own Ziplock [*sic*] bag with the date of the abortion and the name of the mother written on it," she wrote in a blog post on the Pro-Life Action League's website. "Twins were placed together in one bag. They photographed some of the babies to document the atrocity, all while exercising the utmost care and respect. But it was an awful sight. I could not stay very long in the garage."

In 1988, Cardinal Joseph Bernardin officiated a burial service for some 2,000 aborted fetuses at Queen of Heaven Catholic Cemetery in south suburban Hillside, Illinois.[20] Joseph Scheidler had told the *Tribune* that the remains were salvaged in different ways.

"Fifteen bodies from a major hospital were brought to us," he said at the time.[21] "Sometimes employees told us when and where we could pick them up."

The remains were laid to rest in two white caskets and the service was attended by about 500 mourners. In the homily, the cardinal spoke of how "every life, at every stage of development from conception to natural death and in all its circumstances, is sacred and beloved by God."[22]

Reproductive rights advocates were outraged.

Colleen K. Connell of the ACLU of Illinois called the burial a "shameless publicity stunt."[23]

"It's one thing for the cardinal to say the Catholic Church is opposed to abortion," she told the *Tribune* at the time. "But it's quite another for him to participate in an action which demeans the personal privacy and integrity of women who may or may not be churchgoers."

She questioned whether laws were violated in providing and transporting the fetuses—as well as in giving information on the location of the remains—though she conceded there likely wouldn't be legal action without an individual to bring a complaint.

"If these people respect human life, why cart this fetal tissue around the country and save it up for a media stunt?" she said.

Yet to Miller and her supporters, these burials were critical to illustrate that "the unborn are human beings. . . . they are not trash, they are people," she said.

Abortion opposition has been her life's work and many times she's run afoul of the law in her activism: Miller estimated that she's been arrested more than 50 times at abortion protests across the country from 1978 to 2017, often for trespassing or disorderly conduct. She served seven months in jail after a demonstration in Wisconsin in 1989 and 32 more days in jail following a Michigan protest in 2017.[24]

The National Abortion Federation cited an uptick in incidents like trespassing, obstruction and vandalism directed at abortion providers in a 2018 report. The organization attributed the rise to the growing anti-abortion rhetoric of politicians.

"In 2018 the number of individuals attempting to intimidate patients and disrupt patient services continued to increase at an alarming rate," the report said. "We know those who oppose abortion feel emboldened to demonize abortion providers when they see elected officials spreading misleading propaganda and that was true in 2018."[25]

Miller, who serves as the co-director of the National Day of Remembrance, said all her actions and demonstrations at abortion clinics were nonviolent.

"Social justice is not accomplished without radical acts of love, taking risks and making sacrifices on behalf of those who are oppressed," she said.

During her 40 years of anti-abortion activism, Miller never assumed or took for granted that *Roe* would be repealed in her lifetime.[26] When she found out about the Supreme Court's leaked draft opinion, she was "afraid to be happy" and pondered whether the watershed reversal could really be true. While she and fellow abortion opponents rejoiced at the fall of federal abortion protections, she cautioned that much more work still needs to be done.

"We need to convert hearts and minds to create a culture that is truly inclusive of all human beings—and that means honoring the lives of the unborn—to broaden out the boundaries of social justice," she said.

This includes visiting the graves of fetal remains and taking part in memorial services in their memory, according to her organization's website.

"Especially now that *Roe v. Wade* has been overturned, our country must continue to mourn the millions of children killed by abortion as we work state by state to extend legal protection to children in the womb," the website says. "Visiting these gravesites and memorial markers also offers hope and healing to women who have had abortions and people who have been hurt by abortion such as fathers and grandparents who were never allowed to grieve the death of a child hurt by abortion."[27]

Joseph Scheidler didn't live to see the end of *Roe.* At 93, he died of pneumonia in his Chicago home in January 2021, about seventeen months before the Supreme Court decision came down.[28]

"His conviction was that these vulnerable, tiny children deserved to be loved," said Eric Scheidler. "Every single unborn child was precious to him."

* * *

At the 2019 memorial at St. Mary cemetery, participants recited a special prayer to end abortion.

"I commit myself to be active in the pro-life movement and never to stop defending life until all my brothers and sisters are protected," they vowed solemnly, in unison.

Just a few days before the service, authorities in nearby Will County had made a shocking discovery that generated headlines across the nation: The remains of more than 2,000 fetuses were found at a dead abortion doctor's home, roughly 45 miles from Chicago.[29]

Dr. Ulrich Klopfer had performed "tens of thousands of abortions over the course of more than three decades" in Indiana, until the state stripped him of his medical license in 2016 for "poor record keeping, failure to provide appropriate anesthesia to patients and performing abortions on 13-year-old patients without proper reporting to the state," according to a December 2020 report by the Indiana attorney general's office.[30]

After Klopfer died in 2019, his family discovered medically preserved fetal remains in the garage of his house. During a two-day search, local law enforcement found more than 2,000 fetuses "among boxes of personal items, rusting cars, multitudes of soda cans, and other random garbage stacked high to the ceiling in Dr. Klopfer's garage," according to the state report.

"The fetal remains were in various states of decay," the report said. "The remains were mostly found inside molding boxes and old Styrofoam coolers containing large red medical waste bags. It appeared as though each remain had been placed in a small clear plastic specimen bag for purposes of being medically preserved in a chemical suspected to be formalin, a formaldehyde derivative. However, many of the bags had degraded over time and/or suffered damage, resulting in leakage from the individual bags into the outer bag, box, or cooler."

More fetal remains were later found in the trunk of his car. The investigation never uncovered an explanation for the doctor's actions. No one was ever charged with a crime.[31]

But prominent pro-life figures nationwide pointed to the case as evidence of the horrors of abortion.

"[T]his gruesome discovery exposes the reality of the abortion industry, which destroys innocent babies for profit on a similar scale every day, dismantling the lie that abortion is health care," said a statement by the Susan B. Anthony List, a national organization that supports pro-life political candidates.

Vice President Mike Pence posted on Twitter that the findings were "appalling & should shock the conscience of every American."[32]

The former Indiana governor added that the actions of the deceased doctor "should be fully & thoroughly investigated, the remains of the unborn must be treated with dignity & respect & this [abortionist's] defenders should be ashamed. We will always stand for the unborn."

Numerous court battles and public demonstrations have emerged over the disposition of human fetal remains throughout recent history. A few days after the Supreme Court's reversal of *Roe*, a Delaware judge struck down a small town's ordinance requiring burial or cremation of fetal remains.[33] The Seaford City Council had passed the measure in late 2021 after a Planned Parenthood location opened in the town of roughly 8,000 people.[34]

In 2005, a Catholic church in Boulder, Colorado, buried the ashes of hundreds of fetuses; they were obtained from a mortuary contracted to cremate the remains by a local abortion clinic, whose officials didn't know the ashes were being given to the church.[35]

In 1985, after a three-year legal fight, the remains of more than 16,000 fetuses were buried in California and eulogized by President Ronald Reagan, whose remarks were read by a Los Angeles county official at the gravesite.[36] Reagan's speech recalled Abraham Lincoln's Gettysburg Address, drawing parallels to the present-day burial of the fetal remains.

"Just as the terrible toll of Gettysburg can be traced to a tragic decision of a divided Supreme Court, here also can the deaths be mourned," the eulogy said.[37]

Famed pop singer Pat Boone recorded a song that year titled "16,000 Faces," in honor of those fetal remains as well as in protest of abortion. The lyrics begin: "16,000 faces, 32,000 eyes, 64,000 arms and legs, at least 10 million cries."[38]

The fetal remains recovered in 2019 from the doctor's home in suburban Chicago were buried at a cemetery in South Bend, Indiana. Their final resting place is marked by a simple gray headstone etched with the words "In Memory of the 2,411 precious unborn buried here on Feb. 12, 2020."

Hundreds attended the service, including then Indiana attorney general Curtis Hill.[39] In his office's report on the case, Hill wrote that the recovered fetal remains highlighted the need for more measures mandating cremation or burial following an abortion, as in the Indiana statute.

"As Indiana's 43rd Attorney General my goal is to protect the safety and welfare of Hoosiers, and few matters are more important to me than preserving the dignity of human life," Hill wrote. "This case exemplifies the need for strong laws to ensure the dignified disposition of fetal remains, like those passed by the Indiana General Assembly in 2016 and upheld by the U.S. Supreme Court in 2019."

* * *

Near the end of the service at St. Mary cemetery, Jennifer and other mourners lined up to approach the gravesite individually. Each participant left a pink or blue carnation at the headstone. The remains of Jennifer's terminated pregnancy are not buried there.

"I don't know where the remains of my child are," she said. "I assume it's been disposed of."

Yet she takes part in the memorial and pays her respects at the burial site "to honor all the babies lost to abortion everywhere, including my own," she said. "Because of the humanity of those lost lives."

Jennifer recalled meeting her college boyfriend and falling in love for the first time.

"We were quite serious with one another," she said. "Ironically, he said he wanted me to be the mother of his children. He said that was what he wanted for his future."

Three weeks later, she learned she was pregnant. She took a pregnancy test at a women's health center on her college campus and, when it turned positive, she didn't believe the results and made clinicians give her another one.

The second shock was the reaction of her boyfriend, who immediately wanted to terminate the pregnancy, she recalled.

"He basically said, 'You know what I want you to do,' and gave me money," she said. "He distanced himself from me and it was very, very devastating at that time."

One of her close friends offered to help her if she had the baby.

"I was paralyzed with an inability to see how that could work," she said. "How anything could work."

This was about six years after *Roe*. Although abortion was legal, Jennifer said it wasn't really spoken of openly. Her family obstetrician-gynecologist back home referred her to a Chicago hospital.

She didn't tell her parents. The doctor who performed the procedure was very kind, she recalled, asking beforehand if she was certain she wanted to terminate. Even as she said yes, she felt turmoil inside. Looking back, she believes she went through with the procedure because she didn't have the courage to do otherwise.

Still haunted by the memory of the aspiration abortion years ago, Jennifer recalled feeling "my baby" pulled from her body, which she described as traumatizing. The instant the procedure was over, she said she wanted her baby back and sobbed while the physician embraced her.

While Jennifer identified as pro-choice for years following her abortion—in part to not be hypocritical about her own terminated pregnancy—she said she found healing some 30 years later through the pro-life movement.

Jennifer attended a Mass for post-abortive women. She began praying the rosary. She went on a retreat with Rachel's Vineyard, an abortion support group. And she became the Chicago-area regional coordinator for Silent No More Awareness Campaign, a national organization where "Christians make the public aware of the devastation abortion brings to men and women," according to its website.[40]

"It was just layers of healing for me," she said. "I had to accept what I did and go through the pain of acceptance and grasping the gravity of what I had done. During that time, it was a very painful and necessary process."

When the Supreme Court struck down *Roe*, Jennifer initially felt disbelief. Although the decision was expected, it didn't seem possible that nearly 50 years of constitutional protections for abortion could be wiped away in a moment.

Then she was overcome with a strange mix of joy and deep sorrow.

"*Roe v. Wade* being overturned is a glorious, miraculous thing," she said. "Because it was real that it was wrong. I knew it was wrong. I knew what I did was wrong. But when the ruling came down and the world was told from the Supreme Court that it was wrong. I knew that it never should have been."

But if the Supreme Court had never legalized terminating a pregnancy decades prior, Jennifer believes she would not have had access to an abortion.

"Had *Roe v. Wade* never existed, I never would have had that option," she said. "My child should be here right now."

Had she continued the pregnancy, her firstborn would have been 43 years old when *Roe* was struck down. Jennifer has one son and several stepchildren, but none of them have had children yet.

"You realize at a certain age, you didn't just end the life of one," she said. "I wiped out generations that would have come after. . . . I could potentially have a house full of grandchildren now."

This is the deception of abortion, Jennifer said.

"It's supposed to fix our problems," she said. "It's supposed to free us from undesirable responsibility. It's supposed to give us opportunities that we wouldn't have had otherwise. It's supposed to be the answer, the liberating answer, but it does none of those things. It creates a hole in your heart that can never be healed without the mercy of Jesus Christ. He's the only way I found my way through it, is to know I've been forgiven. Even though I can't always find a way to forgive myself."[41]

8.
800 Miles

The expectant mother was overjoyed as a faint pink line appeared on the pregnancy test, a culmination of two years of infertility and in vitro fertilization treatments.[1] But the pregnancy was considered high-risk early on. The 28-year-old woman from southeast Iowa recalled that physicians were initially concerned about the small gestational sac, which can increase the risk of a miscarriage. Later, her amniotic fluid levels were critically low, a dangerous condition called oligohydramnios, which made it impossible to get an accurate ultrasound reading.

At a little after 21 weeks, her medical providers discussed abortion as an option. Yet she and her husband had only 72 hours to make such a grave, life-changing choice: Iowa's gestational limit prohibited terminating a pregnancy past 22 weeks after the last menstrual period or 20 weeks post-fertilization.[2]

They decided to continue the pregnancy, despite the warning signs. She wanted to hold off in case a better ultrasound image might give more information about the health of the son they longed for. If there were medical conditions or anomalies, she hoped they might be treatable or at least allow for a good quality of life.

"We gave the baby every chance," said the woman from Iowa, who asked to remain anonymous due to the divisive climate surrounding reproductive rights. "I needed proof there were actual things wrong, not just 'low fluid, we can't see.'"

It wasn't until after 24 weeks that she and her husband learned the dire state of the fetus, which faced a vast scope of medical problems beyond anything the couple had ever imagined. In spring 2019, they learned their son suffered from heart defects, multiple congenital spinal abnormalities and a head measuring weeks behind the typical circumference, with a deformed skull.

"It was way worse than we thought," she said.

The risk of stillbirth was high, the young woman from Iowa remembered her obstetrician saying, and if she delivered a live baby the choice would be palliative care or multiple surgeries with a very poor prognosis. The range of defects was incompatible with any kind of quality of life, she said.

"I need an abortion, it's not fair to this child," she recalled telling her doctor, who had pamphlets about terminating pregnancy on hand. "At that moment, I was just thinking what's the best thing to do for my unborn child. And I was not going to let him continue and suffer."

By then, the pregnancy was already past Iowa's gestational limit. She began looking at nearby states where she might be able to terminate the troubled pregnancy. Her medical providers initially discussed the possibility of her traveling to neighboring Illinois, a state known for having far fewer barriers to abortion compared to many others in the Midwest.

After checking, though, her physician told her she was too far along to go there: Illinois law banned abortion after fetal viability—the point where a fetus could potentially survive outside the womb, generally considered to be somewhere around 24 to 26 weeks' gestation—unless the woman's health or life was at risk.[3] But the law didn't specify a time frame or specific point in gestation where an abortion would be prohibited.

At the time, even clinics that provided abortions later in pregnancy in Illinois capped the procedure at 24 weeks. (A new Planned Parenthood clinic that opened in late 2019 in Fairview Heights, Illinois, would provide abortions up to 26 weeks after the last menstrual period, but that health center didn't exist when the young woman from Iowa received her pregnancy's devastating diagnosis.)[4]

The young woman from Iowa's pregnancy was a few days past 24 weeks. Her physician gave her brochures for clinics in Colorado and

New Mexico, states that permitted abortion later in pregnancy but were also much farther away, requiring expensive last-minute airfare and more burdensome travel for a very time-sensitive procedure.

"My husband and I were like, is there anywhere closer?" she said. "It would have made it just a little more compassionate if I could have gotten on the train and gone to Illinois."

* * *

As the couple from Iowa prepared to travel to terminate the pregnancy, a controversial bill to protect and expand abortion access was pending in the state legislature just over the border in Illinois.

In January 2019, Governor J.B. Pritzker pledged to make Illinois "the most progressive state in the nation" when it came to guaranteeing women's reproductive rights.[5] Democratic lawmakers in February introduced the Illinois Reproductive Health Act to replace abortion legislation initially adopted in 1975, much of which had been blocked by the courts, including some requiring criminal penalties for physicians who terminate pregnancies.[6] The Reproductive Health Act proclaimed abortion a "fundamental right" statewide. The measure stated that a fertilized egg, embryo or fetus had no independent rights in Illinois.[7]

Anti-abortion activists denounced every part of the proposed law, but one aspect was deemed particularly egregious: An earlier version of the abortion rights bill didn't include post–fetal viability restrictions, potentially allowing a pregnancy to be terminated past that point for reasons other than life or health endangerment, leaving the decision solely up to the patient and health care practitioner.[8]

Illinois abortion foes were incensed, calling the proposed law too permissive and extreme.

"In reading the Reproductive Health Act, one can feel the disdain, indeed, the contempt, the Act has for the unborn child, whose life counts for nothing," read a February 2019 memorandum on the proposed law by the Thomas More Society, a Chicago-based public interest law firm with the mission of "defending laws that protect human life from conception to natural death."[9]

"There would be no requirement that post-viability abortions be limited to therapeutic, not elective, reasons," the memorandum said. "In other words, Illinois would allow abortion on demand."

At the same time, lawmakers were also considering a bill that would repeal Illinois requirements that minors notify a parent or other specified adult family member prior to having an abortion, which wouldn't be signed into law until 2021.

Thousands of pro-life demonstrators protested the two pieces of abortion legislation in Springfield, Illinois, in March 2019, filling the state capitol to capacity, with protesters spilling outside.[10] Several Illinois pro-life organizations put out a joint news release that said busloads of residents would be coming from all over the state to urge lawmakers to drop the measures.

"These bills would allow unregulated abortion up until the moment of birth for any reason, and would strip away all parental rights," the news release said, warning that if the Reproductive Health Act passed, "Illinois would become a third-trimester abortion destination."[11]

But at demonstrations in downtown Chicago in May 2019, hundreds of supporters of the proposed laws implored lawmakers to take action on the bill in the last remaining days of the legislative session.[12] Some donned red *Handmaid's Tale* robes and white bonnets, signifying their fear that the nation was devolving into the dystopian world of Margaret Atwood's best-selling novel.

The Reproductive Health Act was introduced as the nation grew increasingly polarized on abortion rights, particularly in terms of when in a pregnancy the procedure should be permitted or restricted. The protesters expressed alarm as a wave of states passed some of the strictest abortion laws in the country and the makeup of the U.S. Supreme Court drifted further right.

"I'm someone who has a uterus and I'm worried about *Roe v. Wade*," said one of the protesters, an 18-year-old college student. "I don't want my rights or my autonomy for my body infringed upon."[13]

The Illinois Senate passed the Reproductive Health Act in late May 2019, just before the end of the legislative session.[14] But before its passage, the measure was amended to include post-viability restrictions: "If the health care professional determines that there is fetal viability, the health care professional may provide abortion care only if, in the professional judgment of the health care professional, the abortion is necessary to protect the life or health of the patient."[15]

The new language did alter the state's viability restriction to allow abortions in these endangerment cases without the approval of a second physician, which had been a legal requirement prior to the Reproductive Health Act; the Guttmacher Institute praised this change, which the research group said would "ensure that a patient's health needs guide medical decisions."[16]

Governor Pritzker signed the act into law in June 2019, making Illinois abortion statutes among the most liberal in the country.[17]

"When it comes to contraception, abortion, and reproductive care, this law puts the decision-making where it belongs: in the hands of women and their doctors," Pritzker said in a statement. "The Reproductive Health Act ensures that women's rights in Illinois do not hinge on the fate of *Roe v. Wade*, or the whims of an increasingly conservative Supreme Court. In this state, women will always have the right to reproductive health care."[18]

The law repealed the Illinois Abortion Law of 1975, which would have rendered abortion illegal in Illinois once *Roe* was overturned. The four-decade-old law stated that it was "the longstanding policy of this State, that the unborn child is a human being from the time of conception," though the measure had not been enforced in decades.

"No words can express the disappointment and heartache pro-life Illinoisans, like myself, are feeling," Ralph Rivera, legislative chairman for Illinois Right to Life Action, said in a statement.[19]

The Reproductive Health Act eliminated nearly every legal barrier to abortion in Illinois. Only two major restrictions remained. For the time being, the Parental Notice of Abortion Act was still in effect, mandating that a parent or specified adult family member be notified before those under 18 could have an abortion. And Illinois law still prohibited abortion after fetal viability unless the health or life of the pregnant patient was in danger.

But many medical experts say defining when a fetus is viable can become much more complex in practice than laws and political rhetoric might convey.

* * *

At the time of her deepest turmoil and pain, the woman from Iowa said she felt abandoned by her state.

Iowa in 2017 had passed a statute prohibiting most abortions past 20 weeks post-fertilization, or 22 weeks after the last menstrual period, as most physicians and hospitals measure pregnancy. Planned Parenthood of the Heartland also had to close four clinics in Iowa in 2017 due to state defunding after the legislature blocked abortion providers from receiving family planning services money. Three of those clinics were in the eastern side of the state, near the Illinois border.

"When access to abortion is politically restricted, those who have the means to travel will do so, and those without means are left most vulnerable," said Becca Lee, spokeswoman for Planned Parenthood of the Heartland. "If someone can travel, they may be forced to take time from work, incur additional expenses, take time from family and make other sacrifices in order to access a safe, legal abortion procedure—and they shouldn't have to."

Caitlyn Dixson, executive director of Iowa Right to Life, said Iowa abortion numbers were at "historic lows," which she attributed in part to some of these recent anti-abortion measures. The abortion rate in Iowa decreased 15 percent between 2014 and 2017, going from 7.5 terminated pregnancies per 1,000 women of reproductive age to 6.3.[20] While Dixon acknowledged that some women might be heading to other states, she didn't believe travel accounted for the entire drop in abortions.

"I think women are simply choosing not to terminate," she said. "I believe that this decline goes hand in hand with the climate in Iowa," which included voters in 2018 reelecting Republican incumbent governor Kim Reynolds over a pro–abortion rights challenger.

In April 2019, the young woman and her husband quickly made plans to fly to a clinic in Boulder, Colorado, a roughly 800-mile trip. She was just past 25 weeks pregnant.

"I felt him moving," she said. "I don't know how to describe that emotion. And to let him come into this world, that just seems cruel, to make him continue to suffer."

While she could afford to travel for the procedure, she knows that not everyone has the ability or resources to do so.

"Abortion is about geography and monetary means," she said. "And it shouldn't [be]. Reproductive health care should not be about that. It should be between you and your doctor."

She said it would have been much easier to go to a clinic in Chicago, at roughly a third the distance and far less of a financial and emotional burden.

"I felt so scared that I had to go somewhere else, I felt so scared that I had to go on an airplane and go out west," she said. "This became a medical need for my child and me. There was no other way."

Abortions later in pregnancy are exceedingly rare, with only about 1 percent of terminations occurring past 21 weeks of gestation; in contrast, roughly 93 percent of abortions are performed in the first trimester, according to 2019 CDC data.[21]

Fetal viability became a cornerstone of abortion law after *Roe* was handed down in 1973. The decision acknowledged that, throughout history, there have been a wide variety of religious and scientific beliefs on when life begins.[22]

"It should be sufficient to note briefly the wide divergence of thinking on this most sensitive and difficult question," the opinion stated.[23]

The ruling went on to explain that viability is an interim point between conception and live birth where the fetus "is potentially able to live outside the mother's womb, albeit with artificial aid."[24]

"With respect to the State's important and legitimate interest in potential life, the 'compelling' point is at viability," the opinion stated. "This is so because the fetus then presumably has the capability of meaningful life outside the mother's womb. State regulation protective of fetal life after viability thus has both logical and biological justifications. If the State is interested in protecting fetal life after viability, it may go so far as to proscribe abortion during that period, except when it is necessary to preserve the life or health of the mother."[25]

But in practice, the concept of fetal viability can be very complicated, said Dr. Erin King, physician and executive director at Hope Clinic for Women, which performs the procedure up to 24 weeks.

It should take into account the health of the pregnant patient as well as the pregnancy, conditions that can shift quickly moment to moment, she said. King added that these are individual circumstances that fluctuate and can't be held to one set point decided by lawmakers decades ago.

Although cases like the Iowa woman's pregnancy are uncommon, King said she has seen similar cases where tragic circumstances emerged so late in gestation that she feared performing an abortion could violate state law. In those instances, she has had to refer patients out of state, which she calls "heartbreaking."

"The doctors are well-trained, they know the evidence, they know what's safe for their patients," she said. "Let's let them make the decisions about these really difficult times in patients' lives and these difficult and complicated medical problems."

Dr. Karen Deighan, an obstetrician-gynecologist of more than 30 years, was a featured speaker at March for Life Chicago in January 2020. At one point, she specifically addressed medical professionals in the crowd.[26]

"Science is on our side," she said, to cheers. "And who better to understand that than scientists? Life begins at conception. Our collective voice must be heard."[27]

Two years later, Deighan applauded the end of *Roe* as a step in the right direction "for the protection of unborn children."[28] She marveled at how much medicine and technology had improved over the course of her career and since *Roe* was decided some five decades earlier.

"You can see very early the heart, all the organs, the head, the eyes, the movement," said Deighan, associate professor of obstetrics and gynecology at Loyola University Medical Center. "You can see the baby inside. And I don't think earlier ultrasounds could show us all that."

She called fetal viability "a shifting paradigm" due to medical advances, with newborns surviving after shorter gestation periods than they were decades earlier.

Research shows the odds of survival for extremely early preterm births have been increasing over time. A study that appeared in January 2022 in the *Journal of the American Medical Association* analyzed 10,877 births from 2013 to 2018 and found significant improvement in survival rates of those born at 22 to 28 weeks' gestation compared to those born from 2008 to 2012.[29]

Of infants born after 22 weeks in the womb, almost 11 percent of the more recent births survived compared with nearly 7 percent of the births from 2008 to 2012. At 23 weeks' gestation, the study found that "survival increased significantly" to just over 49 percent of the 2013 to 2018 births compared to just over 32 percent of the 2008 to 2012 births.[30]

"Any obstetrician, we are always caring for two patients," Deighan said. "I struggle sometimes because some of my colleagues will work so hard to protect and save a 22-week peri-viable pregnancy and pull out all the medical advances to do that. And don't see a problem with someone choosing to end that pregnancy."

* * *

The woman from Iowa had expected the abortion to be traumatic.

At the clinic in Boulder, on April 23, 2019, a lethal medication was injected to stop the heart of the fetus.

"When they did it, I actually felt very relieved," she recalled. "Not for myself. I was petrified to go through this process. But I felt relieved for my child, that he wasn't going to have to suffer."

Two days later, she had the surgical abortion. At home, she keeps tiny ink prints that were taken of the hands and feet, as well as a blanket the fetus was wrapped in before the remains were cremated.

She planned to bury her son at a cemetery in Utah, beside the grave of her mother, who died when she was 13. Her mom, she says, would have supported her decision and been there for her as she mourned.

"Not to have a child, when that's all we ever wanted, that's a lot to come to terms with," the woman from Iowa said.

The provider, Boulder Abortion Clinic, treats many women and couples who face severe fetal anomalies later in pregnancy. Sometimes patients ask for an intact fetus they can examine and hold as part of their grieving process, according to the clinic's website. Sometimes the woman or the family asks for special procedures like religious ceremonies, autopsies, genetic studies or private cremation.

"One of the most tragic things that can happen to a woman and her loved ones is to discover late in a desired pregnancy that something has gone terribly wrong," the clinic's website says. "The fetus is discovered to have a serious or even fatal problem of development or to have a genetic disorder that will leave it seriously impaired. In spite of everything, nothing can be done to give the baby a chance for a normal life—perhaps not even a chance for life itself."

Diana Greene Foster's book *The Turnaway Study* explores a landmark decade-long study tracking thousands of women nationwide who either received abortions or were turned away, which was conducted by Foster and a team of researchers. In addition to fetal anomalies and dangerous health conditions, Foster lists a number of other circumstances that lead to terminations later in pregnancy.

"But the quiet truth about abortion between 20 and 24 weeks is that it is often a problem of late recognition of pregnancy followed by real obstacles—financial, travel-related, and legal—to getting an abortion," Foster wrote. "Making abortion more difficult to access does not mean that only the morally-deserving get their abortions. It means that only adult women who don't have any physical or mental health issues and have money and social support get their abortions."[31]

New York in January 2019 had enacted one of the nation's strongest abortion rights laws of the time, which included a provision permitting abortions after 24 weeks in the absence of fetal viability or when a woman's life or health was endangered.[32] The previous law allowed the procedure this late in pregnancy only if a woman's life was at risk.

The law ignited much backlash against terminating later in pregnancy, led by President Trump's calling on Congress to pass a ban on what he referred to as "late-term" abortions in his February 2019 State of the Union speech.[33]

"Lawmakers in New York cheered with delight upon the passage of legislation that would allow a baby to be ripped from the mother's womb moments from birth," he said. "These are living, feeling, beautiful babies who will never get the chance to share their love and their dreams with the world. . . . To defend the dignity of every person, I am asking Congress to pass legislation to prohibit the late-term abortion of children who can feel pain in the mother's womb. Let us work together to build a culture that cherishes innocent life."[34]

In response, a letter titled "We Are Later Abortion Patients" was circulated on the internet.

"The decision to terminate a pregnancy is never a political one, it is a personal one," the letter said. "Later abortions stories are often ones of tragedy and loss. For others they are stories of relief. They feature struggles with hope, women betrayed by their bodies and the incredible complexity of pregnancy. Many stories are ones of overcoming the many obstacles and restrictions our states have placed on these procedures."[35]

The message was signed by more than 130 people from across the country.

"We are not monsters," the letter continued. "We are your family, your neighbors, someone you love. We are you, just in different circumstances."

A few months following the fall of *Roe*, a case in many ways similar to the plight of the Iowa woman garnered national headlines: A pregnant woman in Louisiana said she had had to travel 1,400 miles to New York to have an abortion after her fetus was diagnosed with acrania, a rare and lethal congenital disorder where the skull is missing.[36] A state law in effect post-*Roe* prohibited abortion except in cases where continuing the pregnancy risked death or impairment of the woman or in cases of "medically futile pregnancies."[37]

The patient, Nancy Davis, and reproductive rights advocates have criticized Louisiana's law as vague and ambiguous. The website of her attorney, Ben Crump, had an online petition demanding the Louisiana governor—a rare pro-life Democratic office holder—call for a special legislative session to clarify medical exemptions to the state's abortion ban.[38]

"Under Louisiana law, any person who knowingly performs a criminal abortion after 15 weeks of pregnancy—Ms. Davis' current state—can be imprisoned for up to 15 years and/or fined up to $200,000," the petition stated. "What doctor is going to take that risk? Ms. Davis was among the first women to be caught in the crosshairs of confusion due to Louisiana's rush to restrict abortion. But she will hardly be the last."[39]

In October 2022, the Louisiana Department of Health held a public hearing on conditions that would render a pregnancy "medically futile," as defined by the state's abortion law. But the state's list, which included about two dozen medical conditions, was heavily criticized by pro-life and pro-choice advocates.[40]

During an August 2022 news conference, Davis described the fear and pain she felt after her doctors told her that her baby would die soon following birth.[41]

"They told me that I should terminate the pregnancy," she said. "Because of the state of Louisiana's abortion ban they cannot perform the procedure. Basically, they said I had to carry my baby to bury my baby. They seemed confused about the law and afraid of what would happen to them if they perform a criminal abortion, according to the law."

She asked the audience to imagine what it would be like to continue a pregnancy for six weeks after such a horrible diagnosis.

"Being a mother starts when your baby is in the womb," she said. "Not on the outside. The attachment and everything that comes with it. So as a mother, as a parent . . . it's my obligation to have my children's best interest at heart."[42]

9. Help from a Stranger

One woman came to Chicago from Indianapolis by Greyhound bus in mid-2017, pregnant but with medical complications that would have made labor and delivery potentially dangerous.[1] Another pregnant woman traveled from Wisconsin to Illinois in March 2018, seeking an abortion because she didn't have the financial resources to care for a baby.

They both stayed overnight in the home of a Chicago resident they had never met before their interstate trips for abortion care: A volunteer with Midwest Access Coalition, a nonprofit that helps defray costs associated with travel to terminate pregnancies, hosted both of the women in her Chicago apartment before and after their abortions at local clinics. The host let the traveler from Indianapolis have her bedroom; the woman from Wisconsin slept on a futon lent to the host by a friend.

"It seems like a lot of these states have increased the barriers to abortion and other health care for women in the recent years," the volunteer host said. "It doesn't seem right there should be this island of health care access in Chicago."

Midwest Access Coalition was founded in 2014, when its first executive director, Leah Greenblum, saw a need in Chicago for what's known as a practical abortion fund. The nonprofit doesn't pay for the abortion itself but offers logistical support for patients traveling to, from and within the Midwest—everything from finding an abortion provider to booking and funding travel, which can be expensive, complicated and time-consuming for some patients.

While dozens of abortion funds locally and around the country help patients pay for the procedure, Greenblum realized so many additional expenses come with trekking long distances to end pregnancies. Airplane, bus and train tickets. Hotel stays. Meals. Childcare. Taxi and Uber rides. Gasoline for long car trips.

"We are also here to be cheerleaders in a system that is so systematically disenfranchising [to] poor women," Greenblum said. "If they're trying to make a choice and hitting barrier after barrier, we recognize that. We recognize that is so challenging, and we want to help ease some of that burden."

Greenblum started hosting out-of-town abortion seekers in her own Chicago apartment. In 2015, more than 3,200 patients crossed state lines to have an abortion in Illinois, accounting for about 8 percent of the nearly 40,000 terminated pregnancies that year.[2] The number rose to 4,543 out-of-state abortion patients in 2016 and would continue to rise every year thereafter.[3]

By mid-2017, Greenblum had assembled a network of around 90 Chicago-area volunteers, which included hosts and volunteer drivers. Sometimes patients preferred having trained volunteer drivers rather than getting Uber or Lyft rides; in other cases, travelers who came on their own might need a trusted individual to check them out of the clinic, a role the volunteer driver could serve, according to the charity.

The nonprofit ran background checks on volunteer applicants and reviewed their social media sites; car insurance information was checked for drivers. Prospective volunteers were asked to write down their beliefs about reproductive rights to ensure their "values are aligned with us on wanting accessible and safe abortion care for all," according to the organization. Staff also toured the vehicles and homes of volunteers, to make sure these spaces were safe and comfortable for travelers.

The organization had served nearly 200 clients as of June 2017, with 70 percent coming from out of state. In the early years, most of these out-of-town abortion patients came from Indiana and Wisconsin, though some also traveled from Ohio, Iowa, Michigan, Minnesota and other states, Greenblum said.

"We have to ensure people have control of their bodies," she said. "We cannot keep going back. We have to keep moving forward."

* * *

Another Midwest Access Coalition volunteer described feeling deeply troubled by Trump's ascent to the White House after the November 2016 general election; she would stay up at night worrying about how his presidency might alter the course of the nation.[4] Her concerns included protecting reproductive rights, which suddenly seemed much more fragile for large swaths of the country.

"I definitely was feeling very shocked and helpless," she said. "And then the anger kicked in."

She recalled having a series of grave, late-night conversations with her partner about how the couple could fight back against the shifting political tide and help others whose reproductive freedoms might be in jeopardy. While she had previously donated money to Planned Parenthood, the volunteer said she was searching for a more direct and tangible way to be of service. She learned of Midwest Access Coalition through a social media post and attended her first training session in late November 2016.

"I might not have all the money in the world," she said. "But I have time. I have skills. I have a guest bedroom that we rarely use. . . . So there was kind of no question or hesitation at all."

Her first guest arrived in winter 2017. The young woman stayed in the extra bedroom of the volunteer's Chicago loft, with a window overlooking the Kennedy Expressway. The host left a bottle of lotion and a chocolate bar on the nightstand as homey touches.

"I feel that's the least I can do, is make someone feel like, even if there are things happening that are hard and emotional and difficult, that you can still have those comforts around you and feel safe in that way," she said.

A third volunteer host drew some historical parallels between the Midwest Access Coalition and Jane, the underground abortion network founded in the Hyde Park neighborhood during the final years before *Roe* legalized the procedure.

"These women were so brave," she said. "They really stood up for what they believed in and that was very inspiring to me. I was really grateful that people stood up and did what had to be done. I wasn't expecting to keep fighting that fight again as I got older. But I will, because I have to."

In 2017, she hosted a woman from Indiana in the spare bedroom of her small apartment.

"She came to Chicago not knowing what was going to happen, not knowing how long it was going to take, not knowing where she was going to stay," the volunteer recalled. "You have to be a really strong person to get through something like that."

The host said she tried to be perceptive about whether a visitor wanted her to be more present or would prefer their own space and time to be alone.

"I wish this was a time they could be sharing with their family, in their homes, instead," she said. "I hope that I was a good enough substitute, and I hope that in those moments I was able to figure out what they wanted the most. But I wish it was a time they could have been sharing with the people they care about, the people who support them personally. Because I think it's really hard to go through this when you are away from home and with people you don't know."

Before the woman from Indiana left Chicago, the host put together a care package of a few clementine oranges along with a handwritten note listing the train number and some directions.

There were so many other things she wanted to say. *I respect your decision. I think you're a really strong person for doing that. I really wish you didn't have to go through all this just to have a medical procedure. Things will be better once you get home.* But she didn't want to assume how her guest was feeling or project any of her own emotions on someone she barely knew.

So she settled on a simple "Have a safe trip home."

Two other out-of-state women had been scheduled to stay at this volunteer's home but never arrived.

"I don't know if they found a place to stay at the last minute or if they changed their minds," she said. "It could also be they've been pushed by circumstances to take this other path, in a way that wouldn't have occurred if they were able to access abortion in their state more easily early on, if there were better health care for women generally."

She frequently thinks about the two women she never met.

"What I really want is for everyone to be able to make the choice that's right for them," she said. "For that to actually be a choice between you and your doctor, not something that's coerced by really, really punitive laws."

* * *

The fall of *Roe* ignited a wave in folks inquiring about volunteering with Midwest Access Coalition, which by 2023 had served almost 5,000 people from 30 states. The nonprofit temporarily stopped taking on and training new volunteers, which can be time consuming, in order to focus on assisting the soaring number of abortion seekers.

"There was a sudden and large interest from people all over the country wanting to volunteer for us in some capacity," said Diana Parker-Kafka, who took over as executive director in 2020. "Lots of people were angry and scared about [the Supreme Court's] decision and wanting an outlet for that. . . . For people who would like to volunteer their time, the best thing to do right now is spend that time talking to friends, family, and community about the importance of trusting people to make their own reproductive choices that are best for them, including abortion."[5]

As of mid-September 2022, the nonprofit had provided support for more than 1,100 people coming from 26 states so far that year, up from 800 clients served in all of 2021, according to the charity.

"I would like people to know that requiring someone to travel and [stay] overnight in another state away from their family for a medical procedure is cruel," Parker-Kafka said. "Abortion bans are meant to be cruel and to punish people based on a very small group of bad actors using their religious beliefs as an excuse to inflict this cruelty. The stories you hear about children, people with ectopic pregnancies and nonviable fetuses having to travel states away to avoid sepsis, pain and death are true. We see it happen every week."

Even as more states outlawed or severely restricted abortion, the nonprofit was finding innovative ways to continue serving clients.

Midwest Access Coalition announced in summer 2022 that it would be delivering free emergency contraception on request, and in the first month or so it provided kits to 80 individuals around the country. The nonprescription medication, levonorgestrel, also known as Plan B or the morning-after pill, can be taken within 72 hours after unprotected sex to help prevent pregnancy.

The nonprofit's emergency contraceptive kits include the medication, menstrual pads, pregnancy tests, a cup for urine collection, condoms and a snack. The form of contraception is different from a medication abortion and still legal in states where terminating a pregnancy has been outlawed.

Orders are submitted through an online form or a hotline number, and the pills are mailed or delivered to residences via volunteer drivers. Immediate delivery can be requested, or the pills can be ordered in advance and kept on hand for future use. Special requests can be made to keep delivery of the contraception discrete for those with privacy or safety concerns, according to the online submission form.

* * *

Shortly before the end of *Roe*, a new nonprofit of volunteer pilots began offering patients free flights to out-of-state appointments aboard small passenger planes, forging a path to abortion access in the sky.[6]

The first-of-its-kind charity, called Elevated Access, was founded by a Midwest Access Coalition volunteer who was also a licensed pilot and wanted to merge the two interests to help overcome barriers to terminating a pregnancy. He had been working on the concept with Midwest Access Coalition staff for over a year before incorporating his Springfield, Illinois–based charity in April 2022.

"While voting and giving money are important to try and stop this backslide of people's rights in this country, doing something directly to try and help people get out of that burden is very important to me," said the founder and executive director of Elevated Access, who asked to remain anonymous for his safety, citing the heightened threat of violence surrounding reproductive rights.

The charity recruits licensed pilots with access to light aircraft, who volunteer their time and small planes to fly patients heading to abortion clinics, often across state lines.

"We know you are already stressed," the group's website says. "Let us relieve some of that with a free flight from a volunteer pilot."

The new abortion care transportation model was designed to work around some of the barriers to more conventional travel. Sometimes patients are too young to book a rental car. Commercial airlines, trains and buses often have limited schedules, or take too long for patients who need to watch their children or can't miss an extra day of work. Travel by cars and planes can also be expensive due to rising fuel costs, an added burden for patients who aren't wealthy.

In early June 2022, a few weeks before the demise of *Roe*, Elevated Access flew its first abortion patient from Oklahoma to the Kansas City area, enabling the passenger to terminate a pregnancy in Kansas, the executive director said. Just days before the flight, the governor of Oklahoma had signed one of the nation's strictest abortion measures into law, requiring the patient to travel out of state for the procedure at the last minute.

The inaugural Elevated Access patient traveled aboard a Cirrus SR20, a single-engine propeller plane with four seats. It was the first time the passenger had ever flown on an airplane of any kind, the executive director recalled. Driving from Oklahoma City to the Kansas City region would have taken about 10 hours round trip, and the patient had childcare constraints that prohibited overnight travel. Instead, the traveler left home at 8 a.m. to get to the airplane and then returned by 6 p.m. the same day, eliminating the need for multiple days of travel.

"They were able to get back to their life and their kids," the executive director said.

A commercial flight to and from the same two cities would have cost about $900, according to Midwest Access Coalition staff, who coordinated the patient's travel.

The planes used for these flights typically have a single-propeller engine and can fly one to three passengers at speeds over 100 miles per hour. The aircraft are able to take off and land at one of the roughly 3,000 general aviation airports that dot the country. These flights tend to be more flexible and less bureaucratic than those on commercial airlines, and the experience also offers more privacy, the executive director said.

"At most small airports, there is a small office where you can wait for the pilot if they are not already there to greet you," the website says, in a section with information for passengers. "If anyone asks what you are doing, you tell them that you're meeting someone for a flight. You don't need to tell them anything more than that. There is no security to scan your baggage or requirement to show any identification."

Volunteers must be licensed pilots over 21 years old with a minimum of 200 hours of flight experience. There are also Federal Aviation Administration requirements and regulations governing the planes that are used. Applicants are vetted to ensure they support the nonprofit's mission and are required to provide references and statements about their position on abortion rights; their social media profiles are screened as well.

As of the end of May 2023, over 150 pilots from around the country had expressed interest in volunteering, and about a third had completed the vetting process, the executive director said.

"This goes beyond bodily autonomy," he said. "It's trying to help people who are really struggling with equality in our country."

* * *

Vice President Kamala Harris came to Chicago to convene a roundtable on abortion access with Illinois leaders, medical providers and various reproductive rights advocates in September 2022.[7] She opened the discussion by condemning the Supreme Court's reversal of *Roe.*

"The United States Supreme Court, the highest court in the land, took a constitutional right from the people of America, from the women of America," Harris said. "And we are, in the wake of that decision, facing a healthcare crisis in America that requires us all to speak up and do everything we can to ensure that we will fight to protect a woman's right to make decisions about her own body."[8]

The vice president acknowledged the critical role of Illinois in the Midwest and beyond, calling it a "safe haven" for reproductive rights.

"When I look at a map of the country and the neighborhood in which you exist, there's no question to me that you are helping women from states like Indiana and Kentucky and Missouri and Tennessee and Wisconsin, in addition to the women of Illinois," she said. "So I thank you for that. But I also recognize that when we are seeing, as we have been, women from neighboring states going to those states that are protecting the constitutional right of women, that it makes a statement also about the fact that the women in states that are banning reproductive health care need that health care, want that health care and in spite of that are being denied access to that health care in their own states."

One speaker was Dr. Allison Cowett, medical director of the Chicago abortion clinic Family Planning Associates, whose mission includes helping women from other states where abortion services are unavailable or hard to access. Staff assist out-of-state patients with travel arrangements and connect them with nonprofits to help fund the procedure and logistical costs. Patients from out of town can get a special corporate discount at a hotel one block from the clinic, according to the abortion clinic's website.

On the day the Supreme Court overturned *Roe*, "our phone lines blew up and they haven't stopped ringing since," Cowett told the panel.[9]

The number of second-trimester abortions the clinic was performing had increased by 90 percent, she said, adding that conditions for pregnant people had become "dangerous and uncertain."

The physician shared the story of one recent patient, a college student who had come from Alabama to Chicago to terminate a pregnancy but had first gone to an anti-abortion pregnancy center.

"She had large brown eyes and a very frightened looking face," Cowett said. "She was eight weeks pregnant and she had mistakenly gone to a fake clinic, or a crisis pregnancy center, where she heard lies and misinformation about abortion. She told me in the exam room that she was worried we would sedate her for the abortion procedure and then tie her tubes."

The college student desperately wanted to end the pregnancy and finish her education, but she also desired to have children in the future, Cowett recounted.

"She was 800 miles from home and she was terrified," Cowett said. "The abortion bans throughout the South and Midwest have transformed a simple, five-minute procedure in a doctor's office that is 14 times safer than delivering a baby, they have turned that into a public health emergency. Here in Illinois, we want to be part of the solution."

Chicago Abortion Fund executive director Megan Jeyifo told the roundtable that her nonprofit had received calls from more than 4,000 people in over 40 states and two countries in 2022.

"Since *Roe* has fallen, our callers are facing longer journeys and the scale of our logistical support has increased dramatically," she said. "We know that Illinois has long been a regional access point due to less prohibitive costs and fewer restrictions. But in this new reality, as more bans and restrictions are implemented, we are a national access point. We as people in Illinois and Chicago—the birthplace of the reproductive justice movement—have a responsibility to support our neighbors who can no longer access care in their communities."[10]

Another speaker on the panel was Parker-Kafka, of Midwest Access Coalition.

"We cannot let any government, or the police, criminalize abortion seekers and their supporters," Parker-Kafka said. "That will only lead to tragedy. The radical and racist right do not care about those losses. They think it's deserved. So we have to care. We cannot be OK with the criminalization and trauma of abortion bans."[11]

10.
Jane Doe

The teen was known only as Jane Doe, as far as the courts were concerned.

The young woman from Ohio was just two months shy of her eighteenth birthday as she told her story to a judge in Chicago on a winter afternoon in 2015.[1] Each statement was punctuated by the rapid click of the stenographer's keys, chronicling some of her most intimate and private experiences in a court transcript. All documents from the hearing would be sealed, inaccessible to the public without a court order.

"It was a highly potentially dangerous situation for me, for my parents to know about this, especially my father," she recalled telling the judge. "I was afraid that I would be hurt physically by my mother and then disowned completely by my father."

The petite 17-year-old with long, blonde hair had never been to Chicago before. The Daley Center—a 31-floor modern steel courthouse surrounded by sleek skyscrapers—felt intimidating. The hearing was held in the judge's office, a less imposing setting than one of the large, formal courtrooms with high ceilings and a bench. The judge was a tall woman with short, dark hair and a soothing voice, the teen recalled.

But the girl from Ohio still felt embarrassed as she explained that she was just over eight weeks pregnant and had traveled hundreds of miles on her own to have an abortion in another state without her family ever finding out.

"It can be anyone," said the teen, who asked to remain anonymous so her family wouldn't learn of her terminated pregnancy. "It's the girl who has straight As. It's the girl who has a conservative family. It very well could be your daughter, your niece, your granddaughter."

The high school student had bought her bus ticket to Chicago with a gift card to avoid leaving a paper trail. Her parents thought she was still in her hometown, sleeping over at the house of a friend.

"I had no doubt that I wanted an abortion," she said. "I knew that I was just not ready. There was no chance that I could be a good parent to this child, and it would have been a bad situation for everybody."

At the time, Illinois law required anyone under 18 to notify a parent or other specified close adult relative—a grandparent, stepparent who lives in the home or legal guardian—at least 48 hours before having an abortion. Roughly three dozen states required some form of parental involvement before a minor could have an abortion. Some of those statutes mandated parental consent. Others, like Illinois, required that a parent be notified.[2]

But nearly every state with parental requirements offered an alternative process called judicial bypass, which allows minors the legal right to go before a judge and request a waiver of parental involvement. Individual states, though, can have very different legal standards and requirements for granting a waiver.

In Illinois, the judge had to determine either that a minor was mature and well-informed enough to make the decision on her own or that parental notification would not be in the young person's best interest. If either of those standards were met, a waiver could be granted.

"The vast, vast majority of petitions in Illinois were approved," said Emily Werth, staff attorney for the ACLU of Illinois Judicial Bypass Coordination Project, which offered free legal representation to minors seeking judicial waivers.

Parental notification requirements in Illinois went into effect in 2013.[3] During the next nine years, 625 judicial waivers were granted to young people represented by the Judicial Bypass Coordination Project; only one of these waiver requests was ever denied, according to the ACLU of Illinois.[4]

The teen with the long blonde hair said she had never tried to get a judicial bypass in Ohio, which required parental consent before anyone under 18 could terminate a pregnancy. After consulting with an attorney back home, she learned the process would be much more difficult there compared to Illinois. In 2011, Ohio had tightened its criteria for a judicial waiver, including adding a requirement that the courts "specifically inquire about the minor's understanding of the possible physical and emotional complications of abortion" and determine whether the minor had been coached on her answers.[5]

Regardless of age, Ohio law in 2015 also mandated in-person counseling followed by a 24-hour waiting period before an abortion.[6] For the teen this would have required one trip to seek a judicial waiver from the judge and, if one was granted, two more trips to a clinic for counseling and the procedure. That likely would have meant missing more days of school, and it also would have delayed the procedure.

"Illinois was the closest place to me that had really any hope of a judicial bypass," she said. "So that was my last resort."

* * *

The Ohio teen had been experiencing nausea so intense she had to surreptitiously duck out of her Advanced Placement classes to be sick. She took a pregnancy test at her boyfriend's home. Although terrified, she was not entirely surprised when the second pink line appeared. Her boyfriend was initially speechless.

"What are we going to do?" she asked him as she cried.

"We're going to figure something out," she recalled him saying as he hugged her.

They had met six months prior, when the young man with bright blue eyes approached her in the school library and complimented her performance in a recent school play. He was an athlete, the clean-cut type and not a big partier, all traits she liked. The teen said she and her boyfriend were always meticulous about using condoms.

"I thought I'd done everything to prevent this," she said, adding that she was fitted for an intrauterine device after the unplanned pregnancy and continued using condoms as a backup method.

The high school junior had started researching abortion laws in her home state when she learned she was pregnant and then began quietly stashing away several hundred dollars to pay for the procedure. The longer she waited, the more she was worried the pregnancy would start to show.

"I honestly didn't see how I was going to come out of this OK," she recalled. "I was only months away from being a legal adult and this decision could have changed my life forever, just because of a couple months."

She traveled to Chicago seeking the judicial waiver by herself because she and her boyfriend worried it might seem too suspicious if they were both missing at the same time.

The afternoon hearing didn't take very long: The judge granted the teen the waiver the same day. Then she had a second predicament. Her abortion appointment wasn't until the next morning and she had no money left for a hotel room because all her savings would pay for the procedure. A little snow seeped into her shoes as she contemplated sleeping outside the abortion clinic.

"I guess I'm just going to have to wait outside all night," she recalled thinking to herself.

Instead, she found a warm bed and hot meals in the home of a stranger who lived a few miles from the courthouse in the Bridgeport neighborhood on Chicago's South Side. A woman from Midwest Access Coalition, the Chicago practical abortion nonprofit, hosted the girl from Ohio in her house overnight.

The young woman with the long blonde hair recalled feeling scared the morning of the procedure and sharing those fears with her host over bowls of oatmeal with brown sugar. Later that day, she had an aspiration abortion. Because she needed to return home as soon as possible, she decided to forgo anesthesia.

"It was the most horrible pain I could imagine," she recalled. "It felt like my insides were being sucked out and ripped out of my body."

But the procedure lasted only about five minutes. Soon after, she had to hurry to catch her bus back to Ohio. The teen said she had read that some people feel sadness or regret after terminating a pregnancy, but she never experienced any negative emotions.

"I felt like I had taken care of this," she said. "I still don't regret it. I believe it was such a good choice that I made back then."

She doesn't believe age should be a factor in abortion laws.

The teen with the long blonde hair graduated high school a little over a year after her abortion. She went on to attend a university in a coastal city with mountain peaks in the distance, hundreds of miles from her Ohio town.

"More than anything, I wanted to go to college and get a degree, do something I'm passionate about and have a job," she said. "I feel like the people who helped me get through that, even though they were complete strangers, they gave me a rebirth. A second life."

* * *

While most judicial bypass requests were granted in Illinois, this wasn't the case in many other states that offered the alternative. Some state laws required judges to use specific criteria when deciding whether to grant a waiver of parental consent or notification. These factors could include the minor's intelligence, emotional stability and understanding of potential consequences of having an abortion.[7] Fifteen states used a particularly strict legal standard where the judge had to find "clear and convincing evidence" that the young person was mature enough to make the decision and that terminating a pregnancy was in the minor's best interest.[8]

One of those states was Florida, where an orphaned 16-year-old's request for a judicial bypass was denied in summer 2022, shortly after the fall of *Roe*.[9] The trial court found that the teen had not "established by clear and convincing evidence that she was sufficiently mature to decide whether to terminate her pregnancy," according to court records.[10]

An appeals court affirmed that decision in mid-August and remanded the case back to the trial court, allowing the young woman another chance to go before the initial judge. But the teen was already about 11 weeks pregnant. As of July 1, 2022, Florida had banned abortions past 15 weeks' gestation, so the young woman had only a few weeks to seek the time-sensitive procedure before an abortion would be illegal in her home state.

The young woman—identified as Jane Doe 22-B in court documents—had no parents but lived with a relative and had an appointed guardian. She was pursuing a GED through a program "designed to assist young women who have experienced trauma in their lives by providing educational support and counseling," according to court records.

In a handwritten petition to the court, the young woman said she was sufficiently mature to make the decision to have an abortion, adding that she didn't have a job, was still in high school and was "not ready to have a baby." Her statement said her guardian was "fine" with her decision to terminate.

A caseworker and a guardian ad litem child advocate manager were both present during the hearing with the trial court judge; the teen checked a box indicating she did not request an attorney even though one would have been provided for free by the court, according to court records.

The teen had already done Google searches and read a pamphlet given to her and a family member during a medical clinic visit, to better understand her medical options and their potential consequences, court records said.

But the trial court judge seemed concerned that the teen had at one point indicated she was open to carrying the pregnancy to term and that she might also be under stress stemming from the death of a friend shortly before she decided to seek an abortion, court documents said.

"Reading between the lines, it appears that the trial court wanted to give the minor, who was under extra stress due to a friend's death, additional time to express a keener understanding of the consequences of terminating a pregnancy," an appeals court judge said. "This makes some sense given that the minor, at least at one point, says she was open to having a child, but later changed her view after considering her inability to care for a child in her current station in life."

The case sparked a firestorm online, highlighting the extra burden minors often face when seeking abortions—and how the end of federal abortion protections might exacerbate those challenges.

"It is devastating to know that in Florida, a child is 'sufficiently mature' enough to go through childbirth but not mature enough to receive an abortion," the Washington, D.C.–based National Organization for Women posted on Twitter.[11]

California governor Gavin Newsom encouraged the Florida teen and others grappling with the same dilemma to come to his state, which had no parental involvement requirements for minors seeking abortions.

"Important information for Jane Doe 22-B and all the others facing this kind of government-mandated birth: California is not Florida," he tweeted. "California will provide the medical care you seek."[12]

In another Florida case, Hillsborough County Circuit Court judge Jared Smith denied a judicial bypass to a 17-year-old seeking an abortion, citing her grade point average as part of the reason. Court records said the teen told the judge she made B grades in school, but she had a 2.0 grade point average, which indicated an overall C average.[13]

"However, addressing her 'overall intelligence,' the court found her intelligence to be less than average because '[w]hile she claimed that her grades were Bs during her testimony, her GPA is currently 2.0. Clearly, a B average would not equate to a 2.0 GPA,'" court records said.

The judge said the teen's testimony "evinces either a lack of intelligence or credibility, either of which weigh against a finding of maturity pursuant to the statute." The judge added that the teen, known in court documents as "Jane Doe," had "never had any financial responsibilities, even so much as paying her own cell phone bills," according to court records.

In her petition for a waiver, the high school junior said that after graduation she planned to join the military and then go to college. One day, she hoped to become a nurse. She had been working for the past year and had three jobs during that period; over the summer, she worked two of those jobs at once, court records said.

The 17-year-old said she discussed birth control with her mother, but her mom resided out of state. She lived with her father, "who does not believe in abortion except in cases of rape," court records said. The teen testified that she believed both of her parents "would urge her to keep the baby if they found out that she wanted an abortion," court records said.

She told the court she had never been treated for mental illness and that no one was pressuring her to terminate the pregnancy. She added that she had talked about the decision with her best friend, the mother of her best friend and the mother of her boyfriend; she had been with her boyfriend for a year, and he supported her choice to end the pregnancy, according to court records.

In her testimony, she said she had decided to terminate "because she is not yet financially stable and that she wants to be able to be on her own first," according to court records. While the teen told the court that abortion was inconsistent with her religious beliefs, she said she had considered adoption but "decided to do the abortion because I'm not going to have a baby for nine months and then get attached," adding that she felt this "would hurt more mentally" than having an abortion.

In January 2022, two of three judges on an appeals court panel overturned Smith's decision, granting her the judicial bypass and allowing her to have the abortion. The panel majority found the teen's testimony "demonstrates that she possesses an ability to assess the consequences of her choice and the risk it entails, as well as the intention to reassess her decision after direct consultation with her physician."[14]

Hillsborough County voters in August 2022 ousted Smith, a rare election loss for an incumbent circuit judge.[15] Many reproductive rights advocates attributed Smith's defeat to his highly publicized ruling in the judicial bypass case, while celebrating the victory of his challenger, local attorney Nancy Jacobs.

"Turns out that ripping bodily autonomy from Floridians, including young people, is pretty unpopular," Florida Planned Parenthood Action tweeted after the election. "Congratulations to Florida Planned Parenthood PAC-endorsed candidate, Nancy Jacobs!"[16]

Yet Smith was soon back on the bench: Florida governor Ron DeSantis in December 2022 appointed him to serve as judge on the Sixth District Court of Appeal, a higher court than his previous one.[17]

* * *

The judicial bypass system ended in Illinois on June 1, 2022, just a few weeks before the Supreme Court overturned *Roe*.

In December 2021, Governor J.B. Pritzker had signed a controversial measure repealing the state's parental notice law, allowing minors to have an abortion in Illinois without notifying an adult family member.[18] The law went into effect about six months later. There was no longer a need for anyone under 18 to go before a judge and request a waiver because the age barrier to having an abortion had been eliminated.

Reproductive rights advocates had rallied for dismantling parental notice requirements in Illinois for years, asserting that most youths voluntarily involve a parent or another trusted family member in decisions about an unplanned pregnancy. Those who do not inform parents "often fear physical or emotional abuse, being kicked out of the home, alienation from their families or other deterioration of family relationships, or being forced to continue a pregnancy against their will," according to a 2021 Human Rights Watch and ACLU of Illinois report on parental notice laws in Illinois.[19]

Of 192 youths who went through the Illinois judicial bypass process from 2017 to 2020, 40 percent reported concerns about being forced to continue their pregnancies and 40 percent believed they would be kicked out of their homes or cut off financially. Of those surveyed, 30 percent were worried their family relationships would deteriorate and

9 percent feared physical or emotional abuse, according to the report. (Participants were permitted to cite multiple reasons for seeking a judicial waiver.)[20]

The report also included examples of minors who had to involve unsupportive parents or adult family members in their abortion decisions, due to the parental notice law. A University of Chicago obstetrician-gynecologist described performing an abortion on a young person whose mother refused to give her a ride home afterward.

"We had a mom who left her daughter there (at the hospital)," the physician said in the report, adding that the mother told her daughter, "You can get yourself home. Figure it out."[21]

Another abortion provider interviewed in the report described cases where parental notice put youths in physical danger.

"I see it in cases where a patient has come to us and said, 'I notified my parents,' or another adult living in the house that complies with the law, 'and now because of that, I am scared about going home after this procedure,'" the physician said.[22]

A 2021 study of Illinois judicial bypass data published in the *Journal of Adolescent Health* found that the process extended the average number of days it took for youths to get an abortion by a week—extra time that can add risk and difficulty to the procedure as gestational age increases.

"Judicial bypass can offer young people an opportunity to retain autonomy in decision-making, potentially avoiding abuse and other negative outcomes," the study concluded. "However, even in a state with a well-organized network of attorneys, [judicial bypass] contributes one week to minors' abortion-seeking timeline and necessitates traveling long distances."[23]

The American Academy of Pediatrics also opposes measures that mandate parental involvement for minors seeking abortions.

"Most adolescents voluntarily involve parents and other trusted adults in decisions regarding pregnancy termination and should be encouraged to do so when safe and appropriate," an August 2022 policy statement from the American Academy of Pediatrics Committee on Adolescence said. "The legal climate surrounding abortion law is rapidly becoming more restrictive and threatens to adversely impact adolescents. Mandatory parental involvement, the judicial bypass procedure, and general restrictive abortion policies pose risks to adolescents' health by causing delays in accessing medical care, increasing volatility within a family, and limiting their pregnancy options."[24]

Attorney Ameri Klafeta represented young people during the judicial bypass process as part of her work as director of the Women's and Reproductive Rights Project at the ACLU of Illinois. After the Supreme Court overturned *Roe*, she worried about minors in other states. Whenever there are bans or severe restrictions on abortions, the most vulnerable and marginalized groups bear the brunt of the burden, and that includes young people, Klafeta said.

"They may be in unsafe family situations where if their family finds out they are pregnant, they may be at risk of physical harm," she said. "They may get kicked out of their family's house. They may be forced to carry a pregnancy to term when they don't want to. They have hopes and goals and dreams for their future that they wouldn't be able to realize."[25]

* * *

Anti-abortion activists decried the end of the Illinois Parental Notice of Abortion Act.

"This is a tragic day for parents, girls, and preborn babies across the Midwest," said Kevin Grillot, executive director of the March for Life, on the day the mandate was rolled back. "Illinois is now the only state in the Midwest that does not have parental [involvement requirements] in place, an open invitation to out-of-state minors to pursue abortions in Illinois."[26]

Avery Bourne, a Republican state representative from Morrisonville, in central Illinois, defended the parental notice law on the House floor in October 2021. She listed various actions a minor can't take without consent of a parent: Getting a tattoo or a piercing. Going on a field trip.

"We talk about health care—they can't go to their school nurse and get a Tylenol without the consent of their parents," she said. "It's about parents having the basic right to know what is going on in their minor child's life."[27]

Parents should have the right to know if their child is undergoing a serious medical procedure, Bourne said.

"If your child's having their tonsils taken out, setting a broken arm, a ruptured appendix, of course the parent has a right to know what's happening," she said. "But an abortion has so much more of an impact on a minor daughter's mental and physical health than a broken arm. If a parent deserves to know about a broken arm, then holy cow they deserve to know if their daughter is considering an abortion."

Recalling her own teen abortion, Maureen Deitche of northwest suburban Chicago said she too believes that rescinding the parental notice requirement was a mistake.[28]

At the age of 14, she found out she was pregnant and panicked. This was in 1975, decades before parental involvement was mandated by law in Illinois. At-home pregnancy tests didn't exist at the time. She went to an abortion clinic to take a test and recalled crying hysterically by the building's elevators when she learned it was positive. Clinic staff heard her crying and came to console her; they told her she could terminate the pregnancy and wouldn't have to tell her mother and father, she recalled.

"That was the clincher, that I didn't have to tell my parents," she said. "It sounded like life was going to be OK and go on as usual."

The night before the procedure, she spoke to her unborn baby while rubbing her belly, saying she wished she could keep him or her. After the abortion, she sobbed in a recovery room. She recalled an employee at the clinic tried to comfort her, reassuring her there would be other opportunities for motherhood later in life.

She and her boyfriend, who was just a few years older, both believed their lives would continue as if the unplanned pregnancy had never happened. Yet she described a persistent sorrow and anxiety.

"I believe deep down it's something you'll never forget," she said. "You'll always know there was a child in your life who never lived to see the light of day."

The couple didn't begin using birth control after the first unplanned pregnancy. So she said it was no surprise when she became pregnant again shortly after, at the age of 15. In hindsight, she believes she was trying to replace the first baby that had been terminated.

"I guess because I had such a sense of loss," she said, "I felt like, in my heart, that I had hoped to get pregnant again. It made the loss from the first baby more bearable, knowing that I had another chance."

Her mother and other loved ones urged her to end the pregnancy, not knowing about the first abortion that she had kept secret, or the remorse that followed. This time, the teen was adamant she would never terminate another pregnancy. After finishing her sophomore year at a high school for pregnant girls in downtown Chicago, she dropped out. This was her only regret of becoming a mother so young, that she never completed her education.

She and her boyfriend, Paul Deitche, wed at city hall in downtown Chicago, her father signing to give his consent so his underage daughter could legally marry. They celebrated with a backyard wedding party on Maureen's sixteenth birthday, the young bride eight months pregnant in a white maternity outfit, the groom a recent high school graduate.

Four weeks later, Maureen gave birth via cesarean section to a healthy baby girl. Once she was alone in the hospital room and cradling her newborn daughter, she wept. The tears were for her first baby, the one she would never be able to hold.

"There was no replacement," she said. "I was very sad that I had taken a life of someone who was just as precious as the child I was holding in my arms. I realized I was a mother of two. One was dead and one was alive. It made my motherhood to the first child more of a reality."

Maureen said the instant her mother held the newborn, she was thrilled to be a grandmother. After her mom died in 2007, Maureen was shopping for funeral clothes and a comforting thought assuaged her grief: Her mother was now in heaven with her first baby, whom she always believed to be a girl. In her mind, she heard her mother saying, "Maureen, she's beautiful, she's beautiful!"

Decades later, the Deitches shared the story of their abortion in a video posted on the website of the nonprofit organization Priests for Life.

"It's something you'll regret," Maureen said in the recording. "You can't take it back. Once you've done it, it's done. You can't make up for this type of mistake. You will always remember that you had a child."[29]

Maureen and Paul have four children together and many grandchildren. They have attended retreats designed to provide healing for post-abortive couples struggling with grief. They participate in the annual March for Life in Washington, D.C.

The couple also sponsored a memorial brick that's paved into the walkway of a prayer garden at Marytown, a Catholic pilgrimage site that's home to the National Shrine of St. Maximilian Kolbe, located just north of Chicago.

The marker reads "In memory of our aborted child."

"I would like to tell any young man, or any aged man, that this is not what you want to do," Paul said in the video. "This child is yours as much as it is the woman's and you should want that child because that child is part of you and it's a gift from God, as is all life. And you don't want to be the one to take that life away."[30]

"I don't want to see anybody go down that path," Maureen said.[31]

11.
Abortions in the Shadow of Notre Dame

A young woman exited the back door of a northern Indiana abortion clinic in summer 2019, clutching a fistful of crumpled tissues in one hand and some paperwork in the other.[1] A trio of volunteers in bright pink vests labeled "Pro-Choice Clinic Escort" flanked the patient, walking beside her until she reached her SUV. As she drove off the clinic's property, the three escorts deployed rainbow-hued umbrellas and hoisted them over their shoulders, forming a barrier between the patient's vehicle and several pro-life protesters out front.

Some of the anti-abortion demonstrators were praying. Others held signs declaring "Abortion takes a human life" and "It's a child, not a choice."

After the patient drove off the clinic's property, the three escorts folded their umbrellas and returned inside the roughly 1,900-square-foot red-brick medical building, awaiting the arrival or exit of the next patient. The ritual would be repeated about a dozen times throughout the day.

The abortion clinic, Whole Woman's Health of South Bend, opened in June 2019 in a particularly unusual state of limbo. A federal judge had granted a preliminary injunction allowing staff there to perform medication abortions, even as the clinic remained unlicensed by the Indiana Department of Health.

Whole Woman's Health Alliance had applied for a license to open a clinic in South Bend in 2017, but the state health department denied the application, alleging that the medical facility failed to meet the requirement of "reputable and responsible character." The conservative, Republican-led state also said that clinic owners did not release information related to other Whole Woman's Health medical facilities.

Whole Woman's Health officials filed a lawsuit, calling the state's objections "politically motivated" and "medically unnecessary."

The legal battle over the small medical office in Middle America made national headlines, in part because the unlicensed clinic's tenuous survival was championed by Democratic presidential candidate Pete Buttigieg, the mayor of South Bend at the time.

Buttigieg—who ultimately dropped out of the race for president but went on to serve as U.S. secretary of transportation under the Biden administration—was running on a national campaign that included a pro-reproductive-rights platform. He cited the need for greater abortion access around the country as well as in South Bend, a college town with a population of about 103,000 adjacent to the University of Notre Dame.

"The mayor is deeply concerned by what he views as a new and extreme assault on *Roe v. Wade* in legislatures across the country," said his campaign's press secretary. "He believes that the truly radical idea in this debate and around abortion care is one of banning abortion outright. The South Bend clinic would be the only one for a radius of several counties. It is a restriction on a woman's right if she is low-income, or doesn't have a vehicle, and she has to visit multiple times, but the clinic is dozens of miles away."

In granting the injunction that allowed the clinic to open, district judge Sarah Evans Barker noted the burdens of legal restrictions and travel, saying "the obstacles to obtaining abortions in northern Indiana are such that women find it easier to travel out of state to Chicago, bypassing nearby Merrillville, to obtain abortions there."[2]

State officials, however, called it "deeply troubling" to have a medical facility, especially an abortion clinic, open without a state license.

The Indiana Department of Health "has no authority to inspect an unlicensed clinic, meaning that we cannot investigate any complaints that Whole Woman's Health is not operating safely or not following state law," said a spokesman for Attorney General Curtis Hill.

"These provisions are designed to protect the State's interests in women's health and fetal life," the spokesman said. "Without licensing, the state has no way to protect women and babies."

The state official called the lawsuit a "meritless challenge" that diverted government time and resources from other cases.

"The larger toll, however, is on Indiana women, who now have no recourse against an unlicensed and unregulated abortion clinic that may or may not choose to follow state law," he said. "Indiana will stand strong to protect women and unborn children by ensuring that its duly-enacted abortion regulations are properly enforced and defended."

* * *

One clinic escort wiped beads of sweat from her brow and retreated to the shade of a large tree, awaiting the arrival of another patient at Whole Woman's Health of South Bend. There was a weather advisory in effect that afternoon, with the heat index reaching more than 100 degrees. Several anti-abortion demonstrators lingered just past a makeshift fence—a thin rope attached to a few wooden stakes separating the medical facility's property from the public right-of-way. Clinic staffers said protesters were present every day, regardless of the weather.

"No one should have to go through this," said the clinic escort, who trains other volunteers. "We shield the patients. A lot of patients don't understand, they think they're just going to a doctor's appointment. I didn't understand when I was a patient."

She recounted her own medication abortion several years prior at a now-defunct clinic a few miles away. Abortion wasn't a concept she had ever thought much about while growing up in a small town far from South Bend. As a college student still figuring out her life, she said, she was grateful for an abortion clinic close by and the ability to end the pregnancy.

The day of her abortion appointment, mounds of snow had filled the medical facility's parking lot after a winter storm, so she had to park on the street. She was shocked at the crowd of protesters that formed outside despite the icy roads and freezing temperatures.

The demonstrators kept calling her "mom," the clinic escort recalled, which angered her. There were no escorts to walk by her side at that clinic.

"It was the worst part of my abortion experience, having to walk through them," she said. "I felt so shamed. They don't know who I am, they don't know me. Who are they? I thought Jesus said he who is without sin cast the first stone."

About a month after Whole Woman's Health of South Bend opened, more than 50 volunteers had been trained to serve as escorts, and they helped in numerous ways, clinic staff said. When one protester began preaching with a megaphone, the volunteer escorts raised money to buy a few sound machines to drown out the noise. Members of the community also planted and cared for flowers on the property.

Inside the clinic, the walls were painted a soft shade of light purple, laced with various inspirational quotes.

"Liberation must come from within," by Chicago-born writer Sandra Cisneros, was etched above the front desk.

Some women were alone in the clinic waiting room. Some couples embraced or held hands. Occasionally, soft sobs emanated from the clinic's counseling room. Tea and other drinks were available in the corner.

Ten clients came to Whole Woman's Health that weekday, most for state-mandated counseling prior to their medication abortions. The clinic offered only nonsurgical abortions, up to 10 weeks of gestation. Without a state license, the clinic had to send patients to an outside lab for any blood work or other testing, another step that can delay the time-sensitive procedure, said Brenda Morgan, then the acting clinic manager.

Per Indiana law, the medical provider first had to go through an abortion informed consent brochure from the state health department, which includes descriptions and color pictures of the embryo or fetus at the patient's particular point in gestation as well as information about the likelihood of the fetus's survival outside the womb:

> **Six weeks after fertilization**—Facial features are beginning to form, with dark spots where the eyes will eventually be, opening for the nostrils, and pits which will form ears. Arm and leg buds are beginning to protrude. The brain is forming. The heart is beating regularly at about 150 beats per minute and can be seen on an ultrasound. The very earliest blood vessels are formed and blood has begun circulating.
> **Twelve weeks after fertilization**—The basic structure of the brain is complete. The face has a human appearance, and the genitalia begin to show the gender of the embryo. The eyes are now closed and will not reopen until about the 28th week. Vocal cords are formed, and the embryo begins to make sounds.
> **Eighteen weeks after fertilization**—The eyes and ears are in their final position on the face. The fetus begins to develop reflexes, such as blinking. Fingerprints and toe prints develop. Fetal circulation is completely functional at this gestational age. . . . At this time the fetus begins to move actively, a feeling women often describe as "fluttering."[3]

The state's abortion informed consent certification, which had to be signed by the patient and medical provider 18 hours before the abortion, includes the statement that "human physical life begins when a human ovum is fertilized by a human sperm."[4]

Morgan said the clinic provided its own patient counseling, separately from the state-mandated consent.

"You can come in here and know, 'This is not the right time for me to have a baby, I'm in school, I can't afford another baby,'" she said. "But we want to make sure this is not just the head talking, we want to make sure it's the heart talking too. And that you know that you're going to be OK when you walk out of here and you're not pregnant."

In 2018, 8,037 patients terminated a pregnancy in Indiana, an increase over 7,778 in 2017, according to state health department statistics.[5] In 2018, 142 of those abortion patients were residents of St. Joseph County, which includes South Bend.

The clinic served roughly three dozen patients in its first month, an average of about 10 each week, Morgan said.

"We definitely realize the need is here in South Bend," she said. "The need for us to be here."

Back outside, one demonstrator alternated between praying and attempting to pass out literature on alternatives to abortion to passersby.

"We're not here to beat them up, we're here to let them know they have a choice—but to help them make the right choice, the best choice," she said, her cheeks reddened from the severe heat. "I know women who have had abortions who still think about their aborted babies. This is not your only choice."

* * *

As the clinic fought the state for its license, a separate battle waged right next door.

An anti-abortion pregnancy resource center, Women's Care Center, was trying to open a site on property adjacent to the clinic. The strategic location follows a larger pattern that plays out on the streets of cities and suburbs across the country: Once a new abortion clinic opens, a crisis pregnancy center will often settle nearby or next door, in the hope of deterring patients from terminating and instead leading them to carry their pregnancies to term.

After Whole Woman's Health established a clinic in Peoria, Illinois, which offered telehealth abortion services until its 2019 closure, a Women's Care Center had opened in an adjacent building there. Women's Care Center has 34 locations nationwide in 12 states, according to its website. The one in Peoria remained open even after the nearby abortion clinic closed.

"Our locations are very important to us," said Women's Care Center vice president Jenny Hunsberger. "So we have opened up next to, across the street, close to abortion clinics. . . . Often if we are next door to an abortion clinic, women come to us—not because they are coerced, not because they're tricked, not because they don't know—rather because they're unsure or they want a second opinion."

Mayor Buttigieg ignited a firestorm in 2018 when he vetoed a rezoning request by Women's Care Center, which was required for it to use the property next to the South Bend clinic. In a letter to other city leaders, he argued that the neighborhood wouldn't benefit from adjacent organizations with "deep and opposite commitments on the most divisive social issue of our time."[6]

Whole Woman's Health officials in a statement thanked Buttigieg "for standing up for what is right and putting women and families of South Bend first." But abortion opponents denounced the veto as stymieing the work of a local nonprofit that helped women and children in need.[7]

"It's really disappointing to see him or any presidential candidate devalue the life of the unborn," said Jackie Appleman, executive director of St. Joseph County Right to Life, which would later change its name to Right to Life Michiana.

At Women's Care Center's headquarters on Notre Dame Avenue in South Bend, a man in the lobby bounced a baby girl on his knee while reading a magazine. The cream-colored walls and plush couches were designed to feel warm and inviting, like the living room of a home, Hunsberger said. A dresser by the entrance offered baby clothing of all sizes for moms and dads to take on the way out.

Hunsberger estimated that the mothers of roughly half of all babies born annually in surrounding St. Joseph County were assisted by Women's Care Center facilities; in the city of South Bend, it's about two-thirds, she said, adding that she compared state health department data to the organization's records to get those figures. The average client tends to visit eight times a year, Hunsberger said, with centers offering parenting classes, book giveaways and a boutique with free strollers, cribs and car seats.

Some city leaders were concerned the pregnancy center would fuel protests at the abortion clinic, disrupting peace in the neighborhood. Hunsberger stressed that the charity tries to promote an environment of peace for the women they serve and doesn't engage in politics or demonstrations.

"We exist to give women the opportunity to choose life," Hunsberger said. "For some women, it's a second option they don't know they have."

Women's Care Center has strong ties to the University of Notre Dame, the nearby premier Catholic research university. The nonprofit was founded by a Notre Dame professor in 1984. The University of Notre Dame Center for Ethics and Culture in 2019 recognized Women's Care Centers as the recipient of "the nation's most important lifetime achievement award for heroes of the pro-life movement."[8]

The president of Notre Dame University, the Reverend John Jenkins, who serves on the Women's Care Center Foundation's board, expressed deep disappointment in Buttigieg's veto.

"The mayor's decision excludes an important presence from that neighborhood and thwarts plans that had met the criteria for rezoning and had been approved by the Common Council," Jenkins said in a 2018 statement. "Far from enhancing the harmony of the neighborhood, it divides our community and diminishes opportunities for vulnerable women to have a real choice."[9]

The pregnancy center soon found a different site that didn't require zoning changes. A Women's Care Center opened in July 2019 on the property of a former pet boarding business, whose owner learned of the charity's plight.

The new location was just across the street from the South Bend abortion clinic, the two facilities with clashing ideologies in plain sight of one another.

* * *

The clinic remained open unlicensed, under court order, for more than two years. During that time, more changes were shifting the makeup of the Supreme Court further to the right.

On September 18, 2020, U.S. Supreme Court Justice Ruth Bader Ginsburg died at the age of 87.[10]

Abortion providers around the country, including those at Whole Woman's Health, mourned the death of the second woman ever appointed to the bench, a celebrated pioneer in gender equality and defender of reproductive rights.

"All of us at Whole Woman's Health raise a glass to Justice Ginsburg and thank her from the bottom of our hearts for the contributions she made to our equality, our health, and our rights," Whole Woman's Health said in a statement. "Her passing at this time is devastating for the future of the Supreme Court. We must honor her legacy by following her instruction to 'fight for the things you care about and do it in a way that will lead others to join you.'"[11]

Ginsburg's successor has deep roots at the University of Notre Dame and in the South Bend area.

Thirty-eight days before the 2020 general election, President Trump announced his intent to nominate Judge Amy Coney Barrett of the U.S. Court of Appeals for the Seventh Circuit, who at the time lived with her husband and seven children in the Harter Heights neighborhood of South Bend.[12] Barrett had graduated from Notre Dame Law School, where she was first in her class. She later served as a faculty member at the law school, earning several distinguished professor awards.[13]

Leaders at Notre Dame celebrated Barrett's nomination, noting that she was the first alum of the law school and faculty member to achieve such an honor. Jenkins, the university president, attended Barrett's nomination ceremony at the White House Rose Garden.[14]

"Judge Amy Coney Barrett is an absolutely brilliant legal scholar and jurist," said Marcus Cole, dean of the law school, in a written statement. "She is also one of the most popular teachers we have ever had here at Notre Dame Law School. Judge Barrett is incredibly generous with her time and wisdom while mentoring her students."[15]

Yet a few weeks later, hundreds of Notre Dame faculty members signed two letters opposing Barrett's confirmation, asking her to halt the nomination process until after the November 2020 election.[16]

"The rushed nature of your nomination process, which you certainly recognize as an exercise in raw power politics, may effectively deprive the American people of a voice in selecting the next Supreme Court justice," one of the letters said. "You are not, of course, responsible for the anti-democratic machinations driving your nomination. Nor are you complicit in the Republican hypocrisy of fast-tracking your nomination weeks before a presidential election when many of the same senators refused to grant Merrick Garland so much as a hearing a full year before the last election. However, you can refuse to be party to such maneuvers."[17]

Old newspapers from Notre Dame and the South Bend area offered a glimpse into the conservative judge's pro-life stance. In 2006, Barrett signed an ad opposing "abortion on demand," which was part of a two-page spread in a local newspaper around the anniversary of *Roe*. Her name was included on another "right to life" advertisement while she was on the faculty at Notre Dame Law School and a member of the University Faculty for Life group, which sponsored the ad in the student newspaper.[18]

This other ad was not dated but did mention the 40th anniversary of *Roe*.

"We renew our call for the unborn to be protected in law," stated that ad, which was signed by dozens of university faculty and staff.[19]

After Barrett was confirmed to the Supreme Court on October 26, 2020, sealing Trump's third selection to the bench, Notre Dame's president congratulated her.

"Recognized by experts from across the spectrum of judicial philosophies as a superb legal scholar and judge, she is an esteemed colleague and a teacher revered by her students," Jenkins said in a statement. "We join her family and friends in celebrating this momentous achievement, and we assure Justice Barrett and all her colleagues on the nation's highest court of our continued prayers in their work of administering justice and upholding the Constitution."[20]

* * *

A prospective patient called Whole Woman's Health of South Bend on September 14, 2022, hoping to schedule an appointment to terminate her pregnancy.[21] The manager said the health center could provide a pregnancy test but not an abortion. In a matter of hours, terminating a pregnancy would be nearly outlawed across the state of about 6.7 million people.

"On Wednesday night at midnight, abortion becomes illegal in Indiana," Stacie Balentine, the clinic manager at the time, explained to the caller. "For that reason, we don't have any more appointments available here at this clinic. There is information I can give you for other places you can contact."

The caller asked if she would have to go to neighboring Illinois, where abortion was legal and highly protected by state law.

Balentine said that Illinois—Chicago in particular—would be "a good choice."

Whole Woman's Health ultimately won its fight against the Indiana Department of Health, which granted the clinic a license in January 2022 after about two-and-a-half years of operating without a license under court order.

The framed document hangs on a wall near Balentine's desk.

The clinic's victory was short-lived. About five months later, a majority of Supreme Court justices, including Barrett, voted to overturn *Roe*. Many states had preexisting abortion bans or trigger laws that went into effect after the end of federal abortion protections. But in August, Indiana became the first state to pass a near-total abortion ban after the end of *Roe*.[22] The measure outlawed abortion except in very narrow circumstances. Cases of rape and incest before 10 weeks post-fertilization. Instances that endanger the life and physical health of the pregnant patient. Pregnancies where the fetus has a lethal anomaly.

All seven of the state's clinics had to cease performing abortions, according to the law.

The state health department sent a letter to Whole Woman's Health of South Bend in August 2022 stating that the law eliminated the state licensure of abortion clinics; from then on, any pregnancy terminations that were permitted had to be performed in hospitals.

"Therefore, effective at 12 a.m. (Eastern Standard Time) on September 15, the abortion clinic license issued by the Indiana Department of Health to Whole Woman's Health of South Bend will be rendered void," the letter stated.

Several Indiana abortion providers, including Whole Woman's Health, sued in August to try and block the state's ban from taking place. The lawsuit claimed the state abortion ban violated the Indiana Constitution.[23]

The property of the clinic was conspicuously quiet the day before the state ban went into effect. No protesters waved signs out front. No clinic escorts unfurled umbrellas.

The parking lot had been expanded in the spring to accommodate more cars. Now the lot was nearly empty, except for the vehicles driven by a few staff members. In May, Whole Woman's Health had hosted a clinic blessing, where clergy and religious leaders came to "honor the sacred work at Whole Woman's Health of South Bend, the patients who want and need abortions and the healthcare professionals who serve them," an event invitation said.[24]

"The majority of people of faith support access to abortion, and people from all faith traditions seek abortion care," the clinic said in a statement. "Many spiritual and religious people respect and affirm the right to choose abortion as a moral good. Yet anti-abortion religious extremists have been exceptionally loud in condemning abortion as religiously and morally unacceptable. They are in the minority and their religious understanding of abortion is not the only understanding."[25]

The clinic had received a provisional license allowing it to begin performing surgical procedures in April 2022. But a few days later, a draft copy of the Supreme Court decision leaked, indicating the high court's plan to overturn *Roe*. So the clinic never offered in-clinic procedures, although medication abortions were still available.

The space that would have been a recovery room for patients after a procedure held a few cardboard boxes with packed items. The medical instruments that would have been used to provide aspiration abortions were being sent to other Whole Woman's Health clinics in states where terminating a pregnancy was still legal.

The clinic planned to remain open for follow-up visits, pregnancy tests, ultrasounds and other medical services—just not abortions.

After hanging up the phone with the pregnant patient, Balentine appeared despondent. She said she'd been receiving around five dozen calls a week seeking abortion care, evenly divided between in-state and out-of-state residents.

"That's the worst part of the job—telling people no, we can't help," she said. "That's kind of all that's left at the moment, so it's not great."

* * *

The property next door to Whole Woman's Health that spurred so much controversy a few years ago has a new owner—Right to Life Michiana. The anti-abortion group uses the property adjacent to the clinic "for sidewalk advocacy to help women in crisis, connecting them with alternatives and support in the community," the organization said in an email.

Antonio Marchi, executive director of Right to Life Michiana, said he hopes Indiana's ban perseveres.

"Right to Life Michiana is encouraged by the thought of up to 95 percent of abortions being eliminated in the state, and we are continuing work to build consensus around the value of human life," he said in an email.

In 2021, 8,414 pregnancies were terminated in Indiana, according to state health department data.[26] More than 1,100 patients had abortions at Whole Woman's Health of South Bend after the clinic opened in mid-2019, according to staff. In the weeks following the fall of *Roe*, the number of out-of-state patients coming increased, as bans and restrictions in other states went into effect.

"We would see even more patients from other states where it was more restrictive," said Sharon Lau, Midwest advocacy director for Whole Woman's Health Alliance. "Right after *Roe* in June, we were getting patients from Ohio, because they had a trigger law. We were having patients coming from Texas. It was one after another, as the different avenues that were available are falling."

Lau said Whole Woman's Health is looking into opening a clinic in Illinois, but that's still in the planning stages. Staff can still help patients access medication abortions by mail, but patients must be physically in a state where the abortion is legal when the medical provider prescribes the medication, requiring travel for a telehealth visit and access to an out-of-state address where the pills can be delivered. Whole Woman's Health also started a program to assist patients traveling to other states for abortion care, so staff at the South Bend clinic will help folks access those resources.

"What we're going to see in Indiana is people forced to carry a pregnancy against their will that they don't feel ready for or healthy enough for," said Amy Hagstrom Miller, Whole Woman's Health president and CEO. "Or people are going to have to figure out how to travel to another place to get the abortion that, honestly, they should be able to get in their community."

She added that the drive to Illinois or Michigan to terminate a pregnancy is "more risky than the abortion itself."

"It's been a huge fight, but we've had so much support from the community, and we've served a need for that part of Indiana," she said. "So that part of it has been heartbreaking."

* * *

Just a week after the state abortion ban went into effect, it was temporarily halted when an Indiana circuit court judge issued a temporary injunction.[27] Abortions were permitted to resume at clinics across the state as the case continued through the courts.

Right to Life Michiana lamented that "abortion advocates are using stall tactics to block the law."

"We believe that women can get all the help they need right here in our community, without turning to abortion," Marchi said.

The Women's Care Center location was still open across the street from the South Bend clinic. A pink sign out front with a silhouette of a woman cuddling a baby advertised free ultrasounds and free pregnancy tests. Walk-ins were welcome.

The charity's website says its centers serve more than 400 women a day and perform 28,000 ultrasounds a year. Next to a button for donations, the web page reads "17,538 babies saved in last year."

"Regardless of how circumstances play out in the coming weeks, our mission is clear," Marchi said. "We will continue reaching out to women, educating the community, and advocating that all human life gets the respect and protection it deserves."

Just after the ban was blocked by the courts, Whole Woman's Health of South Bend officials said they would begin making plans to once again offer abortion care "in the near future," noting that it wasn't possible for the clinic to resume abortion services immediately, amid so much legal uncertainty.

But in early June 2023, Whole Woman's Health of South Bend closed, citing "years of politically driven and medically unnecessary abortion restrictions" that made it impossible to stay open.

"Even while navigating relentless attacks on our staff, medical providers, and clinic building—we were still able to serve over 1,100 patients for medication abortion care in our small but mighty South Bend clinic," Miller said in a statement.[28]

In August 2023, Indiana's near-total abortion ban took effect, outlawing the termination of a pregnancy except in the narrowest of circumstances.

12.
Saving the Embryo

Rosaries in hand, a small group of abortion opponents gathered outside a medical clinic to pray for the unborn.[1] Under gray skies and a light drizzle, they recited in unison, "May the eyes of all people be transformed, that they may see each and every human life as a reflection of the glory of God himself."

It was a familiar pro-life ritual held at an unconventional location: a fertility clinic located about 30 miles west of Chicago.

The annual Bike for Life fundraiser culminated on a fall Saturday in 2019 with a prayer vigil at the Naperville Fertility Center, a medical facility where science and cutting-edge technology are often heralded for enabling life when it was once deemed impossible.

Yet the demonstrators in front of the clinic expressed concern for the fate of the frozen embryos inside—particularly those that might be destroyed, cryopreserved indefinitely or donated for research as a result of in vitro fertilization treatments.

"When you do IVF, you create a life, but how many lives does it take?" said John Zabinski, founder of the bicycling event. "When you get this life, what happens to the other babies?"

The frozen embryos are only about a tenth of a millimeter in size.[2] But to Zabinski and his fellow bicyclists, an embryo is just as worthy of protection as a fetus of any size or gestational age, based on the moral principle that life begins at conception.

He lamented that some anti-abortion leaders, while fervent about protecting the unborn at later stages of development, often ignore or de-emphasize the potential consequences of IVF. Around the time of the prayer vigil, numerous states had recently passed some of the most restrictive abortion laws in the nation at the time. Among the most stringent was the 2019 near-total ban on terminating a pregnancy that was signed into law in Alabama.[3]

But that measure included a notable exemption—embryos created during in vitro fertilization.

"The egg in the lab doesn't apply," Clyde Chambliss, a Republican state senator and bill sponsor, said during legislative debate. "It's not in a woman. She's not pregnant."[4]

However, that premise has become a glaring point of contention within the pro-life movement as the use of assisted reproductive technology to treat infertility grows increasingly common. About 19 percent of married heterosexual American women of reproductive age who have never given birth will experience infertility—defined as the inability to get pregnant after one year of trying; about 26 percent of women in this category will have difficulty becoming pregnant or carrying a pregnancy to term, according to the CDC.[5]

American Society for Reproductive Medicine spokesman Sean Tipton considers opposition to IVF a fringe crusade among abortion opponents. He noted that battles against fertility treatments tend to be very unpopular; those who oppose terminating a pregnancy are less inclined to take on IVF because "they know they'll lose," he said.

"Even within the anti-choice community, the sanctification of the embryo is far from the mainstream view," he said. "I find it very difficult to follow the logic of groups that purport to be for life objecting to medical facilities whose mission is to help families have babies."

Yet after the Supreme Court overturned *Roe*, many fertility experts expressed concern for how the decision and ensuing state abortion bans might impact fertility patients. Since IVF didn't exist prior to the landmark 1973 decision, "we are in uncharted waters," said Dr. Kara Goldman, associate professor of obstetrics and gynecology in reproductive endocrinology and fertility at Northwestern University Feinberg School of Medicine and medical director of Fertility Preservation at Northwestern Medicine.[6]

"What does this mean for a patient's frozen embryos?" she asked in a university news release.[7] "When a patient has completed their family, embryos are either donated to research or destroyed. If embryo destruction is outlawed, this will have tremendous ramifications for not only the tens of thousands of embryos—and the families who have created those embryos through careful decision-making between the physician and patient—but importantly will have ramifications for the future practice of IVF and the hundreds of thousands of Americans who rely on this technology to build their families."

On the day *Roe* was rescinded, Goldman wrote on Twitter that she'd been asked countless times: What would overturning *Roe* mean for my frozen embryos?[8]

"Each time I'm asked this question I hold back tears, grieving for a freedom we all took for granted," the physician posted on the social media site. "For all who need assisted reproduction to preserve fertility or conceive, for all who need access to abortion, for reproductive rights everywhere: Our grandmothers and mothers are grieving. I grieve for my daughters, I cry for my patients, and I channel my grandmother's fight."

* * *

It's unclear exactly how the end of federal abortion protections might impact fertility treatments in states with abortion bans.

The day after *Roe* was overturned, reproductive rights advocates scrambled to battle a 2021 Arizona "personhood" law with provisions that grant rights to fertilized eggs, embryos and fetuses. The Arizona measure states that "the laws of this state shall be interpreted and construed to acknowledge on behalf of an unborn child at every stage of development, all rights, privileges and immunities available to other persons, citizens and residents of this state." The law defines an unborn child as "the offspring of human beings from conception until birth."[9]

The American Civil Liberties Union of Arizona, the Center for Reproductive Rights and other pro-choice groups filed an emergency motion against the law in late June, and a federal judge temporarily blocked the measure.[10]

While an official from the Arizona attorney general's office told the judge that the law wasn't designed to create any new crime related to abortion, reproductive rights advocates argued the wording and its vague implications spurred more confusion post-*Roe*.[11] Although the measure includes a specific exception for IVF, Arizona Democrats who opposed the law cited in vitro fertilization as a major concern, noting that the scope of the exemption was unclear.[12]

"Does it apply to any nurse, anesthesiologist or technician or office staff that works for an entity that conducts IVF?" said an April 2021 report by Arizona lawmakers in opposition. "What about a company that stores embryos in deep freezers? Would their potential negligence in damaging a test tube containing an embryo or shutting off a freezer subject them to criminal or civil liability and damages?"[13]

After the fall of *Roe*, a law in Georgia took effect granting personhood to fetuses after roughly six weeks of gestation, as soon as a heartbeat can be detected; the provision also grants a $3,000 tax exemption starting at that point in pregnancy and allows parents to claim the embryo or fetus as a dependent on their state taxes.[14] Yet this didn't go far enough for the anti-abortion group Georgia Right to Life, which petitioned the state to convene a special assembly to pass an amendment to the state constitution recognizing the "right to life of all human beings as persons at any stage of development from fertilization to natural death."[15]

"The recent Supreme Court decision on *Dobbs* paves the way for Georgians to take bold, decisive action and leave no child vulnerable to death by abortion," the petition states. "By enacting a Personhood Amendment to the state's constitution, we will lay the foundation to protect all innocent human life, from earliest beginning through natural death—no exceptions. This is the pivotal opportunity we've been praying and working for—to do everything in our power to protect hundreds of thousands of innocent lives."

Even though most state abortion bans don't explicitly target IVF and other forms of assisted reproductive technology, the interpretation of certain definitions of terms within those laws, such as "fertilization" and "unborn," could have an impact on reproductive medicine, according to a July 2022 report by the American Society for Reproductive Medicine, which analyzed abortion trigger laws in roughly a dozen states. The report also noted that IVF patients may be at greater risk for pregnancy complications such as ectopic and heterotopic pregnancy and that state abortion restrictions might have ramifications for care related to these health issues.[16]

A subsequent report on abortion laws by the organization in October 2022 surmised that more fetal personhood laws might be coming in the future, raising additional questions about ramifications for assisted reproductive technology.

"Importantly, in addition to explicit abortion bans, 'fetal personhood' legislation—which confer fetuses and embryos the same legal standing as a human being outside the womb—may become more common in the post-*Roe* world, exposing routine ART (assisted reproductive technology) procedures such as IVF, preimplantation genetic testing, and the donation for research or discarding of unused embryos to legal challenge, and exposing ART providers who practice them to potential liability."[17]

Much of the controversy over IVF stems from embryos that are left over, which can be kept frozen for future use, donated to research, discarded, or adopted by others struggling with infertility. There are an estimated 620,000 embryos cryopreserved in the United States, though many of those will likely be used for future family-building, according a U.S. Department of Health and Human Services report for fiscal year 2019.[18]

"In the course of treatments for infertility, couples usually produce more embryos than they can use," the report said. "These supernumerary embryos are generally frozen while the couple who created them decides about their ultimate disposition."

Margo Kaplan, a professor at Rutgers Law School who had children with the assistance of IVF, found a stark contrast in how the law treats IVF patients versus abortion patients. After her family was complete, she donated a remaining embryo to scientific research. Kaplan noted that she faced no waiting period, state-mandated counseling or any of the other legal barriers women often encounter when terminating a pregnancy.

To Kaplan, this polarity reveals that abortion restrictions are more focused on "controlling women's sexuality and adhering to certain norms of sex and motherhood than preserving life," she said in a telephone interview.

"IVF is different in that women are seeking to become mothers," she said. "Both allow the destruction of an embryo. But only one attracts this vitriol against women who seek it."

* * *

The Washington, D.C.–based Personhood Alliance has long championed the rights of embryos, calling for "equal protection of all human beings," said the group's former president, Gualberto Garcia Jones. To Jones, protecting embryos is akin to the work of other major human rights movements that defend often-marginalized groups.

"Humanity should be concerned about embryos because embryos are human too," he said. "[The] same feeling that leads people to be concerned about any group of vulnerable fellow human beings like orphans, the elderly, minorities of different stripes, is the very same reason we should be concerned about humans at the embryonic stage."

The pro-life organization's mission is "defending innocent human life—from earliest biological beginning to natural death," according to the group's website, which adds that "many existing pro-life organizations are out of touch with their base and are more interested in winning elections than saving lives."[19]

While the Personhood Alliance opposes abortion, the group seems to take even greater issue with reproductive medicine.

"Abortion's devastation is minor when compared to the destruction leveled by the assisted reproductive technology industry," the organization's website says. "From IVF and three-parent embryos to future technologies like self-cloning and artificial wombs, ethics have taken a back seat to the desire to parent, no matter what the cost."[20]

Some scholars, however, caution against the personification of the embryo.

"There are many different stages of development and they are quite different from one another," said Jane Maienschein, director of the Center for Biology and Society at Arizona State University. "Those embryos in the dish are radically different than anything that comes later. . . . Any embryo cannot develop on its own. It has to get nutrients and exchange waste and nutrients with something."

Less than half of all embryos in nature are estimated to survive, because they have a high probability of not developing properly, never implanting or resulting in a miscarriage, among other difficulties, she said.

She added that there are all sorts of problems with granting legal rights to an embryo. One example is the naturally occurring phenomenon of the chimera: There can be instances where two eggs are fertilized at the same time, but one doesn't survive and is absorbed by the other.

"Did the one kill the other one? Is this embryo, is it guilty of manslaughter?" asked Maienschein, author of *Embryos under the Microscope: The Diverging Meanings of Life*. "It's actually a serious question if you take seriously the claim that at the beginning you have a person."

Various court battles over embryos have emerged in recent years, as the law grapples to keep pace with advancements in medicine and technology.

An Ohio couple sued a fertility clinic after thousands of embryos were destroyed due to a storage tank malfunction in 2018. After 11 miscarriages, Wendy and Rick Penniman had two children with the help of the clinic and wanted to have more, but their embryos were no longer viable after the disaster. The lawsuit argued the couple's frozen embryos were people and should be treated as patients.[21]

"The key question we want to be answered is: when does life begin?" the couple's attorney said in a blog post about the case. "The Pennimans believe that life begins at conception, and that means that their embryos that were destroyed . . . are, in fact, people. However, the decision must be based on law, not emotion. If the judge determines that the embryos have the same legal status that people do, then the Pennimans could seek action for wrongful death."[22]

But an Ohio judge in May 2018 ruled that an embryo that hasn't been implanted in the uterus doesn't constitute a "distinct human entity" and isn't entitled to the rights and protections of a person.[23]

"The individuals who have produced the eggs and the sperm that have combined to form that embryo may think of themselves as parents; they may believe that the embryos thus created are already persons—but that is a matter of faith or of their personal beliefs, not of science and not of law," the judge wrote in his opinion, which an appellate court later affirmed. "They are of course entitled to mourn the loss of this potential, and even to feel the anguish of a parent who has lost a child. However, the court can deal only with rights and obligations that the law recognizes, not with emotions, feelings, or beliefs of individuals."

An Illinois appellate court in 2015 affirmed that Chicago cancer survivor Karla Dunston should get "custody" of frozen embryos over the opposition of her ex-boyfriend, in part because the fertilized eggs represented the woman's "last and only opportunity to have a biological child with her own eggs."[24]

In 2009, President Barack Obama was sued by frozen human embryo "Mary Scott Doe" on behalf of other frozen embryos and potential adoptive parents of embryos. The case challenged the morality of federally funded stem cell research on human embryos.

"At the heart of this controversy is one method used by researchers to derive a stem cell line or source from human embryos through a process that necessitates the destruction of the human embryos," a federal judge wrote. "Although some believe the embryo stem cell research has the potential for developing cures to numerous diseases, others believe that the destruction of human embryos in the extraction process equates to killing human life, which the Government should not use tax dollars to support."[25]

The judge dismissed the case, in part because Mary Scott Doe had no legal standing; the ruling cited a previous decision that found embryos are not people, legally.

"This Court agrees and accordingly holds that in order to establish an injury in fact, the embryos must be able to show an 'invasion of a legally protected interest,' which embryos do not possess as they are not considered to be persons under the law," the judge's opinion said.

* * *

At the 2019 Bike for Life rally outside the Chicago-area fertility clinic, about 16 demonstrators formed a circle along the public right-of-way adjacent to the 15,000-square-foot, two-story brick medical building. Some participants wore matching jackets decorated with a logo of a tiny fetus above the phrase "Defend the Unborn."

The roughly 10-mile bike race had begun in the morning outside a Planned Parenthood in neighboring west suburban Aurora, a more typical and routine target of abortion opposition protests. The event concluded with prayers at the fertility clinic in downtown Naperville around noon.

"We're strictly prayerful," Zabinski said, adding that he and his group weren't there to condemn any patients at the fertility clinic. "They're at a crisis decision, wouldn't you want someone to be praying for you? It's a major decision—whether you have an abortion or are doing IVF. It's a life decision that can impact other lives, not just the life that you're living. We're just praying for them."

Zabinski called the embryo and fetus "equally important."

"No matter how microscopic and tiny they are, they are still human embryos," he said. "They are still alive, no matter how small they are. . . . They have laws that protect the bald eagles' eggs. But you can destroy human embryos? It seems ironic."

When asked about the protest, the fertility center's medical director, Dr. Randy Morris, said the clinic and staff "are committed to providing state-of-the-art medical care to women and couples suffering from infertility, recurrent miscarriage and other problems related to the reproductive system."

Morris and the fertility clinic drew intense backlash in 2012, when the medical facility was approved by the Naperville City Council. The Reverend Thomas Milota, then a priest at Saints Peter & Paul Catholic Church in Naperville, in a letter had asked his parishioners to speak out against the development.

"At first glance, this opposition may be confusing for people, because the clinic's stated purpose is assisting well-meaning couples in having a child and the Church certainly supports a parent's desire to have a family," the letter said, but it went on to take issue with the treatment of embryos, among other criticisms.

"Some will be implanted," the letter said. "Some will be donated to science. Some will be discarded. Others will simply be kept frozen indefinitely . . . never being allowed to come to term."

Dozens of clinic supporters gave impassioned speeches before the Naperville City Council in March 2012; many brought along their babies and children who were conceived with the help of IVF.

"I am proud to say that I am the mother of two IVF miracles," said one woman, holding a baby. "I do not wish infertility on anyone. The months and years of trying to conceive my daughter were the hardest of my life. Countless nights I cried myself to sleep and my emotions ate at my heart each day that I was not pregnant. It was not just the pain of the sadness at not being able to conceive the child we so desperately wanted, but the self-blame and guilt that my body—one that was meant to conceive and carry a baby—was failing me."[26]

Another mother specifically thanked Morris for the "two beautiful children I wouldn't have without IVF."

"We support life, and Dr. Morris has helped us raise families," she said. "I guarantee you not one of you could look in my daughter's eyes and not see her as an angel. And she was given to me by Dr. Morris from a God that I prayed to on a daily basis to have. And I don't believe anyone could ever claim she was just manufactured. I love her. And thank you, Dr. Morris, for my son who gave my daughter a brother because of the medical, FDA approved treatment I get to receive from him. . . . People who want to discriminate against us, we haven't done anything wrong. We're loving families."

The Pro-Life Action League's Eric Scheidler spoke out against the clinic at the council meeting, while acknowledging all the children in the audience whose lives began with infertility treatments.

"What's at stake here today is justice," he said. "Among my friends, I count some who were conceived under conditions far less morally ambiguous than in vitro fertilization. Conditions of violence and victimization that all of us would condemn. Their valued membership in our human family does not alter the fact that they were conceived by acts of injustice. Similarly, who could fail to celebrate the humanity of these beautiful children here this evening, whatever the circumstances of their conception? Who does not sympathize with their parents' fervent desire to be mothers and fathers?"

As a father, he said, he certainly appreciated how painful it would be to not be able to conceive a child.

"But as easy as it is to sympathize with those we can see before us today, we must also learn to sympathize with those we cannot see," he said. "The tiniest human beings in their earliest days of life who are victimized by Dr. Morris. Who are destroyed or permanently frozen because they are unwanted or deemed unfit."

He ended by saying there was no moral difference between the treatment of embryos at the fertility clinic "and the children being killed down the road at Planned Parenthood" in Aurora, and announced that there would be public protests at the clinic site if the facility were to be approved, because "justice demands it."

A councilwoman grew visibly angry during his comments comparing the fertility center to an abortion clinic. She noted that many in the room "do not see them as comparable in any sort of way."

"It seems to me that it's a very different sort of facility, of course," she said. "There would be many people who would be sympathetic to the protests in Aurora who would be completely unsympathetic to the protests here."

Morris spoke to the council as well, addressing the opposition of abortion opponents and the local church.

"I support your right to practice your religion and to have your religious beliefs," he said. "Don't stop me and the other members of this community from having our religious beliefs just because they are different from yours."

At one point during the council meeting, an ordained pastor in the Evangelical Lutheran Church in America who served at a Naperville church shared her four-year struggle with infertility.

"I stand here as a woman who has been pregnant twice and who has grieved the loss of both of those pregnancies," she said. "I stand here as a woman for whom IVF is the last grasp at starting a family and a woman who knows the profound disappointment of a failed IVF cycle. I stand here as a Christian woman of deep faith. During my journey of infertility, I have prayed for miracles. I have argued with God in grief and I have looked to God for sustaining hope throughout this struggle to begin our family."

The clergywoman said she was both deeply committed to her faith and very supportive of the work of Morris and other fertility specialists, "who help women live out their hopes and dreams to quote, be fruitful and multiply."

"Those who have opposed this proposed fertility center do not speak for all Christians," she said. "They do not speak for all Naperville citizens and they do not speak for me."

The Reverend Jason Reed, former pastor of a Methodist church in Naperville, later recalled the heated debate over the fertility center, which he supported.

"I saw it as a wonderful means of enabling children to be born into healthy homes," he said. "A fertilized egg is a fertilized egg. It is human tissue, human cells. But it is not a human being."

13.
Booking a Hotel, Plane Ticket and Abortion, in One Spot

The call came in to the southern Illinois abortion clinic on a Friday afternoon in early May 2022: A young woman from Missouri was on the line, frantic because she no longer had the money to pay for her $470 surgical abortion, which was scheduled for the next day.[1]

The caller assumed she'd have to cancel her appointment and reschedule later, whenever she could come up with the money. The prospect of delaying such a time-sensitive procedure was terrifying. But after the call was transferred, a calm voice on the line asked a few questions about the patient, her life and how much of the procedure's cost she could afford at that moment.

The woman said she had just started a new job and insisted she would be getting her first check soon, but the abortion appointment fell in the middle of a pay period. She also mentioned that she had a child and an unexpected bill came up, swallowing the money she had set aside to pay to terminate the pregnancy.

"I don't want you to commit something you don't have," said the staff member who took the call, Kawanna Shannon.

After a few minutes of searching various abortion funds, Shannon came up with enough money to cover the cost of the procedure. Then she went over a few instructions for the caller's appointment, which would continue as scheduled the next day. Shannon asked if the patient needed help booking any transportation to and from the abortion clinic, and the caller said she was already set.

"Thank you, ma'am," the patient repeated several times, her panicked tone melting into relief.

Shannon is the director of patient access at the Regional Logistics Center, a designated call center where dedicated case managers assist abortion patients with travel needs, including arranging transportation to get to the clinic, childcare and hotel lodging for overnight stays, as well as coming up with the money to pay for the procedure through existing nonprofit abortion funds.

The center opened in January 2022 inside the Planned Parenthood in Fairview Heights, Illinois, just on the cusp of the Missouri border.[2] With the end of federal abortion protections looming, the nearby Hope Clinic and the Planned Parenthood affiliate jointly created the call center to prepare for the expected influx of out-of-state patients.

Reproductive rights advocates celebrated the center's opening with a virtual ribbon-cutting ceremony the day before the 49th anniversary of *Roe*, in anticipation that this would be the last year the landmark decision would exist to be commemorated. Governor Pritzker spoke at the event, calling the project "lifesaving and life-changing work."

"With reproductive rights under attack across the United States, it's never been more vital for the state of Illinois to ensure access to reproductive services," he said. "On the 49th anniversary of *Roe v. Wade*, we all thought we would be vigorously celebrating this important milestone. Instead, we are forced to contend with the possibility that there may not be a 50th anniversary of this fundamental right."

Abortion providers had predicted that after the fall of *Roe*, anywhere from 20,000 to 30,000 additional patients would be crossing state lines each year to have abortions across Illinois, where the right to terminate a pregnancy is ensconced in state law.

These two southern Illinois abortion providers estimated an extra 14,000 patients from outside their typical service area would flood their region in the absence of *Roe*; the Planned Parenthood affiliate and Hope Clinic invested $10 million for additional staffing, infrastructure and clinical capacity to "prepare for a post-*Roe* reality," according to a report by Reproductive Health Services of Planned Parenthood of the St. Louis Region.[3]

The new call center in southern Illinois had been in the works for several years as the two local abortion providers saw an increasing number of patients coming from neighboring states as well as from many in the South. After the six-week ban in Texas went into effect in September 2022, terminating a pregnancy was nearly banned in the nation's second largest state. Afterward, Hope Clinic began treating several patients from Texas weekly, as well as more women traveling from other southern states due to a ripple effect from the void of abortion access in Texas, said Erin King, the clinic's executive director.

She described one patient she saw in January 2022: The woman found out she was pregnant on a Wednesday, made the appointment on Friday and flew in on Saturday to have a medication abortion at Hope Clinic. The same day, she flew back to Texas, King recalled.

"And that was her first trip on a plane, ever," King said. "If she had not lived in Texas . . . most of the visit could have happened over the phone, like a telemedicine visit, or a short trip [to the] gynecologist. I think what is so hard for people to understand is that this is care that shouldn't take all of this coordination and all of this funding."

Elisabeth Smith, director of state policy and advocacy for the Center for Reproductive Rights, noted the pivotal role of abortion rights in Illinois amid the increasingly restrictive Midwest, a geographic and legal position that was magnified after the fall of *Roe*.

"Illinois is an incredibly important state for access," she said. "Illinois is surrounded by states that have worked to really limit access to care."

* * *

The after-hours phone line rang at around 3 a.m. on a winter morning, just a few weeks after the Regional Logistics Center was launched. The caller was a woman from Louisiana, desperate to book a ride to the airport that instant to get to her appointment the next day, said Shannon, who took the call.

"I didn't tell people this, but I'm in a very abusive relationship and he just left," Shannon recalled the woman saying. "I don't know if he's gone for a minute or what, but I just want to leave right now."

The Louisiana woman said her partner did not know she was pregnant. Shannon recalled scrambling to book an Uber in the middle of the night and then staying on the phone with the caller until the ride arrived, fearful her partner would return before the Uber's arrival.

"I'm literally packing now," Shannon remembered the woman saying.

The woman from Louisiana flew in and had a surgical abortion. Afterward, Shannon asked the patient if she needed a return ride to the airport.

"No," she recalled the patient saying. "I'm not going back."

"Where are you going?" Shannon said she replied, surprised. "What are you doing?"

The patient said she decided to leave her partner and start a new life, Shannon recalled. Before leaving, the woman from Louisiana said she was going to a shelter.

"She was like, 'Ms. Kawanna, I'm good. I'm going to be fine,'" Shannon said. "That sticks with me. Sometimes I wish she'd call, so I know she's good. I really wholeheartedly believe she's never going back."

Planned Parenthood in late 2019 opened the 18,000-square-foot Fairview Heights site where the Regional Logistics Center operates. The location on the border of Missouri was strategically chosen to serve patients coming from that neighboring state and beyond.

The abortion clinic includes a family room designed for children, equipped with beanbag chairs, books and toys, as well as extra diapers and wipes. So many patients had childcare constraints and were bringing their kids into the regular waiting room, so staff decided to set aside a more comfortable space for families, said Bonyen Lee-Gilmore, a spokesperson for Planned Parenthood of the St. Louis Region.

When one patient from Missouri couldn't find anyone to watch her three children, Shannon said she took the kids to the family room. For about two and a half hours, she watched the baby, toddler and six-year-old during the mother's surgical abortion. The oldest, a little boy, watched TikTok videos on a laptop while performing some of the dances featured in them.

"I even did a couple with him—at least, I was trying to," Shannon said, laughing a little.

Sometimes patients stay with their children in the family room and receive services and information sessions there, until it's time for the parent to go to a procedure room, staff members said. Shannon stressed that the family room isn't a formal day care center.

"But if you happen to come with your child, you have a safe place to go with your child," she said.

* * *

One day in February 2022, an 18-wheeler truck pulled in to the Planned Parenthood parking lot. The big rig looked quite conspicuous alongside all the regular cars and SUVs that typically parked there, Lee-Gilmore recalled. A patient who drove the truck for a living had traveled more than a thousand miles from Arizona to southern Illinois to pick up abortion pills, an appointment that usually takes about 90 minutes, according to staff.

"We get a lot of people who will drive hundreds of miles for a medication abortion," Lee-Gilmore said. "This scheme that politicians have set up is literally a game they put people on. It is an obstacle course."

One young woman traveled about 800 miles from rural Mississippi to southern Illinois to terminate a pregnancy in April 2022. The hardest part of coordinating her trip was scrambling to find a ride from her home to the closest Greyhound station, about 45 minutes away in Memphis, said Kenicia Page, Regional Logistics Center manager.

"It was just very difficult trying to find transportation in the area," she said, noting that there's often a void of taxis, Ubers and most forms of public transit in rural communities, a common challenge in coordinating care for patients who live far from city centers. "It was really crunch time. I think it was 24 to 48 hours to her appointment."

Eventually, the patient found a ride through a nonprofit organization that offers transportation for those in need in the Mississippi Delta region.

The Regional Logistics Center cases cost on average $900 to $1,500, depending on how many services are required, Lee-Gilmore said. She's concerned about how the center will handle the rising need and make sure funding lasts long term.

The young woman from Mississippi was in her second trimester and had a two-day surgical procedure. The patient was unemployed and needed food and sanitary items during her travels, Page recalled. The Regional Logistics Center sent her an electronic gift card and booked her an Uber to take to a Dollar General store, so she could buy a few necessities before heading back to her hotel.

These were small items, but they were critical pieces to her care and stay while far from home, Page said.

"It was just making her feel comfortable while she was here and keeping her uplifted, because she was just so discouraged from having to go through all the hoops," Page said. "But she was able to get everything done and then return home safely afterward."

Brian Westbrook, executive director of the St. Louis–based organization Coalition Life, called the Regional Logistics Center nothing more than a "media ploy."

"Quite frankly, it's nothing more or less than what they've always done, which is provide abortions and take the life of unborn children," he said.

When the center opened, Missouri had the one abortion clinic in St. Louis. In contrast, Westbrook said there were 75 anti-abortion pregnancy resource centers statewide.

"With all of that help and assistance for pregnant women, they don't feel like they have to get an abortion," he said.

Westbrook added that he and other abortion foes had long been confident that *Roe* would eventually fall. But the downfall of federal abortion rights protections would only be the beginning, he predicted.

"It's not a matter of if it will be overturned," he said. "It's a matter of when. The pro-life movement will only do more as a result. This is not necessarily a victory—it's a shifting of work from the federal level down to the state level."

* * *

Although the southern Illinois clinics had been preparing for the Supreme Court to overturn *Roe*, the impact was still formidable. Just a few weeks after the ruling, hundreds more out-of-state patients began traveling to Illinois each day and wait times in the southern portion of the state skyrocketed.[4] Before June 24, 2022, when abortion was still legal nationwide, a patient could schedule an abortion appointment in three or four days in southern Illinois. By late July, terminating a pregnancy was taking on average three weeks or more.

"One month later, I would say that our biggest surprise was really around how quickly our capacity dwindled," Lee-Gilmore said. "Our best guess, before *Roe* was overturned, was that this would happen over time. Especially because we knew that abortion wasn't going to be banned in all the states all at once. It depends on if you have trigger laws, pre-*Roe* bans and some states have litigated their trigger bans. So we knew there was going to be a patchwork and access would fall. But we thought it would fall a little slower than what's happened."

Delaying an abortion can have numerous ramifications, including increasing the gestational age of the pregnancy, potentially complicating the procedure and incurring risk to the patient.

"Time, travel, money, risk, all of it," Gilmore said. "It just makes the whole thing drag out longer and more complicated."

Extended waits can also have a ripple effect if patients have special medical needs or extenuating circumstances. In one instance Lee-Gilmore recounted, an out-of-state patient was anemic and required a blood transfusion prior to the abortion. She was sent to another state to have the transfusion but was turned away. Even though that medical provider wasn't asked to terminate the pregnancy, there was still concern that giving ancillary care might in some way violate the state's abortion ban.

"A lot of hospitals from banned states are trying to get advice from their lawyers about whether they are going to be considered aiding and abetting an abortion and whether it qualifies under the medical emergency exception," Lee-Gilmore said.

The patient ultimately went to a third state to have the blood transfusion and then came back to Illinois to terminate the pregnancy, a confusing and time-consuming web of appointments and multistate travel, Lee-Bonyen said.

"It is getting vastly more complicated than it was pre-*Roe*, in that it isn't just about the logistics of getting a patient in or on a certain time frame," she said. "That patient may need extra support care. . . . And we're now living in a landscape where medical providers in hospital systems and doctors' offices are turning patients away for that care because they don't want to be criminally liable or liable in any other sense in this new hostile landscape, where politicians are trying to criminalize providers."

In the first month after the end of *Roe*, the Fairview Heights clinic saw a roughly 52 percent increase in the number of abortions past 15 weeks of gestation, an early indicator that new state restrictions and increased travel distances might be delaying abortion care.

"At our health center at least, we are seeing the consequences of abortion bans, [which are] pushing people later into pregnancy," she said.

By then, 11 states in the Midwest and South had outlawed abortion in almost all cases or had enacted six-week abortion bans, according to a July 2022 report by the Guttmacher Institute.[5] At least 43 clinics in these states stopped performing abortions, a decrease from 71 before the Supreme Court decision to 28.

"The clinic closures resulting from state-level bans and restrictions in the wake of the June 24 decision will further deepen inequities in access to care as the addition of long travel distances to reach an abortion clinic in another state will be a barrier for many people," the report said.

Lee-Gilmore added that prolonging the time it takes to have an abortion—as well as the sense of uncertainty post-*Roe*—all add to patient stress.

"Once they figure out that yes, you can get an abortion here, we're here to help, they're relieved," she said. "Because they've been navigating a system in a post-*Roe* reality and that can be very scary. A lot of them have been turned away by providers and they've really had to go searching for a place to land."

Students for Life of America on July 24, 2022, celebrated "one month in a nation without *Roe*" on its social media sites.

"One month of celebrating that Life won & thousands of lives are being saved," the national nonprofit posted on Facebook. "America is growing. Our culture is healing from the lie that women need abortion violence in order to have equal footing in society. Women are finding empowerment through embracing the natural functions of their bodies, rather than rejecting them. States are acting to protect life from the moment of conception."[6]

The organization has trained more than 127,000 young pro-life activists and serves 1,245 campus groups at high schools, colleges and universities in all 50 states, according to its website. The nonprofit's stated mission is abolishing abortion.

To that end, the group crafted the campaign "Blueprint for a Post-*Roe* America." The plan includes a half dozen action items, and the first one has already been checked off: reversing *Roe*. Remaining imperatives include advancing pro-life legislation, promoting adoption, supporting pregnant and parenting women, and defunding Planned Parenthood and other abortion providers.[7]

"Protecting the preborn is a moral requirement of a civil society," the website states. "Doing so will have significant, positive consequences for all of us. It will foster mutual respect, advance the dignity of all, and make our American family more closely-knit. This Blueprint is how we can construct our American home for the 21st century."

* * *

Three months after *Roe*'s demise, 66 clinics in 15 states had halted abortion services; 26 of them had shut down and the other 40 were offering other forms of health care. Fourteen of those states had no remaining abortion clinics in operation.[8] Around two dozen clinics provided abortions in Illinois at that point, although most were in the Chicago area.

At the Regional Logistics Center in southern Illinois, calls for assistance surged in just the first few months after *Roe*'s reversal, rising from 648 in May to 1,771 in July to 1,937 in August.

"This is what we mean when we say banning abortion does not eliminate the need for abortion care," said Yamelsie Rodríguez, the Planned Parenthood affiliate's president and CEO.

A hundred days after *Roe* was overturned, Rodríguez and other officials announced plans to launch Planned Parenthood's first mobile abortion clinic, which would drive along the southern Illinois border to help reach traveling patients.[9] A 37-foot recreational vehicle was retrofitted to "create a patient experience similar to what one would experience when they are coming for a medication abortion at one of our health centers," the Planned Parenthood affiliate said in a statement.

They planned for the mobile clinic to initially offer medication abortions and eventually expand to provide first-trimester aspiration abortions as well. The RV design included a standard lab, small waiting room, and two exam rooms that could later be converted to procedure rooms for surgical abortions. Once it was up and running, patients would also be able to get other reproductive health services such as birth control and emergency contraceptives there, as well as testing for sexually transmitted infections, agency officials said.

"Over the past 100 days, I've cared for people from across the country who traveled to southern Illinois for abortion care," said Dr. Colleen McNicholas, the Planned Parenthood affiliate's chief medical officer. "These patients are navigating a politically designed obstacle course to access abortion and other basic health care."

At the Planned Parenthood clinic in Fairview Heights, patients from states other than Missouri and Illinois increased by more than 340 percent after the fall of *Roe*, the agency said.

Eric Scheidler of the Pro-Life Action League likened the mobile clinic to "the mobile meth lab from *Breaking Bad*," referencing an RV used in the popular crime drama series that portrayed a fictional drug-trafficking underworld. He called the mobile unit Planned Parenthood's attempt to "corner the interstate abortion market" and "muscle out the competition."

"Personally, I'm horrified by the bloodthirstiness of this scheme: an RV driving around looking for unborn children to abort," he said.

While he acknowledged that some patients will travel out of state to terminate a pregnancy, he believes prohibitions and limits that states are imposing post-*Roe* "will decrease abortions, though perhaps not dramatically."

"Some women will seek abortions out of state, some will try to access abortion pills illegally, but some will certainly decide not to have abortions," he said. "It's a very fraught decision, as we all know, so in many cases these abortion measures may tip the scales. In addition, many states did not simply ban or limit abortion, they also provided funds to help pregnant women in need, which will also bring down abortion rates."

Reproductive rights advocates say the rollback of abortion rights has made terminating a pregnancy harder and more confusing, but patients and providers will keep finding new avenues of access.

"For the past 100 days—and even longer in some places—we have been living in two Americas: one where abortion is available and one where it is not," said McNicholas. "This post-*Roe* reality was both predictable and preventable: patient confusion, a politically designed patchwork of access across the country and health care systems not knowing how to navigate laws that are not based in science. The list goes on and on."

"One day, we will bring back abortion care to Missourians," Rodríguez said. "Until then, we are committed to protecting and expanding care where and when we can. This is our act of defiance."

* * *

Then, in mid-October 2022, a new clinic opened to offer abortion seekers a third option in the southern region of the state. Choices: Center for Reproductive Health, which is based in Memphis, established a health center in Carbondale, Illinois, after Tennessee's abortion ban went into effect on August 25, 2022.[10] The nonprofit kept open its original health center in Memphis, which continues to provide other sexual and reproductive health services.

The Carbondale location is about a three-hour drive from Memphis and Nashville, providing proximity for Tennessee patients who no longer have abortion access in their state.

"We had to figure out another solution—and Carbondale was the solution we came up with," said Jennifer Pepper, president and CEO of Choices, which opened in Memphis in 1974, a year after the Supreme Court handed down *Roe*. "It is really surreal to be at the helm of this organization when it has to stop providing abortions [in Tennessee] for the first time in its 49-year history."

Choices was among a wave of new abortion providers settling in Illinois. In November 2022, the Alamo Clinic relocated to Carbondale from Oklahoma, and doctors travel there from Montana, Texas and Tennessee to perform abortions.[11] In January 2023, a Wisconsin physician opened an abortion clinic near the Wisconsin border in Rockford, Illinois, the first dedicated abortion provider in that community in over a decade.[12]

An Ohio-based obstetrician-gynecologist founded Equity Clinic in Champaign, Illinois, in February 2023 and began traveling roughly 500 miles round trip from Dayton, Ohio, each week to perform abortions there.[13] Equity Clinic was also established to serve as a training site for doctors; 15 residents and some medical students were planning to travel there from nearby states—and some from as far as Texas—for abortion training amid dwindling options elsewhere in the country due to state bans and restrictions. About 95 percent of patients were from out of state as of late May 2023, according to clinic staff.

Dr. Keith Reisinger-Kindle, Equity Clinic medical director and founder, said he went to medical school in order to perform abortions. He believes the work has a far more profound impact on patients than delivering babies.

"Everyone's excited about a baby. People come out of the woodwork to support and be excited about babies," he said. "Culturally, it's a very big deal for most communities. And it's a very public thing. It's very hard to hide a pregnancy. People know it's coming, usually for months at a time. People in this space, unfortunately, are often shunned and shamed and really stigmatized. There's a lot of secrecy and they don't tell a lot of people. So you as a single human can have so much impact with that patient in this space, destigmatizing and de-shaming this for them."

Around the country, other abortion providers began migrating from states where abortion rights were under fire to open new clinics in states where terminating a pregnancy remained legal. Whole Woman's Health closed several clinics in Texas, where abortion was outlawed at all stages of pregnancy except in life-threatening emergencies. The nonprofit in March 2023 opened a new location in New Mexico—one of the few southern states where abortion was still legal—and set up a GoFundMe to raise donations to help pay for the move.

"Opening a brick-and-mortar clinic site in New Mexico, where we already offer Virtual Services, will allow us to provide first and second trimester abortions to people from Texas, Oklahoma, Arizona and elsewhere in the South where safe, legal abortion care is restricted," the GoFundMe site said. "In addition, New Mexicans are also going to struggle with access as their local clinics book up with patients traveling from out of state."

Another clinic, in late 2022, relocated from Bristol, Tennessee, to a new location about a mile up the street in Bristol, Virginia, where abortion was still legal.[14]

The last abortion clinic in North Dakota, Red River Women's Clinic, in August 2022 moved from Fargo to another site just a few miles over the state border in Minnesota.[15]

"Red River Women's Clinic was the only abortion provider in North Dakota for 20-plus years," the clinic website stated. "After the US Supreme Court overturned *Roe v. Wade* in June of 2022, we made the commitment to continue to provide abortion care to our region, so we moved our services across the river to Moorhead, MN."[16]

After the end of Roe, Wisconsin providers ceased offering abortion services, due to the state's 1849 criminal abortion statute.[17] Even though the measure had been passed before the Civil War—a time when cars didn't exist, slavery was still legal and women weren't allowed to vote—the prohibition remained codified in state law. Wisconsin patients began streaming into neighboring Illinois.[18]

"During this time, we've seen a tenfold increase in patients from Wisconsin coming for care to Illinois," said Jennifer Welch, Planned Parenthood of Illinois president and CEO, during a July 2022 press conference. "This is clear evidence that abortion restrictions and bans do not stop people from having abortions. Restrictions and bans only make it harder for people to access essential reproductive health care where they live."

Welch described the case of one patient who had an abortion scheduled at a Planned Parenthood in Wisconsin the day after *Roe* was overturned. Her appointment had to be canceled, but she still needed care quickly. The patient, a single mom with young twins, had to coordinate childcare in addition to travel arrangements, she said. Planned Parenthood was able to get her an abortion appointment a few days later at the Waukegan, Illinois, clinic. Wisconsin provided support for transportation and gas money, and Illinois provided financial assistance for the abortion, Welch said.

"So that patient got the care she needed," Welch said. "Sadly, this story is not unique. We've seen a tremendous increase in patients coming from Wisconsin to all Illinois Planned Parenthood health centers."

In response to the sudden massive migration of abortion patients, Wisconsin physicians and clinicians began traveling across state lines to provide abortions in Illinois. In July 2022, Planned Parenthood officials in Illinois and Wisconsin announced a new partnership, which involved Wisconsin medical providers working out of a Planned Parenthood in Waukegan, just a few miles from the state boundary line.

All Wisconsin clinicians who were traveling there to work would first be licensed in Illinois, Planned Parenthood officials said.

Wisconsin providers also began offering abortion services through telehealth appointments at the Waukegan clinic, but patients had to physically be in Illinois during the visit.

Planned Parenthood affiliates in both states set up designated "abortion navigators" who help patients with travel arrangements, find funding to cover the cost of the procedure and provide other assistance.

Dr. Kristin Lyerly worked at a Planned Parenthood clinic in Sheboygan, Wisconsin, about 150 miles from Chicago, which suspended abortions a few days before the Supreme Court ruling, in anticipation of it.[19] The obstetrician-gynecologist had performed abortions there for about six months and elsewhere in the state for about a decade.

The physician said she was terrified for patients in Wisconsin and across the country who had suddenly lost access to safe and legal abortion.

"We are devastated," she said. "So many of the patients we see are already at a huge disadvantage, whether that means financial, support, everything. And now they will have to travel and spend more. They just don't have the resources to get the care that they need and deserve. I'm afraid they will do unsafe things out of desperation."[20]

Lyerly began traveling to provide abortions just over Wisconsin's border in Minnesota, one of the few Midwest states besides Illinois where the right to terminate a pregnancy was still intact; but she hopes to one day return to serving patients in her state.[21] She noted that even before the Supreme Court ruling, terminating a pregnancy had become incredibly difficult for so many in Wisconsin.

"Over the last ten years, we have lost so much access," she said. "But this is just a terrible final straw. Because abortion is health care. In greater society we see it as a political issue and it's very polarizing. But within the scope of health care, this is just one of many challenging gray areas we deal with every day."

President Joe Biden and Vice President Kamala Harris convened the Task Force on Reproductive Healthcare Access just after the

Supreme Court overturned *Roe*. The group met at the White House on October 4, 2022, marking 100 days after the end of *Roe*.[22]

"We have doctors here with us today who are on the frontlines of this crisis, and many of these laws would make doctors criminals just for treating a patient," Biden said.[23]

One of those physicians was Lyerly, who noted that, at the time, interpretations of state law could make it a felony for her to provide an abortion, with no exceptions for rape or incest. The only exemption in Wisconsin would be to save the life of the pregnant patient.

"But pregnant people don't have a warning light that comes on when they've crossed that threshold," Lyerly told the president, vice president and other members of the task force. "We have to use our clinical judgment developed through over a decade of formal education, experience and commitment to make those kinds of sensitive, individualized decisions."[24]

Those who can afford the cost and time away from work travel to Illinois or Minnesota, she told the rest of the task force.

"Many, especially in abusive relationships or difficult social situations, they have to continue their pregnancies," she said. "Or they resort to desperate measures."

Then, in September 2023, abortions resumed in Wisconsin after a Dane County judge determined the nineteenth-century ban was referring to feticide and did not apply to consensual abortions.

14.
Weighing the Risk

Mindy Swank learned she was pregnant with her second child while traveling in Germany in 2009. She shared the joyous news with her husband and their young son back home in western Illinois, where they lived at the time, with a postcard written from the perspective of the unborn baby.[1]

> *Dear Daddy and Big Brother Liam,*
>
> *Went on a Rhine River cruise with mommy today. We also explored the biggest castle we've ever seen!! I'll let mommy tell you about it when we get home! We also had lunch at the place on this post card! Can't wait to meet you! Mommy sends her love.*
>
> *Love,*
> *Baby #2*

But at about 20 weeks into pregnancy, Mindy's water broke prematurely, and she was taken to a local hospital.[2] The 24-year-old mother was grief-stricken when physicians told her that not only would her unborn baby not survive due to severe fetal anomalies but a miscarriage could cause life-threatening bleeding and infection, risking her ability to have future children, according to an amicus brief that recounted her treatment.[3]

Mindy and her husband prayed together and, despite her Christian upbringing, they decided that ending the pregnancy was the best decision.[4] The couple asked her doctors to terminate the pregnancy, but they learned that her Catholic hospital would not treat her in this manner because it adhered to the requirements in *Ethical and*

Religious Directives for Catholic Health Care Services, which generally prohibit abortions.[5] These religious restrictions allowed the hospital to terminate the pregnancy only if she was already infected or hemorrhaging; she said she was given no other treatment options.[6]

Mindy said she tried to get medical care elsewhere but learned her insurance would not cover her because her hospital "refused to provide adequate records showing that the procedure was medically necessary," according to the amicus brief.[7] Unable to afford the procedure costs out of pocket, she returned home.

A few weeks later, she woke up bleeding and sought care at a different hospital—but this was another Catholic medical facility, bound by the same religious restrictions.[8]

"The doctors told her that she 'was not sick enough for them to induce labor and help end the pregnancy,'" the amicus brief said. "The doctors told Mindy to come back if she bled more or had a fever. No one offered to help Mindy find a secular health care facility where she could end her pregnancy. Nor did they present her with any options other than waiting to get sick enough to justify ending the pregnancy under the [ethical and religious directives]."

Mindy repeatedly returned to the same hospital over the next five weeks, with increased bleeding. At 27 weeks' gestation, she awakened to severe hemorrhaging.[9]

"Desperate to prove I was sick enough for them to treat me, I brought to the hospital all the pads and clothing I had bled through," she testified before an Illinois Senate committee in 2015. "The doctors decided that I was sick enough to induce delivery."[10]

She gave birth to a baby boy who never gained consciousness. For several hours, the mother watched as the newborn struggled to breathe, until he died as she held him.[11]

"No one should ever have to go through this," she told the state senate committee during her testimony.

Mindy had told her story to Illinois lawmakers to support the passage of a 2016 law that amended the state's Health Care Right of Conscience Act, which protected medical practitioners who would not perform abortions based on objections to terminating a pregnancy. The new law required physicians and nurses to notify pregnant patients of all their available medical options—including abortion, even if medical practitioners had religious or ethical objections to the procedure. The American College of Obstetricians and Gynecologists and the Illinois Academy of Family Physicians cited Mindy's account in an amicus brief supporting the new law when it was challenged in court and later temporarily blocked.[12]

Yet her experience illustrates just how complicated the concept of life endangerment during pregnancy can be. After the fall of *Roe*, about a dozen states began enforcing trigger bans that outlawed abortion in nearly all circumstances. Some state legislatures passed new abortion bans or very early gestational limits, significantly curtailing the procedure.

But most of these laws banning or severely restricting abortion include narrow exceptions for cases where the pregnant person's life is in danger. Some states, such as Texas and Tennessee, also include abortion exemptions when the pregnant person is at risk of "substantial and irreversible impairment of a major bodily function."

Roughly 73 percent of American adults say they believe abortion should be legal when the life or health of a woman is threatened by the pregnancy, according to a Pew Research Center survey released in May 2022.[13] But some medical experts say these exemptions can be vague and unclear. Health risks in real-world situations are often complex and thorny, given the plethora of medical conditions and complications that can arise during pregnancy, with varying levels of severity.

Now physicians in states with abortion bans are left grappling to determine what exactly constitutes life and health endangerment during pregnancy—and how life-threatening a pregnancy must become before it can be ended legally.

* * *

A panel of doctors at Duke University in North Carolina discussed the variety of ways abortion bans complicate disease treatment, as well as the legal risks these emerging laws pose for physicians, during a virtual media briefing in August 2022.

Dr. Beverly Gray, an obstetrician-gynecologist at Duke, said she fears abortion bans will increase maternal deaths and health risks faced by pregnant individuals.

"There's this idea that a ban will make care safer for patients, but that's absolutely not true at all," said Gray, who is also the founder of the Duke Reproductive Health Equity and Advocacy Mobilization team. "In fact, it makes care less safe. It will likely increase maternal mortality in this country, when we already have a maternal mortality crisis."[14]

Even before the end of federal abortion protections, that crisis appeared to be worsening. In 2020, 861 women died of maternal causes in the United States, at a rate of 23.8 deaths per 100,000 live births; this is compared to 754 deaths in 2019, at a rate of 20.1 deaths per 100,000 live births, according to CDC statistics.[15]

American women had the highest rate of maternal mortality compared to women in 10 other high-income nations, according to an April 2022 study by the Commonwealth Fund, a nonprofit foundation that supports independent research on health policy reform.[16]

Dr. Maria Small, a maternal-fetal medicine specialist at Duke, noted during the video conference that there's an inherently greater risk to carrying a pregnancy to term versus having an abortion. The risk of death is about 14 times higher during childbirth compared to having an abortion, according to the American College of Obstetricians and Gynecologists; the professional organization states that only about 2 percent of abortion patients suffer from a complication, and most are minor and easily treatable.

Small said that risk during pregnancy can be exacerbated by other health problems. For example, she said cardiac disease is the leading cause of maternal death, and many heart conditions can result in a much higher chance of death during pregnancy.

"So sometimes individuals who are pregnant with a cardiac condition need to have the option to terminate a pregnancy, to end a pregnancy, as a life-saving action for themselves," she said.[17]

Although legislators and the public might think of life endangerment as a black-and-white concept, health care during pregnancy can be complicated and challenging, Gray said. She said she knew that physicians in other states with bans or severe restrictions often struggle to "determine at what point is someone's life so endangered that we can intervene and help save their lives?"[18]

"We take care of many cases where, unfortunately, a patient will break their water very early in pregnancy and we know that puts their lives at risk for infection, severe infection that can lead to ICU admission and even death, hemorrhage or bleeding," she said. "We know those patients in those situations are in grave danger."

Even those who survive dangerous pregnancies can still experience health complications, including inability to conceive again, after waiting longer for medical intervention. Gray pointed to Texas, where Senate Bill 8, outlawing abortion in almost all cases after fetal cardiac activity could be detected, at roughly six weeks' gestation, went into effect in September 2021. After the end of *Roe*, a trigger ban on abortion in nearly all cases was enforceable in Texas by late August 2022.

"In Texas, with those very strict bans, with very narrow exceptions on saving the life of the patient, they saw a doubling of morbidity of those patients who experienced that very early breaking of water," Gray said. "Essentially, they were having to watch those patients until they were on the brink of a catastrophic outcome and then they could take care of them."

Researchers estimated that Texas abortion restrictions doubled the risk of health problems for pregnant women, according to a study by Parkland Health and the University of Texas Southwestern Medical Center, whose findings were published in the *American Journal of Obstetrics and Gynecology* in October 2022. The study, which analyzed the outcomes of the cases of 28 pregnant women with complications at 22 weeks of gestation or less, found doctors were delaying treatment until patients faced an immediate threat to their lives. One expectant mother was rushed to the intensive care unit; in some cases, the women suffered from infections and hemorrhaging.[19]

"Because of the intense politicization of these issues nationally, some have questioned, 'What does the threat of death have to be?' and 'How imminent must it be?'" researchers said. "As large academic medical centers prepare to navigate the potential for loss of access to services, more questions are raised than answers."[20]

A Texas judge in early August 2023 issued a temporary exemption to the state's abortion ban, allowing patients with medically complicated pregnancies to terminate while protecting health care providers from prosecution in these cases.[21]

The ruling came after the Center for Reproductive Rights filed a lawsuit on behalf of two obstetrician-gynecologists and 13 patients who suffered pregnancy complications but were denied abortions in Texas. The lawsuit was in part asking the court to clarify what circumstances qualify for abortion exemptions, when so many medical providers feared prosecution, prison time, fines and loss of their medical licenses—all potential penalties for violating the state's abortion ban.[22]

Plaintiff Amanda Zurawski described at a July 2023 press conference how she had developed sepsis and almost died; she said she was refused an abortion at 18 weeks pregnant, when her water broke.[23]

"I became so ill that I had to spend a week in the hospital, three days of which were in the intensive care unit," she said. "This was all because doctors weren't allowed to give me an abortion until my life was on the line, despite the fact that there was absolutely no way my daughter would survive."

Within hours, though, the state attorney general appealed the decision, blocking the judge's ruling.

"Texas pro-life laws are in full effect. This judge's ruling is not," the attorney general's office said in a press release. "Protecting the health of mothers and babies is of paramount importance to the people of Texas, a moral principle enshrined in the law which states that an abortion may be performed under limited circumstances, such as in the event of 'a life-threatening physical condition aggravated by, caused by, or arising from a pregnancy' that places the pregnant woman 'at risk of death or poses a serious risk of substantial impairment of a major bodily function unless the abortion is performed or induced.'"[24]

Gray pointed out that it can be difficult to determine in each individual situation what constitutes enough illness for legal exemptions. There isn't a test that physicians can give patients that will clearly show "OK, you're sick enough that we can take care of you now," she said.[25]

"So it is a spectrum," she said. "Do you need one organ failing? Do you need two organs failing? Do you need to be to the point where you're bleeding, where you need a blood transfusion? What are those questions and how do we ask them? That's not written into the law. So patients are confused. Physicians are confused. . . . That makes it complicated to give patients the best advice and the best care—the best evidence-based care. And that's being limited."

The medical experts from Duke noted that there can be a variety of health concerns that impact people of reproductive age, from mid-pregnancy cancer diagnoses to preexisting conditions to unexpected emergencies that afflict the pregnant patient or fetus.

"Until people have an understanding of what individuals are facing, it's really hard to comprehend," Gray said. "We all know or love or care for someone who has had an abortion. And I think when we're allowed through that window in people's lives and we understand what they are facing, we're able to appreciate how decisions are made—how folks are approaching their lives and their futures."[26]

* * *

Dr. Megan Clowse is a rheumatologist at Duke who treats patients who are pregnant or trying to get pregnant while having a rheumatic disease—a collection of autoimmune conditions where the immune system attacks the body, which can pose numerous complications during pregnancy. Some examples include rheumatoid arthritis and lupus. During the video conference, Clowse said abortion bans have significantly altered the landscape of rheumatic disease care for women of reproductive age.[27]

"We see high rates of pregnancy loss, preterm birth, still birth, preeclampsia and severe health consequences in the short term and long term for both the mother and for the baby," she said. "Pregnancies that threaten the life of a woman with rheumatic disease are surprisingly common."[28]

Clowse said she typically treats one or two women annually who conceive when their rheumatic disease is active, which might lead to kidney damage or harm to another organ, or could drive up the patient's blood pressure dangerously high, putting her at risk of a stroke or a heart attack. Often in these circumstances, the health of the fetus is also threatened, with a high potential for early delivery, lower survival rates and long-term medical complications.

These patient conversations can be extremely challenging, she said.

"It's not like a woman can walk in very early in pregnancy and I can say, 'You for sure are going to have a very catastrophic outcome,'" she said. "Instead, it's a lot of, 'Here's the situation, here are the risks. How do you want to weigh the risks? Where do you personally draw the line of your safety, of your ability to mother your existing children, your ability to survive this pregnancy versus your desire to continue this specific pregnancy?' How they weigh this specific pregnancy, that will likely end in catastrophe, versus a future pregnancy that could be very well planned and lead to a successful delivery."

Different women make different choices in these cases, Clowse said, adding that it's hard for her to predict which patients will choose to carry a pregnancy to term and which ones will terminate.

"Often, I see women who are so hopeful that they can make this pregnancy survive and are so hopeful that they can become a mother that they will continue in what I know as a physician is a really low chance of success," she said. "These are, for me, the hardest pregnancies to watch and care for the women after they deliver and have infants and then children who have devastating complications. It's really heartrending for me. Taking away the ability of women to make that challenging decision for themselves, I find particularly tragic here."

She added that abortion bans can complicate treatment for all patients of reproductive age with rheumatic disease, regardless of whether the individual is pregnant or trying to conceive. Some standard medications that treat rheumatic disease can cause complications during pregnancy, such as methotrexate and mycophenolate, which are known to increase birth defects when there's first-trimester exposure, Clowse said. Methotrexate is also used, at higher doses, to treat ectopic pregnancy.[29]

"I'm particularly concerned that the use of these medications is going to decrease in women of reproductive age who are not trying to get pregnant, leading to increased medical complications and disability, organ failure and, in some cases, premature death in these women," she said.

The Arthritis Foundation released a statement that said arthritis patients have reported difficulty accessing methotrexate since the Supreme Court overturned *Roe* and states began enacting abortion bans and severe restrictions.[30]

"Many of these state laws specifically list certain medications as 'abortion-inducing drugs,' which bans their use without necessarily distinguishing by condition or diagnosis," the statement said.

Conversations about reproductive health between physicians and patients that take some of these medications are already changing post-*Roe*, Clowse said.[31]

"We used to talk a lot about how they really needed to avoid pregnancy," she said. "But we gave them some leeway in how they did that. We trusted them to really make those decisions for themselves. And we are wrestling amongst ourselves as rheumatologists as to how much freedom do we give women in those situations to make their own reproductive health choices versus where do we need to step in and not allow them to get pregnant, by using more strongly effective contraceptives that might have more side effects but the tradeoff is we avoid these catastrophic pregnancies."

This is an uncomfortable position for a physician, she added.

"I don't think I should be making choices for other women about their reproductive health and their reproductive health capacity," she said. "But that's the situation we are in. I also know the catastrophe of people conceiving in those situations if abortion is not available to them."

With the end of federal abortion protections, all three physicians from Duke worried that criminalization of terminating pregnancy could harm doctor-patient relationships and result in subpar care. Small predicted that abortion bans will only worsen health disparities that already exist across the nation, particularly for people of color.

"You have a scenario where you've placed individuals in an adversarial position that may even involve law enforcement, and I think that's a very dangerous situation for communities of color," she said. "I think this environment of placing pregnant and potentially pregnant individuals in this kind of toxic relationship with health care providers is one that is going to only worsen maternal mortality and worsen the disparities and inequities in maternal mortality for Black women in America."[32]

She added that many medical providers are concerned that patients won't alert clinicians if they are having complications.

A June 2022 article in the *New England Journal of Medicine* covered a variety of scenarios health care providers, particularly in emergency departments, should prepare for post-*Roe*. Patients using unsafe abortion methods might need lifesaving care for conditions like sepsis, pelvic-organ injury, bleeding and toxic exposures. In cases where patients use mifepristone and misoprostol on their own, "the biggest risks to patients may be legal ones: threat of reporting, arrest, and detention," and those risks will likely be higher for Black and low-income patients, the article said.[33]

"Pregnant patients who have bleeding in pregnancy or pregnancy loss may be vulnerable to reporting and criminal prosecution, whether they took measures to end the pregnancy or are having a miscarriage; spontaneous pregnancy loss and self-managed abortion with medications are virtually indistinguishable," the article said. "Data show that health care providers are most likely to report Black pregnant patients and those living on low incomes to the authorities."

Gray also expressed concern that medical students and residents in states with abortion bans will receive subpar training, weakening reproductive health care in those parts of the country.

"There are so many downstream ramifications that we've only started to see the tip of the iceberg," she said. "And over these next decades, if we don't protect reproductive health in our country, the crisis is going to continue and worsen."[34]

* * *

Mindy Swank's traumatic pregnancy was one of more than a dozen cases highlighted in the 2016 ACLU report *Health Care Denied*, which focused primarily on reproductive rights decisions made at Catholic hospitals around the country.[35] Many of these stories show how subjective life-endangerment cases can be, depending on a medical provider's views on abortion or their religious affiliation.

In spring 2015, Dr. AuTumn Davidson rushed to the University of Illinois Hospital in Chicago in the early hours of one morning to perform an emergency abortion, according to the report. A 19-year-old patient was about 19 weeks pregnant and bleeding profusely from a subchorionic hemorrhage, a pregnancy complication where blood collects under one of the membranes that surround the fetus in the uterus.

"The patient had sought emergency care at two different Catholic hospitals during the previous week, but neither would perform an abortion—even though she was bleeding so heavily that one of the hospitals gave her a blood transfusion before sending her home," the ACLU report said.[36]

The patient said someone at the second hospital whispered to her that if she wanted an abortion, she could go to another hospital, according to the report. That's when the patient went to the University of Illinois Hospital to terminate the pregnancy.

"She and her partner just kept saying that they thought she was going to die," Davidson recalled in the report.[37]

The report recounted another case, from 2010, when St. Joseph's Hospital and Medical Center in Phoenix was stripped of its official Catholic status after providing an emergency abortion to a mother who was 11 weeks pregnant with her fifth child and suffered from hypertension.[38]

Linda Hunt, president and CEO of St. Joseph's Hospital at the time, defended the decision to terminate.

"If we are presented with a situation in which a pregnancy threatens a woman's life, our first priority is to save both patients," she said in a statement. "If that is not possible, we will always save the life we can save, and that is what we did in this case."[39]

Bishop Thomas Olmsted, then the leader of the Roman Catholic Diocese of Phoenix, said in a statement that the abortion was a clear violation of the requirements in *Ethical and Religious Directives for Catholic Health Care Services*.[40]

"When I met with officials of the hospital to learn more of the details of what had occurred, it became clear that, in the decision to abort, the equal dignity of mother and her baby were not both upheld; but that the baby was directly killed, which is a clear violation of [ethical and religious directives, number 45]," he said in a statement.

Olmsted added that exceptions mentioned in the directives were not met.

"[T]hat is, there was not a cancerous uterus or other grave malady that might justify an indirect and unintended termination of the life of the baby to treat the grave illness," he said. "In this case, the baby was healthy and there were no problems with the pregnancy; rather, the mother had a disease that needed to be treated. But instead of treating the disease, St. Joseph's medical staff and ethics committee decided that the healthy, 11-week-old baby should be directly killed. This is contrary to the teaching of the Church."

The bishop added that longtime nurse and hospital administrator Sister Margaret McBride, who in consultation with the hospital's ethics committee determined the abortion was necessary, had incurred an excommunication. The excommunication was lifted in 2011.

McBride received a leadership award from the Catholic social justice organization Call to Action in 2011 for her role in permitting the emergency abortion. In her acceptance speech, McBride said she found healing through the patient whose life was likely saved that day. Yet McBride added that reconnecting with the Catholic church and taking Holy Communion once again were still very important to her.[41]

"The word excommunication has a very powerful meaning when you're sitting in the midst of being excommunicated," she said. "It's when you want the Eucharist, it's when you want to be in the presence of the Catholic community and it's suddenly denied to you. So it is in that excommunication that I moved forward. . . . I want you to know that in my journey I did reconcile with the church. The church means something very different to me today. Something has to be taken away sometimes for you to appreciate it even more."[42]

In another case featured in the ACLU study, Dr. Colleen Krajewski of Pennsylvania recounted treating a pregnant patient whose water broke dangerously early, at the beginning of her second trimester. The woman went to the nearest hospital, which was Catholic, the report said.

"Although it was apparent to all that the (much desired) pregnancy had no chance of survival, the patient was left in a hospital bed for two days to passively wait for a spontaneous miscarriage," the report said. "The patient was devastated that she was losing the pregnancy, and her trauma was compounded each time the hospital staff came to check if there was still a fetal heartbeat."[43]

Physicians petitioned the hospital's ethics committee to permit an abortion, but the request was denied, the report said. The patient was transferred to Krajewski's hospital, which terminated the pregnancy.

"The hours-long, middle-of-the-night transfer added to the patient's experience of fear and abandonment," Krajewski, an obstetrician-gynecologist, recalled in the report.

The ACLU report culminated by acknowledging that American religious freedom protects everyone's right to their religious beliefs.

"But it does not give us the right to use our religion to discriminate against and impose those beliefs on others who do not share them—especially when doing so comes at the expense of women's health and lives," the report concluded.

15. Violence and Faith

A white pickup truck with red doors and a noticeably loud exhaust pulled up near a central Illinois abortion clinic late at night on Sunday, January 15, 2023.[1] The Planned Parenthood Health Center of Peoria, located about 170 miles southwest of Chicago, wasn't scheduled to be open for business for another eight hours or so.

A man in a hooded coat exited the vehicle and approached the clinic carrying a bottle roughly the size of a laundry detergent container, as video surveillance of the scene showed.[2] He lit a rag on fire on one end of the bottle and then smashed a window of the health center, placing the Molotov cocktail inside the building before fleeing on foot, according to a criminal complaint.[3]

Flames engulfed the abortion clinic a little before midnight.

While no patients or staff were inside the building and no one was injured in the blaze, the firebombing caused about a million dollars in destruction to the health center; Planned Parenthood of Illinois officials predicted the abortion clinic—the only one at the time in the college town with a population of 112,000—wouldn't be able to reopen for months.[4]

That was, apparently, the point of the fire.

Authorities in late January arrested and charged 32-year-old Tyler Massengill of Chillicothe with "malicious use of fire and an explosive to damage, and attempt to damage" the Planned Parenthood Health Center, according to a Justice Department statement.[5]

Initially, Massengill denied responsibility. But he later told investigators that his ex-girlfriend had had an abortion in Peoria three years earlier, which "upset Massengill," according to the complaint.

The man said he had been working in Alaska when his girlfriend told him over the phone that she had become pregnant but chose to terminate.

On or around the day of the fire, "Massengill heard or saw something that reminded him of the abortion, again upsetting him," the complaint stated.

The suspect told investigators that if the fire caused "a little delay" in a person receiving services at the health center, it might have been "all worth it," according to the complaint.

Massengill pleaded guilty on February 16, 2023, according to the Justice Department.[6] In August 2023, Massengill was sentenced to 10 years in prison and ordered to pay $1.45 million in restitution. The fire occurred days after Illinois officials passed highly publicized reproductive rights legislation to widen the pool of abortion providers as well as to protect in-state health care workers and traveling patients, a measure spurred by the recent spike in out-of-state abortion seekers.[7]

Besides abortion care, Planned Parenthood of Illinois ticked off many reproductive and health services the clinic once provided for the Peoria area, which wouldn't be available there for some time.

"This senseless act of vandalism has robbed the community of access to birth control, cancer screenings, [sexually transmitted infection] testing and treatment, and gender-affirming care as well as medication abortion services," said the agency's president and CEO, Jennifer Welch, in a written statement. "We appreciate the outpouring of support from the community, state, and nation as we continue to meet our patients' needs through telehealth and at our other 16 health centers across the state."[8]

About six miles away from the abortion clinic, another suspicious fire had engulfed a building with an opposing mission about two years prior. In May 2021, flames erupted in the early morning hours one day at the Peoria Women's Care Center, an anti-abortion pregnancy resource center.[9]

The nonprofit was able to reopen in August 2022 at a new, larger location in Peoria—just down the street from the Planned Parenthood clinic that would be set ablaze in January 2023.

"Because of you, our center continues to set new records for women served and babies saved," the website states, on a page with a button for donations. "And today 1 in 5 babies born in Peoria County start with Women's Care Center. You are touching the lives of so many women . . . and saving so many babies."[10]

Although Peoria Fire Department investigators determined the cause of the fire was arson, no arrests have been made; the case is still open, but no leads or new information has emerged since the fire, according to Peoria fire officials.[11]

The two parallel suspected arsons in one Illinois city illustrate the kind of violence and acts of intimidation abortion-related causes have endured for years across the country. Yet reproductive rights organizations and anti-abortion groups alike say they've experienced unprecedented levels of vandalism, threats and acts of destruction since the high court overturned *Roe*.

Carol Tobias has served as the president of the Washington, D.C.–based National Right to Life for 12 years. While she said pro-life organizations have always risked reprisal, "the assault, the violence against pro-life facilities has greatly escalated" since the end of *Roe*.

"Pro-life pregnancy centers and churches, and pro-life organizations, have been firebombed and vandalized," she said. "I think society has just gotten meaner, angrier."

The FBI announced in early 2023 that it was offering $25,000 rewards for information leading to the arrest and conviction of anyone responsible for a series of recent attacks on reproductive services organizations across the country that were set on fire, vandalized or defaced. Nine of the listed targets were anti-abortion groups and one was a Planned Parenthood medical building in California.

"Today's announcement reflects the FBI's commitment to vigorously pursue investigations into crimes against pregnancy resource centers, faith-based organizations and reproductive health clinics across the country," FBI director Christopher Wray said in a statement on the FBI's website. "We will continue to work closely with our national, state, and local law enforcement partners to hold responsible anyone who uses extremist views to justify their criminal actions."[12]

In the early hours of May 8, 2022, police and firefighters were dispatched to a suspicious fire at the Wisconsin Family Action executive office in Madison, Wisconsin, where two Molotov cocktails had been thrown inside the office. Graffiti on the outside of the building near a broken window read, "If abortions aren't safe then you aren't either," according to the FBI.

At around 1:30 a.m. on June 30, 2022, someone threw a Molotov cocktail through the front window of the pro-life organization Hope Clinic for Women in Nashville; the words "Jane's Revenge" were painted on the building's exterior, the FBI site said.

To Tobias of National Right to Life, this kind of attack on pro-life nonprofits "wreaks of cruelty and insensitivity, an uncaring nature."

"There are just some elements of this society that don't think choosing life for an unborn child is acceptable," Tobias said. "And they're doing everything they can to shut down the places that provide free help to a woman who needs it. And wants it."

* * *

Pro-choice groups have faced similar peril for years. The Justice Department website lists more than 30 criminal and civil cases of violence, threats and harassment targeted at abortion providers and reproductive health facilities going back more than a decade.[13]

In 2021, a man was accused of using a slingshot to fire metal ball bearings at the glass door of the Planned Parenthood Health Center in the Edgewater neighborhood of Chicago. A Michigan man in October 2022 pleaded guilty to setting a July fire at a Planned Parenthood clinic in Kalamazoo. The defendant had "breached the fence surrounding the building, used a combustible fuel to ignite the exterior bushes of the building, lit a fireplace starter log, and then threw the burning log onto the roof of the building, ultimately starting two separate fires," according to a federal prosecutors.[14]

Authorities alleged the Michigan man had made proclamations about abortion in videos he posted online.

"Right now we have a genocide happening, genocide of babies," he said in one of those recordings.[15]

The National Abortion Federation's *2022 Violence and Disruption Statistics* showed a surge in arsons, burglaries, death threats and clinic invasions compared to 2021.[16] Clinic invasions—perpetrators making fake appointments to access the health centers or forcing their way in and refusing to leave—can disrupt abortion providers and delay patient care, according to the report.

"In a year marked by a devastating Supreme Court decision that overturned *Roe v. Wade*, and subsequent state abortion bans, anti-abortion extremists were emboldened and traveled to states where abortion remained legal to target clinics there," the report said.

There was an alarming rash of online threats reported in 2022 compared to the previous four years; the report cited examples of threats posted online including:

"Me and the boys about to bomb a planned parenthood."

"This is 2022. Its [*sic*] time to take all the abortionists and burn them at the stake. They are witches."

"The abortion clinic is now a free fire zone."

Melissa Fowler, chief program officer for the National Abortion Federation, said the agency "saw an immediate uptick in online harassment and threats against abortion providers and clinics" in the days following the leaked Supreme Court ruling in May.[17]

"People who felt emboldened by the decision, who were celebrating it and, in some cases, not wanting to wait until it was delivered," she said. "People that wanted clinics to shut down immediately."

Fowler cited various threatening and inflammatory social media posts that emerged just after the decision to overturn *Roe* became public.

"It's time to firebomb abortion clinics," read one Twitter message on May 12, 2022. "It's too late to be 'civil' about murdering babies."[18]

"The Buffalo shooter should have started a Planned Parenthood Clinic," another person posted on Twitter on May 15, 2022. "That way it would have been legal to murder Black people and brown people."[19]

While this type of incendiary rhetoric intensified with the news of *Roe*'s reversal, Fowler said it isn't new. But she urged the public not to accept threats against abortion clinics and pro-choice organizations as commonplace or normal.

"It shouldn't be seen as just part of the job of an abortion provider to deal with threats and harassment every day, on top of everything else they do to . . . help as many patients as they can in a landscape where access is dwindling," she said. "It's not surprising to me, because I know when there are things that abortion opponents see as victories—such as the Supreme Court decision and the passage of abortion bans—that can lead to an increase in this type of activity."

On May 20, 2022, police in Danville, Illinois, responded around 4:30 a.m. to an alarm blaring at the site of a future abortion clinic that had been the center of controversy earlier that month, when the city passed an ordinance banning the shipping and mailing of abortion pills.[20]

A maroon Volkswagen Passat had rammed backward into the brown brick building and was still sticking out of the front entrance when law enforcement arrived; the driver, 73-year-old Philip Buyno of Prophetstown, Illinois, told an officer that he had intentionally crashed his car into the structure "because he had recently learned that it was going to be used as an abortion clinic and his intent was to destroy the building so it could not be used for that purpose," according to a criminal complaint.[21] Buyno also told law enforcement that he had filled the Passat with tires, firewood and a can of gasoline and planned to set the car on fire once it was completely in the building, the complaint said.

"Buyno told us that he intended to burn his own car, along with the building, but he never got the chance because he got stuck inside the Passat and then the police arrived," the complaint said.

Video surveillance showed the car backing into the building many times; photos of the scene revealed major damage to the structure, particularly the front entrance, according to the complaint.

The driver, who was charged with attempted arson, told federal authorities that he had been active in the pro-life movement in the

1980s and 1990s and had been arrested multiple times for anti-abortion activities, the complaint said.

"If I could sneak in with a gas can and a match, I'd go in there again," Buyno told authorities, according to the complaint.

Buyno pleaded guilty to attempting to use fire to damage a building used in interstate commerce in September 2023, according to the Justice Department.

* * *

The sign outside the church pronounced, "We Support Abortion on Demand Without Apology."

In August 2022, shortly after the fall of *Roe*, the sign's glass casing and a stained-glass window on the side of the church were shattered by vandals. Leaders at First Unitarian Church of Chicago in the East Lakeview area said neighbors caught on video a recording of two women throwing rocks and pieces of fencing to smash the glass features, after allegedly commenting negatively on the pro-choice message on the sign.[22]

A Chicago Police Department spokesperson said two female offenders threw unknown objects at the church on August 24, 2022, "breaking the stained-glass picture and sign," but no suspects were arrested.

A few days later, the church responded by hosting an interfaith rally in support of abortion rights. Under a light drizzle, about 200 supporters gathered outside the house of worship, some holding posters reading "Parents' heartbeats matter" and "Roe has fallen, we have not."

The Reverend Alka Lyall, pastor at Broadway United Methodist Church in Chicago, invoked her own two abortions while speaking at the event. Both pregnancy terminations were deeply difficult but "equally deeply believed to be the right decision," she said.

"I know the general feeling is that religious institutions are anti-abortion," she said. "Well, we stand here together to say that these religious institutions and their leaders support every human's right to choose. . . . We support abortion rights for all people."

Speaker Rabbi Steven Philp said there's a "prevailing rhetoric" that pits progressive values against traditional religious values—and he said he strives to "rewrite that narrative."

Philp, of Mishkan Chicago, a synagogue on the city's North Side, added that intertwining religion and reproductive rights is not a new theological concept.

"Lest people think we are just inserting our modern interpretation into very ancient traditions, I also want to say, actually, we draw these values in fact from our traditions themselves," he said. "Judaism has long held that access to abortion is a vital and necessary human right. And not just a hundred years ago, not just 500 years ago; we were writing about this about 2,000 years ago."

* * *

> *Listen to me, O coastlands, and hearken, you peoples from afar. The LORD called me from the womb, from the body of my mother he named my name.*[23]

On January 22, 2023, the nation marked what would have been the 50th anniversary of *Roe v. Wade*. The half-century milestone fell on a Sunday: Across the country, many clergy members and their faithful commemorated the now-defunct landmark ruling in disparate ways, often in accordance with their theological beliefs on abortion.

For those opposed to abortion, it was a moment to celebrate the fall of *Roe* and pray for an end to abortion. Shortly before the anniversary, the annual National March for Life in Washington, D.C., took on a decidedly more victorious tone than the events of past years, when *Roe* was still intact. The Reverend Franklin Graham, president and CEO of Samaritan's Purse, offered a prayer before the crowd.

"Father, we've come today to say thank you for Donald J. Trump and Mike Pence for nominating judges who believed in the sanctity of life," he said.[24]

Bishops and priests from around the Archdiocese of Chicago held an overnight vigil at St. John Paul II Newman Center Chapel at the University of Illinois at Chicago in the days leading up to the anniversary. The 12 hours of prayer followed by early morning Mass were part of the National Prayer Vigil for Life, an annual event to "pray for an end to abortion and a greater respect for all human life."[25]

On the anniversary, worshippers at Good Shepherd Lutheran Church in the Chicago suburb of Elgin celebrated National Sanctity of Human Life Day, which has been recognized by abortion opponents on the third Sunday in January since 1984, when it was designated by President Ronald Reagan.[26]

"Now it's a whole new reality, that *Roe v. Wade* is not the law of the land," said Steve Maske, a Lutheran Church–Missouri Synod pastor who serves at Good Shepherd. "So that's a good thing to celebrate. But unfortunately, the state of Illinois in essence is a pro-abortion state. So there's still work for Christians to do to support life."

The pastor said Good Shepherd took up special collections to help a local pregnancy resource center and maternity home as part of the Sanctity of Human Life observance, which often extends through the month of January. Members also made donations to an interfaith food pantry and distributed "blessing bags" filled with toiletries, food and other necessities to those in need, he added.

The pastor said this is part of the mission of supporting "life at any age, from conception to when the heart stops beating."

Around the time of the anniversary of *Roe* in 2021, Maske posted on social media a video of a 4D ultrasound, a clear image of a fetus kicking, waving its fingers and moving its lips in utero.

"Life is a miracle!" the caption read. "Life is a gift from God!"

Over the years, Maske said, he has counseled those who suffered from guilt and sorrow following an abortion.

"The pain of abortion is unique," he said. "You're taking a human life. And that's a pain that lingers in a person's life."

Yet he added that everyone is sinful and falls short of the glory of God; as a pastor, he's there to "share the grace and mercy of Jesus Christ that covers every sin."

"We still have work to do to protect life, to support life and to protect moms and families that are struggling with this decision," he said. "And to show mercy and forgiveness to those who have struggled with the decision for the last 50 years."

* * *

The LORD God formed the man from the dust of the ground and breathed into his nostrils the breath of life, and the man became a living being.[27]

About 25 miles away from Good Shepherd, a different clergy member decorated another suburban Chicago church with signs declaring "abortion is a human right" and "be faithfully pro-choice" for the Sunday worship service, which honored *Roe*.[28]

The Reverend Denise Cawley, who once served as an abortion clinic chaplain, said she approached the day with deep sadness, lamenting the loss of abortion rights across large sections of the United States. Themes of bodily autonomy and reproductive justice were laced into the service, the hymns and her sermon.

"I believe that everyone has inherent worth," said Cawley, interim minister at Countryside Church Unitarian Universalist in northwest suburban Palatine. "And if I believe that everyone has inherent worth, then I believe that all the people walking around living on this planet deserve health care, so they are best able to make health care decisions for themselves. My faith teaches me this."

The minister added that there are many religions that support reproductive choice; for her, legal and accessible abortion is rooted in the core beliefs and principles of Unitarian Universalism.

In the years before *Roe*, the Clergy Consultation Service on Abortion—an organization of Protestant and Jewish religious leaders—helped women with unwanted pregnancies get abortions. These religious denominations "openly lined up to support abortion law reform and appeal" by the early 1960s, according to historian Gillian Frank.[29]

A few days before *Roe*'s 50th anniversary, more than a dozen clergy members from six faith traditions filed a lawsuit in Missouri challenging the state's bans on abortion and other reproductive rights restrictions as unconstitutional, claiming these laws impose one religious doctrine and violate the separation of church and state.

"Missouri's abortion bans contradict, devalue and disrespect my religious beliefs that the life and health of a pregnant person take precedence over a fetus," said Maharat Rori Picker Neiss, executive director of the Jewish Community Relations Council of St. Louis and a plaintiff in the suit. "Jewish law mandates the termination of a pregnancy if the life of the person carrying the fetus is in jeopardy. The claim that life begins at conception is a statement of theological belief, and that belief is explicitly not a Jewish one."[30]

As Cawley, the minister, recalled her experience as a chaplain from late 2017 to 2019 at a Planned Parenthood clinic in Wisconsin, where she offered patients spiritual care and emotional support, there were moments when patients had needs that weren't directly related to terminating a pregnancy.[31]

On one occasion, Cawley encountered a 13-year-old pregnant girl who was scared because clinicians had just diagnosed her with a uterine infection. She had to go to the hospital immediately for treatment, but the girl said she was scared because she hadn't been to church recently; she worried that if she died at the hospital she would go to hell.

"We can take care of that right now," Cawley recalled telling her. "God will forgive you right now for not going to church. You and I can pray right here and everything will be fine and you will be able to go the hospital and get care."

So Cawley, the pregnant girl and her foster mother prayed for forgiveness for her absence at church and that her infection would be healed, just before the patient was rushed to the hospital.

"She was so much more at peace," the minister said. "So that was a blessing, that's what she needed."

Cawley doesn't know if that patient ever did end up having an abortion.

In another instance, the chaplain met an expecting Hindu couple who desperately wanted a baby, but the mother suffered from a medical condition that threatened her health and life. After the abortion, the patient asked to see the remains and requested that Cawley bless them. So the chaplain found prayers from the couple's faith and offered a blessing during their time of grief.

"It's too bad we can't put this in someone else who wants a baby, because we can't use it right now," Cawley recalled the husband saying, as he looked upon the remains of the pregnancy.

Cawley said she doesn't think of these "products of conception" as unborn babies. To her they are "a grouping of cells that were in various stages of growth and they were not meant to come to be."

"For centuries and centuries, people have had pregnancies that were not meant to complete, and that don't complete, through various means," she said.

At the worship service on January 22, 2023, Cawley told the congregation that there's no doubt a loved child is a gift and desired pregnancies are blessings.[32]

"Yet, not every pregnancy is welcomed," she said. "As a minister, I know a child being raised by people without access to good housing and educational opportunities and health care, for me that's a far bigger ethical issue than when cells divide and start to pulse. As a Unitarian Universalist, I trust people. I trust you; I trust me to make moral decisions that are best for ourselves. I believe in you."

Later in the service, Cawley said she has come to see the matter of abortion as "a holy conversation between a person and their circumstances and their beliefs."[33]

"I can support and walk people through that and accompany them," she said. "But abortion is complex. . . . My aim is to love people into finding their own voice. Their own way."

Notes

1. CROSSING THE MISSISSIPPI RIVER

1. Angie Leventis Lourgos, "'My Last Resort'—Thousands Come to Illinois to Have Abortions," *Chicago Tribune*, July 14, 2017.

2. "Presidential Nominees Debate at the University of Nevada, Las Vegas," October 19, 2016, C-SPAN video, 12:07, https://www.c-span.org/video/?414228-1/presidential-nominees-debate-university-nevada-las-vegas.

3. Erica Werner, "Gorsuch Confirmation Rolls Supreme Court to the Right," Associated Press, April 7, 2017.

4. Lisa Mascaro, "Barrett Confirmed as Supreme Court Justice in Partisan Vote," Associated Press, October 26, 2020.

5. Mary Ziegler, *Dollars for Life: The Anti-Abortion Movement and the Fall of the Republican Establishment* (New Haven: Yale University Press, 2022), 199.

6. Jill Colvin, "Trump, a Late Convert to Cause, Attends Anti-Abortion Rally," Associated Press, January 24, 2020.

7. Donald Trump, "Remarks by President Trump at the 47th Annual March for Life," January 24, 2020, https://trumpwhitehouse.archives.gov/briefings-statements/remarks-president-trump-47th-annual-march-life/.

8. "'March for Life' Rally," January 24, 2020, C-SPAN video, 31:51, https://www.c-span.org/video/?468482-1/march-life-rally.

9. Kansas Legislative Research Department, "Evolution of Kansas Laws concerning Abortion," July 26, 2022, https://www.kslegresearch.org/KLRD-web/Publications/FedStateAffairs/2022_EvolutnKsLawsReAbortns.pdf.

10. David A. Lieb, "Missouri Enacts 72-Hour Abortion Waiting Period," Associated Press, September 11, 2014.

11. "Counseling and Waiting Periods before an Abortion," Guttmacher Institute, September 1, 2022, https://www.guttmacher.org/state-policy/explore/counseling-and-waiting-periods-abortion.

12. Ashoka Mukpo, "TRAP Laws Are the Threat to Abortion Rights You Don't Know About," American Civil Liberties Union, March 3, 2020, https://www.aclu.org/news/reproductive-freedom/trap-laws-are-the-threat-to-abortion-rights-you-dont-know-about.

13. Elizabeth Nash and Joerg Dreweke, "The U.S. Abortion Rate Continues to Drop: Once Again, State Abortion Restrictions Are Not the Main Driver," *Guttmacher Policy Review*, September 18, 2019.

14. Angie Leventis Lourgos, "Nearly 10,000 Women Traveled from Out of State to Have an Abortion in Illinois in 2020—a 29% Increase," *Chicago Tribune,* January 25, 2022.

15. "Illinois Abortion Statistics 2017," Illinois Department of Public Health (IDPH), November 19, 2018, https://dph.illinois.gov/content/dam/soi/en/web/idph/files/publications/publicationsoppsillinois-abortion-statistics-2017.pdf.

16. "Abortion Statistics," IDPH, 2022, https://dph.illinois.gov/data-statistics/vital-statistics/abortion-statistics.html.

17. "Abortion Statistics," IDPH, 2022.

18. Mikaela H. Smith, Zoe Muzyczka, Payal Chakraborty, Elaina Johns-Wolfe, Jenny Higgins, Danielle Bessett and Alison H. Norris, "Abortion Travel within the United States: An Observational Study of Cross-State Movement to Obtain Abortion Care in 2017," *Lancet Regional Health–Americas*, March 3, 2022, https://www.thelancet.com/journals/lanam/article/PIIS2667-193X(22)00031-X/fulltext.

19. Smith et al., "Abortion Travel."

20. Smith et al., "Abortion Travel."

2. A DOCTOR WITHOUT A NAME

1. Angie Leventis Lourgos, "My Illegal Abortion: One Chicago Woman Recounts Ending Her Pregnancy Pre–*Roe v. Wade*, as More States Pass Near-Bans on the Procedure," *Chicago Tribune*, July 5, 2019.

2. Audiey Kao, "History of Oral Contraception," *AMA Journal of Ethics*, June 2000, https://journalofethics.ama-assn.org/article/history-oral-contraception/2000-06.

3. "The Thin Blue Line: The History of the Pregnancy Test," National Institutes of Health, https://history.nih.gov/display/history/Pregnancy+Test+-+A+Thin+Blue+Line+The+History+of+the+Pregnancy+Test.

4. Gillian Brockell, "An Early U.S. Pregnancy Test Involved Sacrificing Rabbits," *Washington Post*, October 17, 2021.

5. Leslie J. Reagan, *When Abortion Was a Crime: Women, Medicine, and Law in the United States, 1867–1973* (Berkeley: University of California Press, 1997), 8.

6. James C. Mohr, *Abortion in America: The Origins and Evolution of National Policy, 1800-1900* (New York: Oxford University Press, 1978), 6.

7. "To Married Women—Madame Restell, Female Physician," photograph of advertisement in *New York Herald*, April 13, 1840, Library of Congress, https://www.loc.gov/item/2002719608/.

8. "Mrs. Bird, Female Physician; To the Ladies—Madame Costello," photograph of two advertisements in *New York Sun*, February 24, 1842, Library of Congress, https://www.loc.gov/item/2002719613/.

9. *Dobbs v. Jackson Women's Health Organization*, No. 19-1392, 597 U.S. ___ (2022), appendix A.

10. *Dobbs v. Jackson*, appendix A.

11. "Police Spring Trap on Two in Abortion Deal," *Chicago Tribune*, May 7, 1966.

12. "Woman Links Two Doctors to Abortion," *Chicago Tribune*, September 8, 1966.

13. "Nurse, 70, Found Guilty of Abortion on Girl, 18," *Chicago Tribune*, December 7, 1966.

14. Shirley Motter Linde, "The Facts, the Controversy, the National Dilemma: In Application, the Laws Are Uncertain. At What Moment Does Life Begin?" *Chicago Tribune*, February 13, 1966.

15. Linde, "The Facts."

16. Kristin Luker, *Abortion and the Politics of Motherhood* (Berkeley: University of California Press, 1984), 104.

17. Lourgos, "My Illegal Abortion."

18. Cheryl terHorst, "Abortion in the Underground. Before *Roe v. Wade*, the Group 'Jane' Gave Women a Choice," *Chicago Tribune*, September 15, 1999.

19. TerHorst, "Abortion."

20. Dylon Jones, "Inside the 1970s Abortion Underground," Politico Magazine, Politico, May 6, 2020, https://www.politico.com/news/magazine/2022/05/06/jane-abortion-network-chicago-00030433.

21. "Biographical Note," Dr. T.R.M. Howard Papers, Vivian G. Harsh Research Collection of Afro-American History and Literature, Chicago Public Library.

22. "Biographical Note," Howard Papers.

23. "Biographical Note," Howard Papers.

24. "Accepts $500 for Abortion, Police Charge. Agents, Woman Trap South Side Doctor," *Chicago Tribune*, September 24, 1965.

25. "Accepts $500."

26. "Hawaii Legislature OKs Legal Abortions," *Chicago Tribune*, February 25, 1970.

27. "N.Y. Starts New Legal Abortions," *Los Angeles Times*, July 20, 1970.

28. Glen Elsasser, "Top Court Strikes Down Abortion Laws: Supreme Court Rules Laws Banning Abortions Are Invalid," *Chicago Tribune*, January 23, 1973.

29. Ronald Kotulak and Marcia Opp, "20,000 Operations a Year Predicted. Lunch Hour Abortions Expected as Part of the Boom Here," *Chicago Tribune*, March 3, 1973.

30. Kotulak and Opp, "20,000 Operations."

31. Kotulak and Opp, "20,000 Operations."

32. "Excerpts of the Court's Opinion—and Dissent," *Chicago Tribune*, July 4, 1989.

33. Lourgos, "My Illegal Abortion."

34. Ben Nadler and Sanya Mansoor, "Georgia Governor Signs Restrictive 'Heartbeat' Abortion Ban," Associated Press, May 7, 2019.

35. Kim Chandler and Blake Paterson, "Alabama Governor Invokes God in Banning Nearly All Abortions," Associated Press, May 16, 2019.

36. Kay Ivey, "Governor Ivey Issues Statement after Signing the Alabama Human Life Protection Act," Office of Alabama Governor, May 15, 2019, https://governor.alabama.gov/newsroom/2019/05/governor-ivey-issues-statement-after-signing-the-alabama-human-life-protection-act/.

37. "Missouri Governor Mike Parson Signs 'Missouri Stands for the Unborn Act,' SS SCS H.B. 126," press release, Missouri Right to Life, May 24, 2019, https://missourilife.org/wp-content/uploads/2020/02/Missouri-Governor-Mike-Parson-Signs-Missouri-Stands-For-The-Unborn-Act-SS-SCS-HB-126-May-24-2019.pdf.

38. K.K. Rebecca Lai, "Abortion Bans: 9 States Have Passed Bills to Limit the Procedure This Year," *New York Times*, May 29, 2019.

39. *Dobbs v. Jackson*.

40. *Dobbs v. Jackson*, 6.

41. *Dobbs v. Jackson*.

42. *Dobbs v. Jackson*, Brief for Amici Curiae American Historical Association and Organization of American Historians, September 20, 2021.

43. Donald Trump, "Statement by Donald J. Trump, 45th President of the United States," June 24, 2022.

44. Josh Gerstein and Alexander Ward, "Supreme Court Has Voted to Overturn Abortion Rights, Draft Opinion Shows," Politico, May 2, 2022, https://www.politico.com/news/2022/05/02/supreme-court-abortion-draft-opinion-00029473.

45. Government of Brazil, "Brazil Defends Life from Its Conception and Strengthens Family Ties," June 24, 2022.

46. Jair M. Bolsonaro (@jairbolsonaro), Twitter, June 24, 2022, 7:17 p.m., https://twitter.com/jairbolsonaro/status/1540489412064251907.

47. Emmanuel Macron (@emmanuelmacron), Twitter, June 24, 2022, 12:57 p.m., https://twitter.com/emmanuelmacron/status/1540393817609740288.

48. Justin Trudeau (@JustinTrudeau), Twitter, June 24, 2022, 10:51 a.m., https://twitter.com/justintrudeau/status/1540362024051408897.

49. Angie Leventis Lourgos, "Abortion Profoundly Shaped the Lives and Work of These 8 Illinois Women. Here Are Their Stories," *Chicago Tribune*, June 24, 2022.

50. Lourgos, "Abortion Profoundly Shaped."

3. TAXPAYER-FUNDED ABORTION

1. Angie Leventis Lourgos, "Woman Who Had Tax-Funded Abortion Says They 'Help People in Bad Situations,' but Critics Decry Public Money for 'Immoral Act,'" *Chicago Tribune*, June 25, 2018.

2. Kim Geiger and Rick Pearson, "Rauner Signs Controversial Abortion Bill, Angering Conservatives," *Chicago Tribune*, September 29, 2017.

3. Geiger and Pearson, "Rauner Signs."

4. Geiger and Pearson, "Rauner Signs."

5. Geiger and Pearson, "Rauner Signs."

6. Rick Pearson and Kim Geiger, "Ives' Anti-Rauner Ad Ripped as 'Racist, Sexist, Homophobic,'" *Chicago Tribune*, February 3, 2018.

7. Mayor's Press Office, "Mayor Lightfoot and the Chicago Department of Public Health Announce Delegate Agencies for 'Justice for All' Initiative," Chicago Department of Public Health, Chicago (website), August 31, 2022, https://www.chicago.gov/city/en/depts/cdph/provdrs/health_protection_and_response/news/2022/august/mayor-lightfoot-and-the-chicago-department-of-public-health-anno.html.

8. Mayor's Press Office, "Mayor Lightfoot."

9. Dan Petrella and Jeremy Gorner, "In Call with Biden, Gov. J.B. Pritzker Asks for Increased Federal Funding to Help States Where Abortion Remains Legal," *Chicago Tribune*, July 1, 2022.

10. "VA Will Offer Abortion Counseling and—in Certain Cases—Abortions to Pregnant Veterans and VA Beneficiaries," VA News, September 2, 2022, https://news.va.gov/press-room/va-will-offer-abortion-counseling-and-in-certain-cases-abortions-to-pregnant-veterans-and-va-beneficiaries/.

11. Alina Salganicoff, Laurie Sobel and Amrutha Ramaswamy, "The Hyde Amendment and Coverage for Abortion Services," KFF, March 5, 2021, https://www.kff.org/womens-health-policy/issue-brief/the-hyde-amendment-and-coverage-for-abortion-services/.

12. Al Weaver, "Senate GOP Fails to Overturn VA Abortion Policy," *The Hill*, April 19, 2023.

13. Executive Office of the President, "Statement of Administration Policy: S.J. Res. 10—Providing for Congressional Disapproval under Chapter 8 of Title 5, United States Code, of the Rule Submitted by the Department of Veterans Affairs Relating to 'Reproductive Health Services,'" April 19, 2023.

14. "Whose Choice: A Timeline of the Hyde Amendment and Its Impact on Abortion Funding," Center for Reproductive Rights, September 17, 2010, https://reproductiverights.org/whose-choice-a-timeline-of-the-hyde-amendment-and-its-impact-on-abortion-funding/.

15. Mary Ziegler, *Roe: The History of a National Obsession* (New Haven: Yale University Press, 2023), 18.

16. Steve Daley, "New Politics on Abortion Leave Rep. Hyde Diminished," *Chicago Tribune*, October 29, 1989.

17. Salganicoff, Sobel and Ramaswamy, "The Hyde Amendment."

18. "State Funding of Abortion Under Medicaid," Guttmacher Institute, August 31, 2023. https://www.guttmacher.org/state-policy/explore/state-funding-abortion-under-medicaid.

19. Salganicoff, Sobel and Ramaswamy, "The Hyde Amendment."

20. Jean Latz Griffin, "Case History of Abortion at County," *Chicago Tribune*, August 3, 1992.

21. Griffin, "Case History."

22. Storer Rowley, "County Hospital Bans Abortion-on-Request. Dunne's Order Cites Public Cost," *Chicago Tribune*, October 10, 1980.

23. Rowley, "County Hospital."

24. Rowley, "County Hospital."

25. Rowley, "County Hospital."

26. Jean Latz Griffin, "500 Callers Seek Abortions at Cook County Hospital," *Chicago Tribune*, September 15, 1992.

27. Griffin, "500 Callers."

28. Griffin, "500 Callers."

29. Andrew Fegelman and William Grady, "Cook County Quietly Marks One Year of Abortion Service," *Chicago Tribune*, September 19, 1993.

4. LAST CLINIC STANDING

1. Angie Leventis Lourgos, "Inside the Illinois Abortion Clinic That Could Become the Nearest Option for Women in St. Louis and Beyond," *Chicago Tribune*, June 10, 2019.

2. Summer Ballentine, "Missouri Governor Signs Bill Banning Abortions at 8 Weeks," Associated Press, May 24, 2019.

3. Mike Parson (@GovParsonMO), Twitter, May 15, 2019, 11:14 a.m., https://twitter.com/govparsonmo/status/1128695074253099009?lang=en.

4. Holly Yan, "These 6 States Have Only 1 Abortion Clinic Left. Missouri Could Become the First with Zero," CNN, June 21, 2019, https://www.cnn.com/2019/05/29/health/six-states-with-1-abortion-clinic-map-trnd/index.html.

5. "Planned Parenthood Files Unprecedented Lawsuit against Missouri Department of Health and Senior Services with Licensure Renewal Process Still Ongoing," Missouri Department of Health and Senior Services, May 29, 2019, https://health.mo.gov/news/newsitem/uuid/bfbb2a45-3bf9-4b1b-9fa1-d53d3ff4e1ba.

6. Jim Salter and David A. Lieb, "Judge Issues Order Ensuring Missouri's Only Abortion Clinic Can Continue Providing Abortions—for Now," Associated Press, May 31, 2019.

7. Jessica Arons, "The Last Clinics Standing," American Civil Liberties Union, last accessed September 15, 2021, https://www.aclu.org/issues/reproductive-freedom/abortion/last-clinics-standing.

8. Arons, "Last Clinics."

9. Arons, "Last Clinics."

10. Arons, "Last Clinics."

11. Summer Ballentine, "Federal Judge Allows Missouri to Enforce Abortion Rules," Associated Press, September 10, 2018.

12. Summer Ballentine, "Missouri Down to 1 Abortion Clinic amid Legal Battle," Associated Press, October 3, 2018.

13. Luke 1:41–43, KJV.

14. Alice F. Cartwright, Mihiri Karunaratne, Jill Barr-Walker, Nicole E. Johns and Ushma D. Upadhyay, "Identifying National Availability of Abortion Care and Distance from Major U.S. Cities: Systematic Online Search," *Journal of Medical Internet Research* 20, no. 5 (May 2018), https://doi.org/10.2196/jmir.9717.

15. Cartwright et al., "Identifying National Availability."

16. Jim Salter, "New Abortion Clinic Being Built in Illinois, Near St. Louis," Associated Press, October 2, 2019.

17. Elizabeth Nash, Lizamarie Mohammed, Olivia Cappello and Sophia Naide, "State Policy Trends 2019: A Wave of Abortion Bans, but Some States Are Fighting Back," Guttmacher Institute, December 10, 2019, https://www.guttmacher.org/article/2019/12/state-policy-trends-2019-wave-abortion-bans-some-states-are-fighting-back.

18. Emily Wagster Pettus and Leah Willingham, "Mississippi Clinic Ends Challenge of Near-Ban on Abortion," Associated Press, July 19, 2022.

19. Marielle Kirstein, Rachel K. Jones and Jesse Philbin, "One Month Post-*Roe*: At Least 43 Abortion Clinics across 11 States Have Stopped Offering Abortion Care," Guttmacher Institute, July 28, 2022, https://www.guttmacher.org/article/2022/07/one-month-post-roe-least-43-abortion-clinics-across-11-states-have-stopped-offering.

20. Angie Leventis Lourgos, "With *Roe* Overturned, Illinois—a Midwest Refuge for Abortion Care—Prepares for Influx of Patients from Other States," *Chicago Tribune*, June 24, 2022.

21. Mike Parson (@GovParsonMO), Twitter, June 24, 2022, 10:17 a.m., https://twitter.com/govparsonmo/status/1540353447203000320.

22. Lourgos, "With Roe Overturned."

5. ABORTION BY IPAD, PHONE OR MAIL

1. Angie Leventis Lourgos, "Abortions Provided via Telehealth," *Chicago Tribune*, January 19, 2018.

2. "Mifeprex (Mifepristone) Information," U.S. Food and Drug Administration, December 16, 2021, https://www.fda.gov/drugs/postmarket-drug-safety-information-patients-and-providers/mifeprex-mifepristone-information.

3. Jeremy Manier and Barbara Brotman, "FDA Gives Final OK to Abortion Pill," *Chicago Tribune*, September 29, 2000.

4. Beth Fouhy, "Gore, Bush Weigh In on Abortion Pill Debate," CNN, September 29, 2000, https://www.cnn.com/2000/ALLPOLITICS/stories/09/29/abortion.politics.goresound/index.html.

5. Fouhy, "Gore, Bush."

6. Fouhy, "Gore, Bush."

7. Manier and Brotman, "FDA Gives Final OK."

8. Manier and Brotman, "FDA Gives Final OK."

9. "Medication Abortion," Guttmacher Institute, September 1, 2022, https://www.guttmacher.org/state-policy/explore/medication-abortion.

10. Daniel Grossman and Kate Grindlay, "Safety of Medical Abortion Provided through Telemedicine Compared with In Person," *Obstetrics and Gynecology* 130, no. 4 (October 2017): 778–782, https://doi.org/10.1097/AOG.0000000000002212.

11. Mark Sherman, "Texas Illegally Curbs Abortion Clinics, Supreme Court Rules," Associated Press, June 27, 2016.

12. *A Woman's Right to Know*, Texas Health and Human Services Commission and Texas Department of State Health Services, December 2016, https://www.hhs.texas.gov/sites/default/files/documents/serviceshealth/women-children/womansright-to-know.pdf.

13. Tony Leys, "Iowa Supreme Court: Ban on Telemedicine Unconstitutional," *Des Moines Register*, June 19, 2015.

14. "Iowa 'Defunding' Law to Force Closure of Four Planned Parenthood Health Centers, Cutting Off Health Care for More Than 14,600 Women," Planned Parenthood, May 19, 2017, https://www.plannedparenthood.org/about-us/newsroom/press-releases/iowa-defunding-law-to-force-closure-of-four-planned-parenthood-health-centers-cutting-off-health-care-for-more-than-14-600-women.

15. Laurie Sobel, Amrutha Ramaswamy, Brittni Frederiksen and Alina Salganicoff, "State Action to Limit Abortion Access during the COVID-19 Pandemic," KFF, August 10, 2020, https://www.kff.org/coronavirus-covid-19/issue-brief/state-action-to-limit-abortion-access-during-the-covid-19-pandemic/.

16. "Health Care Professionals and Facilities, Including Abortion Providers, Must Immediately Stop All Medically Unnecessary Surgeries and Procedures to Preserve Resources to Fight COVID-19 Pandemic," Ken Paxton, Attorney General of Texas, March 23, 2020, https://www.texasattorneygeneral.gov/news/releases/health-care-professionals-and-facilities-including-abortion-providers-must-immediately-stop-all.

17. "COVID-19 Litigation," Center for Reproductive Rights, https://reproductiverights.org/case/covid-19-cases-and-resources/.

18. Sobel et al., "State Action."

19. "ACOG Suit Petitions Court to Remove FDA's Burdensome Barriers to Reproductive Care during COVID-19," American College of Obstetricians and Gynecologists, May 27, 2020, https://www.acog.org/news/news-releases/2020/05/acog-suit-petitions-the-fda-to-remove-burdensome-barriers-to-reproductive-care-during-covid-19.

20. "ACOG Suit."

21. "Using Telehealth to Expand Access to Essential Health Services during the COVID-19 Pandemic," Centers for Disease Control and Prevention, updated June 10, 2020.

22. Rachel K. Jones, Elizabeth Nash, Lauren Cross, Jesse Philbin and Marielle Kirstein, "Medication Abortion Now Accounts for More Than Half of All U.S. Abortions," Guttmacher Institute, February 24, 2022, https://www.guttmacher.org/article/2022/02/medication-abortion-now-accounts-more-half-all-us-abortions.

23. *Food and Drug Administration et al. v. American College of Obstetricians and Gynecologists et al.*, 592 U.S. ___ (2021).

24. Ted Cruz et al., letter to Stephen Hahn, Commissioner, Food and Drug Administration, September 1, 2020, https://www.cruz.senate.gov/imo/media/doc/Letters/2020.09.01%20--%20Pro-Life%20Mifeprex%20Letter%20to%20FDA%20-%20FSV.pdf.

25. Alice Miranda Ollstein and Darius Tahir, "FDA Lifts Curb on Dispensing Abortion Pills during Pandemic," Politico, April 12, 2021, https://www.politico.com/news/2021/04/12/abortion-pills-481092.

26. "ACOG Applauds the FDA for Its Action on Mifepristone Access during the COVID-19 Pandemic," American College of Obstetricians and Gynecologists, April 12, 2021, https://www.acog.org/news/news-releases/2021/04/acog-applauds-fda-action-on-mifepristone-access-during-covid-19-pandemic.

27. Angie Leventis Lourgos, "FDA Permanently Eases Abortion Pill Restrictions," *Chicago Tribune*, December 16, 2021.

28. Lourgos, "FDA."

29. Nisha Verma and Vanessa Wellbery, "Understanding the Practical Implications of the FDA's December 2021 Mifepristone REMS Decision," American College of Obstetricians and Gynecologists, March 28, 2022, https://www.acog.org/news/news-articles/2022/03/understanding-the-practical-implications-of-the-fdas-december-2021-mifepristone-rems-decision.

30. Verma and Wellbery, "Understanding."

31. "U.S. Bishops' Pro-Life Chairman Denounces FDA Decision on Chemical Abortion Pill," United States Conference of Catholic Bishops, December 16, 2021, https://www.usccb.org/news/2021/us-bishops-pro-life-chairman-denounces-fda-decision-chemical-abortion-pill.

32. Elizabeth Nash, Lauren Cross and Joerg Dreweke, "2022 State Legislative Sessions: Abortion Bans and Restrictions on Medication Abortion Dominate," Guttmacher Institute, March 16, 2022, https://www.guttmacher.org/article/2022/03/2022-state-legislative-sessions-abortion-bans-and-restrictions-medication-abortion.

33. Nash, Cross and Dreweke, "2022 State."

34. Chloe Murtagh, Elisa Wells, Elizabeth G. Raymond, Francine Coeytaux and Beverly Winikoff, "Exploring the Feasibility of Obtaining Mifepristone and Misoprostol from the Internet," *Contraception* 97, no. 4 (April 2018): 287–291, https://doi.org/10.1016/j.contraception.2017.09.016.

35. Murtagh et al., "Exploring the Feasibility."

36. Murtagh et al., "Exploring the Feasibility."

37. S.B. 24, "College Student Right to Access Act," 2018, https://services.statescape.com/ssVersions/2466000/2466880/u_20191014.htm.

38. Angie Leventis Lourgos, "Planned Parenthood Offers Abortion Pills by Mail," *Chicago Tribune*, May 23, 2022.

39. Lourgos, "Planned Parenthood."

40. Lourgos, "Planned Parenthood."

41. Angie Leventis Lourgos, "In Sign of a New Frontier, Online Clinic Offering Abortion Pills to Patients in Illinois and Elsewhere Who Aren't Pregnant to Save for Future Use," *Chicago Tribune*, September 7, 2022.

42. Lourgos, "In Sign."

43. Lourgos, "In Sign."

44. Lourgos, "In Sign."

45. Paul J. Weber, Matthew Perrone and Lindsay Whitehurst, "Access to Abortion Pill in Limbo after Competing Rulings," Associated Press, April 8, 2023.

46. Comstock Act of 1873, 18 U.S. Code § 1461.

47. James C. Mohr, *Abortion in America: The Origins and Evolution of National Policy* (New York: Oxford University Press, 1978), 196–199.

48. "Judge in Washington Orders Feds to Keep Abortion Pill Access," Associated Press, April 7, 2023.

49. Angie Leventis Lourgos, "As Court Battle over Abortion Drug Mifepristone Continues, Some Illinois Clinics Have a Backup Plan," *Chicago Tribune*, April 13, 2023.

50. "Medication Abortion up to 70 Days of Gestation," American College of Obstetricians and Gynecologists, Practice Bulletin, no. 225, October 2020.

51. "California Announces Emergency Stockpile of Abortion Medication, Defending against Extreme Texas Court Ruling," Office of Governor Gavin Newsom, April 10, 2023, https://www.gov.ca.gov/2023/04/10/california-announces-emergency-stockpile-of-abortion-medication-defending-against-extreme-texas-court-ruling/.

52. Maura Healey (@MassGovernor), Twitter, April 10, 2023, 12:19 p.m., https://twitter.com/MassGovernor/status/1645476714737172489.

53. Mark Sherman, "Supreme Court Preserves Access to Abortion Pill for Now," Associated Press, April 21, 2023.

54. "Planned Parenthood of Illinois Pleased Supreme Court Protects Abortion Pill," Planned Parenthood of Illinois, April 21, 2023, https://

www.plannedparenthood.org/planned-parenthood-illinois/newsroom/planned-parenthood-of-illinois-pleased-supreme-court-protects-abortion-pill.

55. Angie Leventis Lourgos, "Downstate Danville Approves Ban on Mail ing Abortion Pills. But Attorney General, Civil Liberties Experts Say Ordinance is Illegal," *Chicago Tribune*, May 3, 2023.

56. Illinois Family Institute, "Danville Abortion Mill Press Conference," March 2023, YouTube video, 7:51, https://www.youtube.com/watch?v=KOmUyVuWBh8&t=497s.

57. "Attorney General Raoul Issues Statement That Symbolic Danville Ordinance Is Not in Effect and Will Not Take Effect," Office of the Illinois Attorney General, Kwame Raoul, May 3, 2023, https://illinoisattorneygeneral.gov/news/story/attorney-general-raoul-issues-statement-that-symbolic-danville-ordinance-is-not-in-effect-and-will-not-take-effect.

58. Susan Montoya Brian, "New Mexico Supreme Court Blocks Local Abortion Ordinances," Associated Press, March 31, 2023.

6. TINY FOOTPRINTS

1. Angie Leventis Lourgos, "'My Last Resort'—Thousands Come to Illinois to Have Abortions," *Chicago Tribune*, July 14, 2017.

2. "Hypoplastic Left Heart Syndrome," Indiana Department of Health, last accessed October 16, 2022, https://www.in.gov/health/gnbs/files/hypoplastic-left-heart-syndrome_READ6.4.pdf.

3. "State Facts about Abortion: Indiana," Guttmacher Institute, June 2022, https://www.guttmacher.org/fact-sheet/state-facts-about-abortion-indiana.

4. "State Laws and Policies: State Bans on Abortion throughout Pregnancy," Guttmacher Institute, October 6, 2022, https://www.guttmacher.org/state-policy/explore/state-policies-later-abortions.

5. Katherine Kortsmit et al., "Abortion Surveillance—United States, 2019," *CDC Surveillance Summaries* 70, no. 9 (November 26, 2021): 1–29, http://dx.doi.org/10.15585/mmwr.ss7009a1.

6. "Bans on Abortion at 20 Weeks," Planned Parenthood Action Fund, last accessed October 16, 2022, https://www.plannedparenthoodaction.org/issues/abortion/federal-and-state-bans-and-restrictions-abortion/20-week-bans.

7. "20-Week Ultrasound (Anatomy Scan)," Cleveland Clinic, https://my.clevelandclinic.org/health/diagnostics/22644-20-week-ultrasound.

8. Mitch Smith, "Indiana Governor Signs Abortion Bill with Added Restrictions," *New York Times*, March 24, 2016.

9. Mike Pence (@GovPenceIN), Twitter, March 24, 2016, 3:57 p.m., https://twitter.com/govpencein/status/713107554558025728.

10. Lawrence Hurley, "U.S. Supreme Court Takes No Action in Indiana Abortion Cases," Reuters, May 20, 2019.

11. *Box v. Planned Parenthood of Indiana and Kentucky, Inc.*, No. 18-483, 587 U.S. ___, 139 S. Ct. 1780 (2019).

12. "Banning Abortions in Cases of Race or Sex Selection or Fetal Anomaly," Guttmacher Institute, January 11, 2020, https://www.guttmacher.org/evidence-you-can-use/banning-abortions-cases-race-or-sex-selection-or-fetal-anomaly (removed from site).

13. "NIPT Summary of Recommendations," Current ACOG Guidance, American College of Obstetricians and Gynecologists, last accessed June 19, 2023, https://www.acog.org/advocacy/policy-priorities/non-invasive-prenatal-testing/current-acog-guidance.

14. Elizabeth Nash, Lizamarie Mohammed, Olivia Cappello and Sophia Naide, "State Policy Trends 2019: A Wave of Abortion Bans, but Some States Are Fighting Back," Guttmacher Institute, December 10, 2019, https://www.guttmacher.org/article/2019/12/state-policy-trends-2019-wave-abortion-bans-some-states-are-fighting-back.

15. Mabel Felix, Laurie Sobel and Alina Salganicoff, "A Review of Exceptions in State Abortions Bans: Implications for the Provision of Abortion Services," KFF, May 18, 2023, https://www.kff.org/womens-health-policy/issue-brief/a-review-of-exceptions-in-state-abortions-bans-implications-for-the-provision-of-abortion-services/.

16. Megan B. Raymond et al., "Implications for Prenatal Genetic Testing in the United States after the Reversal of *Roe v. Wade*," *Obstetrics and Gynecology* 141 (March 2023): 445–454.

17. Raymond et al., "Implications."

18. "Statement Re: Supreme Court Decision on *Dobbs v. Jackson Women's Health Organization*," American Society of Human Genetics, June 24, 2022, https://www.ashg.org/publications-news/ashg-news/statement-dobbs-v-jackson-womens-health-organization/.

19. Angie Leventis Lourgos, "'Just Seems Cruel': 800-Mile Trip to End Severely Troubled Pregnancy Illustrates Divide on Abortion Laws," *Chicago Tribune*, May 25, 2019.

20. "Abortion of Down's Babies Rising," Reuters, October 26, 2009.

21. Icelandic Ministry of Welfare, "Facts about Down's Syndrome and Pre-Natal Screening in Iceland," Government of Iceland, March 26, 2018, https://www.government.is/diplomatic-missions/embassy-article/2018/03/26/Facts-about-Downs-syndrome-and-pre-natal-screening-in-Iceland/.

22. "Facts About Down Syndrome," Centers for Disease Control and Prevention, October 10, 2023, https://www.cdc.gov/ncbddd/birthdefects/downsyndrome.html.

23. CBS News (@CBSNews), Twitter, August 14, 2017, 7:30 p.m., https://twitter.com/cbsnews/status/897254042178650113?lang=en.

24. Ted Cruz (@tedcruz), August 15, 2017, 9:42 a.m., https://twitter.com/tedcruz/status/897468446111395840?lang=en.

25. Patricia Heaton (@PatriciaHeaton), August 14, 2017, 9:56 p.m., https://twitter.com/patriciaheaton/status/897290974262472704.

26. Martha MacCallum, "Sarah Palin Slams Controversial Down Syndrome Policy," Fox News, August 16, 2017, https://www.foxnews.com/transcript/sarah-palin-slams-controversial-down-syndrome-policy.

27. Icelandic Ministry of Welfare, "Facts about Down's."

28. Susan Mizner and Alexa Kolbi Molinas, "Offensive Hypocrisy of Banning Abortions for a Down Syndrome Diagnosis," *The Hill*, December 24, 2019.

29. Mizner and Molinas, "Offensive Hypocrisy."

7. FUNERALS FOR FETAL REMAINS

1. Angie Leventis Lourgos, "Abortion Opponents Hold Memorials at Fetal Burial Sites amid Battle over How These Remains Should Be Treated: 'They Are Not Trash, They Are People,'" *Chicago Tribune*, September 20, 2019.

2. *Box v. Planned Parenthood of Indiana and Kentucky, Inc.*, No. 18-483, 587 U.S. ___, 139 S. Ct. 1780 (2019).

3. Mike Pence (@VP45), Twitter, May 28, 2019, 12:57 p.m., https://twitter.com/VP45/status/1133432082917711872.

4. *Box v. Planned Parenthood.*

5. Julie Carr Smith, "Judge Again Blocks Ohio Law Regulating Aborted Fetal Remains," Associated Press, February 2, 2022.

6. Kevin McGill, "Texas Hoping to Revive Law on Burial of Fetal Remains," Associated Press, September 5, 2019.

7. *Doe et al. v. Attorney General of Indiana et al.*, 1:20-cv-03247-RLY-MJD, Doc. 98 (2022).

8. McGill, "Texas Hoping."

9. McGill, "Texas Hoping."

10. Mary Anne Pazanowski, "Supreme Court Denies Review in Indiana Fetal Remains Lawsuit," Bloomberg Law, May 1, 2023, https://news.bloomberglaw.com/litigation/supreme-court-denies-review-in-indiana-fetal-remains-law-suit.

11. Debra Goldschmidt and Susan Scutti, "Trump Administration Limits Research Using Fetal Tissue," CNN, June 5, 2019, https://www.cnn.com/2019/06/05/health/hhs-fetal-tissue-research-bn/index.html.

12. Letter to U.S. Department of Health and Human Services Secretary Alex Azar, July 11, 2019, https://www.cogr.edu/sites/default/files/2019%20Coalition%20Fetal%20Tissue%20Letter%20re%20HHS%20Policy%20-%20July%2011%202019.pdf.

13. Amy Goldstein, "Trump Ban on Fetal Tissue Research Blocks Coronavirus Treatment Effort," *Washington Post*, March 18, 2020.

14. Alice Miranda Ollstein, "Biden Administration Reverses Trump Restrictions on Fetal Tissue Research," Politico, April 16, 2021, https://www.politico.com/news/2021/04/16/biden-reverses-fetal-tissue-research-restrictions-482503.

15. "U.S. Bishops' Pro-Life Committee Chairman Denounces Reversal of Limits on Human Fetal Tissue Research," United States Conference of Catholic Bishops, April 20, 2021, https://www.usccb.org/news/2021/us-bishops-pro-life-committee-chairman-denounces-reversal-limits-human-fetal-tissue.

16. Monica Migliorino Miller, *Abandoned: The Untold Story of the Abortion Wars* (Charlotte: St. Benedict Press, 2012), 223.

17. Jack Houston, "Abortion Protesters Parade Fetuses Outside Clinic," *Chicago Tribune*, May 7, 1987.

18. Houston, "Abortion Protesters."

19. Ann Scheidler, "Burying the Dead: The Recovery and Burial of 500 Victims of Abortion," Pro-Life Action League, September 5, 2014, https://prolifeaction.org/2014/michiganavevictims/.

20. Michael Hirsley, "Abortion Foes Hail Cardinal for Fetus Rite," *Chicago Tribune,* August 5, 1988.

21. Hirsley, "Abortion Foes."

22. Hirsley, "Abortion Foes."

23. Hirsley, "Abortion Foes."

24. Lourgos, "Abortion Opponents."

25. *2018 Violence and Disruption Statistics*, National Abortion Federation, 2019, https://prochoice.org/our-work/provider-security/.

26. Angie Leventis Lourgos, "Abortion Profoundly Shaped the Lives and Work of These 8 Illinois Women. Here Are Their Stories," *Chicago Tribune*, June 24, 2022.

27. "About the National Day of Remembrance," National Day of Remembrance, https://nationaldayofremembrance.org/about/.

28. Angie Leventis Lourgos, "Joe Scheidler, of Chicago, 'Godfather of Pro-Life Activism,' Dies at 93," *Chicago Tribune,* January 19, 2021.

29. Faith Karimi, "The Thousands of Fetal Remains Found in a Doctor's Illinois Garage Date to 2000, Authorities Say," CNN, September 20, 2019, https://www.cnn.com/2019/09/20/health/indiana-doctor-fetal-remains-trnd/index.html.

30. Curtis T. Hill, Jr., "Final Report on the Investigation of Dr. Ulrich Klopfer," Office of the Indiana Attorney General, December 28, 2020, https://www.in.gov/attorneygeneral/files/KLOPFER-Final-Report-12-28.pdf.

31. Hill, "Final Report."

32. Mike Pence (@VP45), Twitter, September 16, 2019, 6:09 p.m., https://twitter.com/VP45/status/1173720469452873730.

33. Amanda Fries, "Court Rules against Seaford's Effort to Require How Fetal Remains Are Disposed," *Delaware News Journal*, June 29, 2022.

34. Fries, "Court Rules."

35. David Kelly, "Church to Bury Abortion Ashes," *Los Angeles Times*, January 22, 2005.

36. Linda Rapattoni, "16,000 Fetuses Buried, Eulogized by Reagan," UPI, October 6, 1985.

37. Rapattoni, "16,000 Fetuses."

38. Allon Jalon, "Fetuses Left Unburied Prompt Song by Pat Boone," *Los Angeles Times*, May 14, 1985.

39. Meredith Colias-Pete, "Hundreds Attend Burial in South Bend for Fetuses Stored in Will County Garage by Late Abortion Doctor Ulrich Klopfer," *Post-Tribune*, February 12, 2020.

40. "What Is the Silent No More Awareness Campaign?," Silent No More Awareness Campaign, http://www.silentnomoreawareness.org/about-us/.

41. Jennifer Shea, interview by author, September 8, 2022.

8. 800 MILES

1. Angie Leventis Lourgos, "'Just Seems Cruel': 800-Mile Trip to End Severely Troubled Pregnancy Illustrates Divide on Abortion Laws," *Chicago Tribune*, May 25, 2019.

2. Barbara Rodriguez, "Iowa Lawmakers OK 20-Week Abortion Ban, 3-Day Wait," Associated Press, April 18, 2017.

3. "Abortion Care," Chicago Department of Public Health, Chicago (website), accessed October 16, 2022, https://www.chicago.gov/city/en/depts/cdph/provdrs/healthy mothers_and_babies/svcs/abortion-care.html.

4. "Abortion Services in Fairview Heights, IL," Planned Parenthood, last accessed October 16, 2022, https://www.plannedparenthood.org/health-center/illinois/fairview-heights/62208/fairview-heights-health-center-2712-90770/abortion.

5. Tina Sfondeles, "Pritzker Vows 'Most Progressive State' on Abortion—GOP Sees 'Left Wing' Agenda," *Chicago Sun-Times*, January 22, 2019.

6. Angie Leventis Lourgos, "Illinois Democrats Propose Laws Expanding Abortion Access," *Chicago Tribune*, February 14, 2019.

7. Reproductive Health Act, 775 ILCS 55/1-25(a) (2019), https://www.ilga.gov/legislation/ilcs/ilcs5.asp?ActID=3987&ChapterID=64.

8. Reproductive Health Act, H.B. 2495, 101st Gen. Assembly, State of Illinois (2019).

9. Paul Benjamin Linton, "Memorandum Re: Analysis of H.B. 2495, S.B. 1942 (the 'Reproductive Health Act')," February 20, 2019, https://www.ilcatholic.org/wp-content/uploads/Analysis-of-HB-2495-SB-1942-Final.pdf.

10. Rebecca Anzel, "Big Crowd Fills Capitol to Protest Abortion Bills," *Capitol News Illinois*, March 20, 2019.

11. "Illinoisans Descend on Springfield to Defend Life and Stop New Abortion Bills," Illinois Right to Life Action, March 19, 2019, https://illinoisrighttolifeaction.org/2019/03/19/illinoisans-descend-on-springfield-to-defend-life-and-stop-new-abortion-bills/.

12. Alice Yin, "Hundreds Protest Abortion Bans, Show Support for Illinois Reproductive Rights Bill at Federal Plaza Rally," *Chicago Tribune*, May 20, 2019.

13. Yin, "Hundreds Protest."

14. Cassie Buchman, "Illinois Senate Approves Legislation to Protect Abortion Procedures," *State Journal-Register*, May 31, 2019.

15. Reproductive Health Act, 775 ILCS 55/1-25(a).

16. Elizabeth Nash, Lizamarie Mohammed and Olivia Cappello, "Illinois Steps Up as Other States Decimate Abortion Rights," Guttmacher Institute, June 12, 2019, https://www.guttmacher.org/article/2019/06/illinois-steps-other-states-decimate-abortion-rights.

17. Lolly Bowean, "Gov. J.B. Pritzker Signs Abortion Rights Law Making Procedure a 'Fundamental Right' for Women in Illinois," *Chicago Tribune*, June 12, 2019.

18. "Gov. Pritzker Signs Reproductive Health Act, Making Illinois a National Leader amid Flurry of Attacks on Reproductive Rights," press release, Illinois.gov (website), https://www.illinois.gov/news/press-release.20199.html.

19. "BREAKING: Illinois House Passes Extreme Abortion Bill," Illinois Right to Life Team, May 28, 2019.

20. "State Facts about Abortion: Iowa," Guttmacher Institute, June 2022, https://www.guttmacher.org/fact-sheet/state-facts-about-abortion-iowa.

21. Katherine Kortsmit et al., "Abortion Surveillance—United States, 2019," *CDC Surveillance Summaries* 70, no. 9 (November 26, 2021): 1–29, http://dx.doi.org/10.15585/mmwr.ss7009a1.

22. *Roe v. Wade*, 410 U.S. 113 (1973), https://tile.loc.gov/storage-services/service/ll/usrep/usrep410/usrep410113/usrep410113.pdf.

23. *Roe v. Wade.*

24. *Roe v. Wade.*

25. *Roe v. Wade.*

26. Illinois Family Institute, "March for Life Chi Full Rally," January 11, 2020, YouTube video, https://www.youtube.com/watch?v=kf3_QnnRHzA.

27. Illinois Family Institute, "March," 35:00.

28. Angie Leventis Lourgos, "Abortion Profoundly Shaped the Lives and Work of These 8 Illinois Women. Here Are Their Stories," *Chicago Tribune*, June 24, 2022.

29. E.F. Bell et al., "Mortality, In-Hospital Morbidity, Care Practices, and Two-Year Outcomes for Extremely Preterm Infants in the United States, 2013–2018," *Journal of the American Medical Association,* January 2022.

30. Bell et al., "Mortality."

31. *Diana Greene Foster, The Turnaway Study: Ten Years, a Thousand Women, and the Consequences of Having—or Being Denied—an Abortion* (New York: Scribner, 2020), 87–88.

32. David Klepper, "New York Enacts New Protections for Abortion Rights," Associated Press, January 22, 2019.

33. Donald Trump, "Remarks by President Trump in State of the Union Address," Trump White House Archives, February 5, 2019, https://trumpwhitehouse.archives.gov/briefings-statements/remarks-president-trump-state-union-address-2/.

34. Trump, "Remarks."

35. "We Are Later Abortion Patients," Abortionpatients.com, January 23, 2020, https://www.abortionpatients.com/.

36. "Louisiana Woman Carrying Unviable Fetus Forced to Travel to New York for Abortion," *Guardian*, September 14, 2022.

37. Sara Cline, "Louisiana Woman Denied Abortion Wants 'Vague' Ban Clarified," Associated Press, August, 26, 2022.

38. Ben Crump, "Vague Laws Put Pregnant Women at Risk," Ben Crump Trial Lawyer for Justice, https://act.bencrump.com/a/nancy-davis?utm_source=twitter.com&utm_medium=referral&utm_campaign=social_organic&utm_content=083022.

39. Crump, "Vague Laws."

40. Sam Karlin, "Doctors Say Louisiana's Abortion Exceptions List Has Created an 'Atmosphere of Terror,'" *Advocate*, October 25, 2022.

41. The Recount, "Nancy Davis Speaks after She Was Denied Abortion in Louisiana Despite a Non-viable Fetus #shorts," 2022, August 26, YouTube video, 0:19, https://www.youtube.com/watch?v=vgoTDXqfWtY.

42. The Recount, "Nancy Davis."

9. HELP FROM A STRANGER

1. Angie Leventis Lourgos, "More than 5,500 Women Came to Illinois to Have an Abortion Last Year amid Growing Restrictions in the Midwest," *Chicago Tribune*, November 30, 2018.

2. "Illinois Abortion Statistics 2015," Illinois Department of Public Health, December 15, 2016.

3. "Illinois Abortion Statistics 2016," Illinois Department of Public Health, December 5, 2017.

4. Angie Leventis Lourgos, "'My Last Resort'—Thousands Come to Illinois to Have Abortions," *Chicago Tribune*, July 14, 2017.

5. Diana Parker-Kafka, email interview by author, September 19, 2022.

6. Angie Leventis Lourgos, "With *Roe* Overturned, a New Illinois Nonprofit Has Begun Providing Free Light Aircraft Flights for Patients Traveling to Get an Abortion," *Chicago Tribune*, June 24, 2022.

7. Dan Petrella, "Vice President Kamala Harris Rallies with Fellow Democrats in Chicago over Abortion Rights as Midterms Near," *Chicago Tribune*, September 16, 2022.

8. Fox 32 Chicago, "Kamala Harris, Illinois Leaders Talk Reproductive Rights," September 16, 2022, YouTube video, 1:00, https://www.youtube.com/watch?v=iBrY3calVZ0.

9. Fox 32 Chicago, "Kamala Harris," 18:54.

10. Fox 32 Chicago, "Kamala Harris," 15:39.

11. Fox 32 Chicago, "Kamala Harris," 24:30.

10. JANE DOE

1. Angie Leventis Lourgos, "'My Last Resort'—Thousands Come to Illinois to Have Abortions," *Chicago Tribune*, July 14, 2017.

2. "Parental Involvement in Minors' Abortions," Guttmacher Institute, September 1, 2022, https://www.guttmacher.org/state-policy/explore/parental-involvement-minors-abortions.

3. Naomi Nix, "Illinois Supreme Court Backs Parental Notification for Abortions," *Chicago Tribune*, July 11, 2013.

4. "Illinois Expands Access to Abortion Care, Ends Enforcement of Parental Notice Law," ACLU Illinois, June 1, 2022, https://www.aclu-il.org/en/press-releases/illinois-expands-access-abortion-care-ends-enforcement-parental-notice-law.

5. Unlawful Abortion upon Minor, H.B. 63, 129th Gen. Assembly, Ohio Rev. Code Sec. 2919.121 (2012), https://codes.ohio.gov/ohio-revised-code/section-2919.121.

6. Information Provided before Abortion Procedure, S.B. 27, 133rd Gen. Assembly, Ohio Rev. Code Sec. 2317.56 (2021), https://codes.ohio.gov/ohio-revised-code/section-2317.56.

7. "Parental Involvement," Guttmacher Institute.

8. "Parental Involvement," Guttmacher Institute.

9. Arek Sarkissian, "Florida Court Says Teen Isn't Mature Enough to Get an Abortion," Politico, August 16, 2022.

10. *In re Jane Doe 22-B*, No. 1D22-2476 (Fla. Ct. App. August 15, 2022), https://law.justia.com/cases/florida/first-district-court-of-appeal/2022/22-2476.html.

11. National NOW (@NationalNOW), Twitter, August 18, 2022, 11:51 a.m., https://twitter.com/NationalNOW/status/1560308468275625985.

12. Gavin Newsom (@GavinNewsom), Twitter, August 18, 2022, 4:55 p.m., https://twitter.com/GavinNewsom/status/1560384950347583488.

13. *In re Petition for Judicial Waiver of Parental Notice and Consent or Consent Only to Termination of Pregnancy, Jane Doe*, No. 2D22-51 (Fla. Ct. App. January 18, 2022), https://law.justia.com/cases/florida/second-district-court-of-appeal/2022 /22-0051.html.

14. *In re Petition for Judicial Waiver.*

15. William March, "Did Anti-Abortion Ruling Lead to Sitting Hillsborough County Judge's Defeat?" *Tampa Bay Times,* August 5, 2022.

16. Florida Planned Parenthood Action (@FAPPA), Twitter, August 25, 2022, 8:47 a.m., https://twitter.com/FAPPA/status/1562798834866343940.

17. "Governor Ron DeSantis Makes Three Judicial Appointments," Office of Governor Ron DeSantis, December 20, 2022, https://www.flgov.com/2022/12/20/governor-ron-desantis-makes-three-judicial-appointments-6/.

18. Jeremy Gorner, "Gov. Pritzker OK's Repeal to Law That Required Parents of Minors to Be Informed When Their Child Seeks an Abortion," *Chicago Tribune*, December 17, 2022.

19. "'The Only People It Really Affects Are the People It Hurts': The Human Rights Consequences of Parental Notice of Abortion in Illinois," Human Rights Watch, March 11, 2021, https://www.hrw.org/report/2021/03/11/only-people-it-really-affects-are-people-it-hurts/human-rights-consequences.

20. "The Only People" Human Rights Watch.

21. "The Only People," Human Rights Watch.

22. "The Only People," Human Rights Watch.

23. Lee Hasselbacher and Amber Truehart, "Forced Parental Involvement in Youth Abortion Creates Obstacles to Access, Even with Judicial Bypass," *Journal of Adolescent Health* 68, no. 1 (January 2021): 5–6, https://www.jahonline.org/article/S1054-139X(20)30611-X/fulltext.

24. "The Adolescent's Right to Confidential Care When Considering Abortion," American Academy of Pediatrics, Committee on Adolescence, August 29, 2022, in *Pediatrics* 150, no. 3 (September 2022), https://doi.org/10.1542/peds.2022-058780.

25. Angie Leventis Lourgos, "Abortion Profoundly Shaped the Lives and Work of These 8 Illinois Women. Here Are Their Stories," *Chicago Tribune*, June 24, 2022.

26. Kevin Grillot, "March for Life Chicago Responds to Governor Pritzker's Signing of the Repeal of Parental Notification," March for Life Chicago, December 17, 2021, https://illinoismarchforlife.org/press-coverage.

27. IL House GOP, "Rep. Bourne Defends Parental Notification Act in Light of Push to Repeal," October 28, 2021, YouTube video, 2:20, https://www.youtube.com/watch?v=govXIq7VLuQ.

28. Maureen Deitche, interview by author, September 28, 2022.

29. Maureen Deitche and Paul Deitche, "Beauty of Life—Pro-Life Testimony Video," Priests for Life, February 5, 2020, 23:52, https://www.priestsforlife.org/frontlines/trip-home.aspx?tripid=1683.

30. Deitche and Deitche, "Beauty of Life," 24:10.

31. Deitche and Deitche, "Beauty of Life," 16:37.

11. Abortions in the Shadow of Notre Dame

1. Angie Leventis Lourgos, “South Bend at Center of Abortion Debate as Unlicensed Clinic Supported by Mayor Pete Buttigieg Is Allowed to Open via Court Injunction,” *Chicago Tribune*, August 6, 2019.

2. *Whole Woman's Health All. v. Hill*, No. 1:18-cv-01904-SEB-MJD, 388 F. Supp. 3d 1010 (S.D. Ind.), May 31, 2019, https://casetext.com/case/whole-womans-health-all-v-hill-1.

3. *Abortion Informed Consent Brochure*, Indiana State Department of Health, June 29, 2020.

4. “Abortion Informed Consent Certification,” State Form 55320 (R2/6-20), Indiana State Department of Health – IC 16-34-2-1.1(a).

5. “Terminated Pregnancy Report,” Indiana State Department of Health, June 30, 2019.

6. Lourgos, “South Bend.”

7. “Whole Woman's Health Alliance Supports Mayor Buttigieg's Decision to Veto Organization's Attempt to Open,” Whole Woman's Health, April 27, 2018, https://www.wholewomanshealth.com/uncategorized/whole-womans-health-alliance-supports-mayor-buttigiegs-decision-to-veto-organizations-attempt-to-open/.

8. Kenneth Hallenius, “DCEC Presents Notre Dame *Evangelium Vitae* Medal to Women's Care Center,” DeNicola Center for Ethics and Culture, April 29, 2019, https://ethicscenter.nd.edu/news/de-nicola-center-for-ethics-and-culture-presents-notre-dame-evangelium-vitae-medal-to-womens-care-center/.

9. “Statement from Notre Dame's President, Father John Jenkins,” Notre Dame News, April 27, 2018, https://news.nd.edu/news/statement-from-notre-dames-president-father-john-jenkins/.

10. Mark Sherman, “Ruth Bader Ginsburg Dies at 87,” Associated Press, September 19, 2020.

11. “Whole Woman's Health Reacts to Ruth Bader Ginsburg's Death,” Whole Woman's Health, https://www.wholewomanshealth.com/uncategorized/whole-womans-health-reacts-to-ruth-bader-ginsburgs-death/.

12. Tucker Higgins, “Trump Nominates Amy Coney Barrett to Supreme Court, Setting Up Election Year Confirmation Battle,” CNBC, September 25, 2020, https://www.cnbc.com/2020/09/25/trump-is-expected-to-nominate-amy-coney-barrett-to-fill-ginsburg-supreme-court-vacancy-.html.

13. “Amy Coney Barrett CV,” https://law.nd.edu/assets/71337/original/.

14. Elyssa Cherney, “University of Notre Dame President Tests Positive for COVID-19 after Attending White House Rose Garden Ceremony with President Trump,” *Chicago Tribune*, October 2, 2020.

15. Dennis Brown, “Notre Dame Law School Professor Barrett Nominated to US Supreme Court,” Notre Dame News, September 26, 2020, https://

news.nd.edu/news/notre-dame-law-school-professor-barrett-nominated-to-us-supreme-court.

16. Susan Adams, "Hundreds of Notre Dame Faculty Sign Letters Opposing Amy Coney Barrett Nomination," *Forbes*, October 14, 2020, https://www.forbes.com/sites/susanadams/2020/10/14/hundreds-of-notre-dame-faculty-sign-letters-opposing-amy-coney-barrett-nomination.

17. "An Open Letter to Judge Amy Coney Barrett from Your Notre Dame Colleagues," October 10, 2020, https://teacher-scholar-activist.org/2020/10/13/an-open-letter-to-judge-amy-coney-barrett-from-your-notre-dame-colleagues/.

18. Lisa Mascaro, "Supreme Court Pick Amy Coney Barrett Signed Second Anti-Abortion Ad While at Notre Dame: 'We Renew Our Call for the Unborn to Be Protected in Law,'" Associated Press, October 10, 2020.

19. Mascaro, "Supreme Court."

20. "Statement from Rev. John I. Jenkins, C.S.C., on Justice Amy Coney Barrett," Notre Dame News, October 26, 2020, https://news.nd.edu/news/statement-from-rev-john-i-jenkins-c-s-c-on-justice-amy-coney-barrett/.

21. Angie Leventis Lourgos, "South Bend Clinic Fought Hard for the Right to Provide Abortions, but Indiana's Ban Brings a New Reality—and More Patients to Illinois," *Chicago Tribune*, September 22, 2022.

22. Arleigh Rodgers, "Indiana Becomes 1st State to Approve Abortion Ban Post-*Roe*," Associated Press, August 5, 2022.

23. Tom Davies and Arleigh Rodgers, "Indiana Abortion Clinics Sue to Block State Ban Set to Take Effect," Associated Press, August 31, 2022.

24. "Religious Leaders Come Together to Bless South Bend's Lone Abortion Clinic," Whole Woman's Health Alliance, May 2022.

25. "This Abortion Clinic is Now Blessed," Whole Woman's Health, https://www.wholewomanshealthalliance.org/this-abortion-clinic-is-now-blessed/.

26. "2021 Terminated Pregnancy Report," Indiana Department of Health, June 30, 2022.

27. *Planned Parenthood Great Northwest, Hawai'i, Alaska, Indiana, Kentucky, Inc. et al. v. Members of the Medical Licensing Board of Indiana et al.*, Cause No. 53C206-2208-PL-001756, Order Granting Plaintiffs' Motion for Preliminary Injunction (September 22, 2022), https://www.aclu-in.org/sites/default/files/field_documents/pi_granted.pdf.

28. Whole Woman's Health Alliance, "After Years of Relentless Attacks on Abortion Care, Whole Woman's Health Alliance Announces Closure of Indiana Clinic," June 5, 2023.

12. SAVING THE EMBRYO

1. Angie Leventis Lourgos, "As Abortion Opposition Rallies, Some Activists Are Taking Aim at In Vitro Fertilization, Frozen Embryos," *Chicago Tribune*, October 8, 2019.

2. "How Do Embryos Survive the Freezing Process?" *Scientific American*, June 13, 2005, https://www.scientificamerican.com/article/how-do-embryos-survive-th/.

3. Kim Chandler and Blake Paterson, "Alabama Governor Invokes God in Banning Nearly All Abortions," Associated Press, May 16, 2019.

4. Arwa Mahdawi, "'Consensual Rape' and 'Re-Implantation': The Times Lawmakers 'Misspoke' on Abortion," *Guardian,* May 18, 2019.

5. "Reproductive Health—Infertility FAQs," Centers for Disease Control and Prevention, March 1, 2022, https://www.cdc.gov/reproductivehealth/infertility/index.htm.

6. Marla Paul, "'I'm Afraid for My IVF Patients' after Roe v. Wade Dismantling, Fertility Doctor Says," Northwestern Now, Northwestern University Media Relations, June 30, 2022, https://news.northwestern.edu/stories/2022/06/in-vitro-fertilization-after-roe-v-wade-dismantling/.

7. Paul, "I'm Afraid."

8. Kara N. Goldman (@KaragoldmanMD), Twitter, June 24, 2022, 11:52 a.m., https://mobile.twitter.com/karagoldmanMD/status/1540377391251410945.

9. Abortion; Unborn Child; Genetic Abnormality, S.B. 1457, State of Arizona Senate, 55th Leg., 1st reg. sess. (2021), https://www.azleg.gov/legtext/55leg/1R/bills/SB1457P.pdf.

10. Bob Christie, "Federal Judge Blocks Arizona 'Personhood' Abortion Law," Associated Press, July 11, 2022.

11. Bob Christie, "Arizona Says 'Personhood' Abortion Law Can't Lead to Charges," Associated Press, July 8, 2022.

12. Minority Report, Conference Committee to S.B. 1457, Abortion; Unborn Child; Genetic Abnormality, April 20, 2021, https://www.azleg.gov/ccminrpt/55LEG/1R/s.1457%20MINORI TY%20REPORT.pdf.

13. Minority Report.

14. Sharon Bernstein, "Georgia Anti-Abortion Law Allows Tax Deductions for Fetuses," Reuters, August 2, 2022.

15. "Georgians Ending Abortion: Petition to Gov. Kemp to Convene Special Session to End Abortion Now," Georgia Right to Life, June 27, 2022, https://www.grtlpetitions.online/ (site discontinued).

16. "State Abortion Trigger Laws: Potential Implications for Reproductive Medicine," American Society for Reproductive Medicine Center for Policy and Leadership, July 1, 2022, https://www.asrm.org/globalassets/asrm/asrm-content/news-and-publications/dobbs/cpl-report_impact-of-state-trigger-laws-on-reproductive-medicine_final.pdf (no longer available).

17. "States' Abortion Laws: Potential Implications for Reproductive Medicine," American Society for Reproductive Medicine Center for Policy and Leadership, October 2022, https://www.asrm.org/advocacy

-and-policy/reproductive-rights/summary-reports/state-abortion-laws-potential-implications-for-reproductive-medicine/.

18. Department of Health and Human Services, "Justification of Estimates for Appropriations Committees," Fiscal Year 2019, https://www.hhs.gov/sites/default/files/fy19-departmental-management-cj-4-10-18.pdf.

19. "Personhood Alliance Officially Launched," Personhood Alliance, October 13, 2014, https://personhood.org/media/press-releases/personhood-alliance-launched/.

20. "Science and Technology," Personhood Alliance, https://personhood.org/issues/science-technology/.

21. "Couple Settles Lawsuit over Destruction of Embryos," Associated Press, July 14, 2019.

22. Bruce Taubman, "When Does Life Begin? Taubman Law Says a Judge Needs to Decide," Taubman Law, April 3, 2018, https://taubmanlaw.net/life-begin-taubman-law-says-judge-needs-decide/.

23. *Penniman v. University Health Hospital System, Inc.*, CV-18-895503 (2018).

24. Angie Leventis Lourgos, "Judge Gives Embryos to Woman over Objections from Her Ex-Boyfriend," *Chicago Tribune*, May 16, 2014.

25. *Doe v. Obama*, 670 F. Supp. 2d 435 (2009).

26. Naperville City Council Meeting, "Open Session for Public," April 3, 2012.

13. BOOKING A HOTEL, PLANE TICKET AND ABORTION, IN ONE SPOT

1. Angie Leventis Lourgos, "Missouri. Louisiana. Arizona. Patients Are Already Traveling Hundreds of Miles to Have Abortions in Illinois," *Chicago Tribune*, May 12, 2022.

2. Angie Leventis Lourgos, "With *Roe v. Wade* at Risk, Illinois Abortion Providers Open Center to Help Out-of-State Patients and Other Resources," *Chicago Tribune*, January 21, 2022.

3. "The Future of Abortion Access in Illinois," Reproductive Health Services of Planned Parenthood of the St. Louis Region, October 13, 2021, https://www.plannedparenthood.org/planned-parenthood-st-louis-region-southwest-missouri/blog/report-the-future-of-abortion-access-in-illinois.

4. Angie Leventis Lourgos, "Abortions for Out-of-State Patients Have Skyrocketed," *Chicago Tribune*, August 4, 2022.

5. Marielle Kirstein, Rachel K. Jones and Jesse Philbin, "One Month Post-*Roe*: At Least 43 Abortion Clinics across 11 States Have Stopped Offering Abortion Care," Guttmacher Institute, July 8, 2022, https://www.guttmacher.org/article/2022/07/one-month-post-roe-least-43-abortion-clinics-across-11-states-have-stopped-offering.

6. Students for Life of America, "Today marks one month since *Roe v. Wade* was reversed," Facebook, July 24, 2022, https://www.facebook.com/profile/100064414135042/search/?q=One%20month%20of%20celebrating%20that%20Life%20won%20%26%20thousands%20of%20lives%20are%20being%20saved.

7. "Blueprint for a Post-Roe America," Students for Life of America, last accessed October 16, 2022, https://www.postroeblueprint.com/.

8. Marielle Kirstein, Joerg Dreweke, Rachel K. Jones and Jesse Philbin, "100 Days Post-*Roe*: At Least 66 Clinics across 15 U.S. States Have Stopped Offering Abortion Care," Guttmacher Institute, October 6, 2022, https://www.guttmacher.org/2022/10/100-days-post-roe-least-66-clinics-across-15-us-states-have-stopped-offering-abortion-care.

9. Angie Leventis Lourgos, "Planned Parenthood Launching Mobile Abortion Unit in Southern Illinois as Number of Out-of-State Patients Skyrockets," *Chicago Tribune*, October 3, 2022.

10. "Carbondale CHOICES Location Opens to Patients," CHOICES Center for Reproductive Health, October 11, 2022.

11. Amanda Seitz, "As South Bans Abortion, Thousands Turn to Illinois Clinics," Associated Press, March 25, 2023.

12. Jeff Kolkey, "New Abortion Clinic Opens; Second Location Gets Building Permit," *Rockford Register Star*, January 9, 2023.

13. Angie Leventis Lourgos, "One Year Post-*Roe,* a Wave of New Abortion Providers Has Come to Illinois. A Doctor at One Clinic Calls the Work 'Life-Changing,'" *Chicago Tribune*, June 18, 2024.

14. Gabriella Borter, "Abortion Clinic Moves Up the Street to Escape Tennessee's Ban," Reuters, September 13, 2022.

15. "North Dakota Abortion Clinic Opens at New Minnesota Site," Associated Press, August 10, 2022.

16. "Red River Women's Clinic," Red River Women's Clinic, https://www.redriverwomensclinic.com/.

17. Scott Bauer and Todd Richmond, "Wisconsin Doctors Halt Abortions following Court Ruling," Associated Press, June 24, 2022.

18. Angie Leventis Lourgos, "Planned Parenthood of Wisconsin Physicians Are Traveling to Illinois to Provide Abortions, Increasing Access to the Procedure after the Fall of *Roe v. Wade*," *Chicago Tribune*, July 15, 2022.

19. Angie Leventis Lourgos, "With *Roe* Overturned, Illinois—a Midwest Refuge for Abortion Care—Prepares for Influx of Patients from Other States," *Chicago Tribune*, June 24, 2022.

20. Lourgos, "With *Roe*."

21. Kristin Lyerly, Twitter post, "This Wisconsin doctor spent the day in Minnesota, providing abortion care and looking forward to the day when I can once again serve my patients back home," September 9, 2022, 6:50 p.m., https://twitter.com/KristinLyerly/status/1568386460457238529.

22. Joseph Biden, "Remarks by President Biden and Vice President Harris at the Second Meeting of the Task Force on Reproductive Healthcare Access," October 4, 2022, https://www.whitehouse.gov/briefing-room/speeches-remarks/2022/10/04/remarks-by-president-biden-and-vice-president-harris-at-the-second-meeting-of-the-task-force-on-reproductive-healthcare-access/.

23. Biden, "Remarks by President Biden."

24. "President Biden Remarks at Task Force on Reproductive Healthcare Access Meeting," October 4, 2022, C-SPAN video, 19:10, https://www.c-span.org/video/?523406-1/president-biden-remarks-task-force-reproductive-healthcare-access-meeting.

14. WEIGHING THE RISK

1. ACLU of Illinois, "Mindy and Adam's Story," March 5, 2015, YouTube video, 0:52, https://www.youtube.com/watch?v=SCcvfgFZCF4&t=3s.

2. ACLU of Illinois, "Mindy."

3. *National Institute of Family and Life Advocates v. Schneider*, Brief of Amici Curiae American College of Obstetricians and Gynecologists, Illinois Academy of Family Physicians, et al., in Opposition to Plaintiffs' Motions for Summary Judgment, 16-cv-50310, doc: 154-1, November 21, 2019.

4. Steve Schmadeke, "Christian Crisis Pregnancy Centers Sue Illinois over New Abortion Notice Law," *Chicago Tribune*, July 5, 2017.

5. United States Conference of Catholic Bishops, *Ethical and Religious Directives for Catholic Health Care Services*, 6th ed., June 2018.

6. *National Institute of Family and Life Advocates v. Schneider*, Brief of Amici.

7. *National Institute of Family and Life Advocates v. Schneider*, Brief of Amici.

8. *National Institute of Family and Life Advocates v. Schneider*, Brief of Amici.

9. *National Institute of Family and Life Advocates v. Schneider*, Brief of Amici.

10. Schmadeke, "Christian."

11. *National Institute of Family and Life Advocates v. Schneider*, Brief of Amici.

12. Lori Chaiten, "Illinois Health Care Right of Conscience Act Amendment Protects Patients," ACLU of Illinois, August 10, 2017, https://www.aclu-il.org/en/news/letter-illinois-health-care-right-conscience-act-amendment-protects-patients.

13. "America's Abortion Quandary," Pew Research Center, May 6, 2022, https://www.pewresearch.org/religion/2022/05/06/americas-abortion-quandary/.

14. Duke University, "How Abortion Bans Complicate Disease Treatment During Pregnancy—Media Briefing," August 2022, YouTube video, 50:00, https://www.youtube.com/watch?v=ugbspn1fbIQ&t=28s.

15. Donna L. Hoyert, "Maternal Mortality Rates in the United States, 2020," Centers for Disease Control and Prevention, February 23, 2022, https://www.cdc.gov/nchs/data/hestat/maternal-mortality/2020/maternal-mortality

-rates-2020.htm#:~:text=In%202020%2C%20861%20women%20were,20.1% 20in%202019%20(Table).

16. “Health and Health Care for Women of Reproductive Age,” Commonwealth Fund, April 5, 2022, https://www.commonwealthfund.org/publications/issue-briefs/2022/apr/health-and-health-care-women-reproductive-age.

17. Duke University, “How Abortion,” 3:58.

18. Duke University, “How Abortion,” 14:20.

19. Anjali Nambiar, Shivani Patel, Patricia Santiago-Munoz, Catherine Y. Spong and David B. Nelson, “Maternal Morbidity and Fetal Outcomes among Pregnant Women at 22 Weeks' Gestation or Less with Complications in 2 Texas Hospitals after Legislation on Abortion,” *American Journal of Obstetrics and Gynecology* 227, no. 4 (October 2022): 648–650, https://www.ajog.org/article/S0002-9378(22)00536-1/fulltext#secsectitle0025.

20. Nambiar et al., “Maternal Morbidity.”

21. Sarah McCammon and Emma Bowman, “Texas Abortion Bans Are Back in Place after State Appeals Judge's Order,” NPR, August 5, 2023, https://www.npr.org/2023/08/04/1192324395/texas-abortion-bans-lifted-temporarily-for-medical-emergencies.

22. Center for Reproductive Rights, “Texas Judge Rules in Favor of Women Denied Abortions,” press release, August 4, 2023.

23. Center for Reproductive Rights, “Hearing Wrap-Up: *Zurawski v. State of Texas*: Texas Women Denied Abortion Care Give Riveting Testimony while the State Tries to Dismiss the Lawsuit,” press release, July 21, 2023.

24. Ken Paxton, Attorney General of Texas, “Office of the Attorney General Files Appeal to Texas Supreme Court, Blocking District Judge's Ruling and Leaving Abortion Law in Place,” press release, August 5, 2023.

25. Duke University, “How Abortion,” 15:31.

26. Duke University, “How Abortion,” 6:03.

27. Duke University, “How Abortion,” 1:58.

28. Duke University, “How Abortion,” 7:45.

29. Duke University, “How Abortion,” 2:29.

30. “Arthritis Foundation Statement on Methotrexate Access,” Arthritis Foundation, last accessed October 16, 2022, https://www.arthritis.org/about-us/news-and-updates/statement-on-methotrexate-access.

31. Duke University, “How Abortion,” 20:15.

32. Duke University, “How Abortion,” 38:33.

33. Lisa H. Harris, “Navigating Loss of Abortion Services—A Large Academic Medical Center Prepares for the Overturn of *Roe v. Wade*,” New England Journal of Medicine 386 (June 2, 2022): 2061–2064, https://doi.10.1056/NEJMp2206246.

34. Duke University, “How Abortion,” 51:05.

35. Julia Kaye, Brigitte Amiri, Louise Melling and Jennifer Dalven, *Health Care Denied*, American Civil Liberties Union, May 2016, https://www.aclu.org/wp-content/uploads/legal-documents/healthcaredenied.pdf.
36. Kaye et al., *Health Care Denied.*
37. Kaye et al., *Health Care Denied.*
38. Kaye et al., *Health Care Denied.*
39. Amanda Lee Myers, "Phoenix Hospital Loses Catholic Status over Surgery," Associated Press, December 21, 2010.
40. "St. Joseph's Hospital No Longer Catholic. Statement of Bishop Thomas J. Olmsted," Roman Catholic Diocese of Phoenix Communications Office, December 21, 2010.
41. NCRonline, "Sister of Mercy McBride Receives Leadership Award at Call to Action 2011," 2011, YouTube video, 0:20, https://www.youtube.com/watch?v=SVbIfjRRSf4.
42. NCRonline, "Margaret McBride Accepts Award at Call to Action 2011," 2012, YouTube video, https://www.youtube.com/watch?v=IaUdxXIZ5pE&t=2s.
43. Kaye et al., *Health Care Denied.*

15. VIOLENCE AND FAITH

1. Angie Leventis Lourgos, "Arson. Vandalism. Threats. Abortion Clinics, Abortion Opponents Face Violence after the Fall of *Roe*," *Chicago Tribune*, February 5, 2023.
2. "Chillicothe, Illinois, Man Charged with Setting Fire to Planned Parenthood," press release, U.S. Attorney's Office, Central District of Illinois, January 25, 2023.
3. Complaint, *U.S. v. Massengill*, No. 1:23-MJ-06018 (C.D. Ill.), January 25, 2023.
4. Jennifer Welch, "Planned Parenthood of Illinois Responds to Arrest Made in the Peoria Health Center Fire Bombing," Planned Parenthood of Illinois, January 25, 2023, https://www.plannedparenthood.org/planned-parenthood-illinois/newsroom/planned-parenthood-of-illinois-responds-to-arrest-made-in-the-peoria-health-center-fire-bombing.
5. "Illinois Man Charged with Setting Fire to Planned Parenthood," press release, U.S. Department of Justice Office of Public Affairs, January 25, 2023, https://www.justice.gov/opa/pr/illinois-man-charged-setting-fire-planned-parenthood.
6. "Chillicothe, Illinois, Man Pleads Guilty to Setting Fire to Planned Parenthood," press release, U.S. Attorney's Office, Central District of Illinois, February 17, 2023, https://www.justice.gov/usao-cdil/pr/chillicothe-illinois-man-pleads-guilty-setting-fire-planned-parenthood.

7. Angie Leventis Lourgos, "Pritzker Signs Law Safeguarding Abortion Protections in Illinois amid Surge in Out-of-State Patients," *Chicago Tribune,* January 13, 2023.

8. Welch, "Planned Parenthood."

9. Andy Kravitz, "Arson Blamed in Fire That Caused $250,000 in Damage to Peoria Women's Care Center," *Peoria Journal Star*, May 3, 2021.

10. "Peoria, Illinois," Women's Care Center, last accessed April 29, 2023, https://supportwomenscarecenter.org/locations/peoria/.

11. Lourgos, "Arson."

12. "FBI Offering $25,000 Rewards for Information in Series of Attacks against Reproductive Health Service Facilities," FBI National Press Office, January 19, 2023, https://www.fbi.gov/news/press-releases/fbi-offering-25000-rewards-for-information-in-series-of-attacks-against-reproductive-health-service-facilities.

13. "Recent Cases on Violence against Reproductive Care Providers," U.S. Department of Justice Civil Rights Division, last accessed April 29, 2023, https://www.justice.gov/crt/recent-cases-violence-against-reproductive-health-care-providers.

14. "Paw Paw Man Pleads Guilty to Arson, Admits Setting Fire at Kalamazoo Planned Parenthood," press release, U.S. Attorney's Office, Western District of Michigan, October 12, 2022, https://www.justice.gov/usao-wdmi/pr/2022_1012_Brereton#:~:text=GRAND%20RAPIDS%2C%20MICHIGAN%20%E2%80%94%20U.S.%20Attorney,Parenthood%20clinic%20in%20Kalamazoo%2C%20Michigan.

15. "Man Charged in Planned Parenthood Clinic Fire in Michigan," Associated Press, August 4, 2022.

16. *2022 Violence and Disruption Statistics Report*, National Abortion Federation, May 11, 2023, https://prochoice.org/wp-content/uploads/2022-VD-Report-FINAL.pdf.

17. Lourgos, "Arson."

18. Lourgos, "Arson."

19. Lourgos, "Arson."

20. Angie Leventis Lourgos, "Man Allegedly Rammed Car into Prospective Danville Abortion Clinic While Trying to Set It on Fire, Feds Say," *Chicago Tribune*, May 23, 2023.

21. Complaint, U.S. v. Philip J. Buyno, No. 23-MJ-7063 (C.D. Ill.), May 22, 2023.

22. Angie Leventis Lourgos, "Vandals Shattered an Abortion Rights Sign at an East Lakeview Church. Clergy Responded with a Rally Supporting the Right to Choose," *Chicago Tribune*, September 4, 2022.

23. Isa. 49:1, RSV.

24. March for Life Education and Defense Fund, "2023 March for Life LIVESTREAM," January 2023, YouTube video, 2:42:50, https://www.youtube.com/watch?v=ENjxe71KcVA.

25. Angie Leventis Lourgos, "50th Anniversary of *Roe v. Wade*: Some Pray for End to Abortion, while Others Mourn Loss of Reproductive Rights," *Chicago Tribune*, January 22, 2003.

26. Ronald Reagan, "Proclamation 5147—National Sanctity of Human Life Day, 1984," Office of the Federal Register, January 16, 1984.

27. Gen. 2:7, NIV.

28. Lourgos, "50th Anniversary."

29. Gillian Frank, "The Religious Network That Made Abortion Safe When It Was Illegal," The Gender Policy Report, University of Minnesota, August 17, 2022, https://genderpolicyreport.umn.edu/the-religious-network-that-made-abortion-safe-when-it-was-illegal/.

30. "Missouri Faith Leaders File Lawsuit Challenging State Abortion Bans That Violate Church-State Separation," Americans United for Separation of Church and State, January 19, 2023, https://www.au.org/the-latest/press/missouri-faith-leaders-challenge-abortion-bans/.

31. Lourgos, "50th Anniversary."

32. Countryside Church Unitarian Universalist, "2023-01-22 *Roe v. Wade* Anniversary," January 2023, YouTube video, 8:59, https://www.youtube.com/watch?v=XkySc12G6-o&t=561s.

33. Countryside Church Unitarian Universalist, "2023-01-22," 56:20.

Permissions

Portions of *Life-Altering: Abortion Stories from the Midwest* have been published previously in similar form by Angie Leventis Lourgos in articles in the *Chicago Tribune*. They are reprinted here with permission.

Abortion laws—and legal challenges—are constantly shifting; regulations and ordinances were described as accurately as possible at the time of the book's publication. Updated versions will reflect changes in laws since that time.

Angie Leventis Lourgos, "'My Last Resort'—Thousands Come to Illinois to Have Abortions," *Chicago Tribune*, July 14, 2017.

Angie Leventis Lourgos, "Abortions Provided via Telemedicine: Illinois, Other States Allow Procedure to Bridge Limits, Miles," *Chicago Tribune*, January 19, 2018, page 1.

Angie Leventis Lourgos, "6 Months in, Abortion Law Having Impact: 'Immoral Act' to Some Is a Help and a Relief to Others," *Chicago Tribune*, June 25, 2018, page 1.

Angie Leventis Lourgos, "'Just Seems Cruel': 800-Mile Trip to End Severely Troubled Pregnancy Illustrates Divide on Abortion Laws," *Chicago Tribune*, May 25, 2019.

Angie Leventis Lourgos, "Inside the Illinois Abortion Clinic That Could Become the Nearest Option for Women in St. Louis and Beyond," *Chicago Tribune*, June 10, 2019.

Angie Leventis Lourgos, "Abortion in Chicago before *Roe v. Wade*: As More States Pass Curbs on Procedure, 1 Woman Recounts Hers," *Chicago Tribune*, July 5, 2019, page 1.

Angie Leventis Lourgos, "South Bend at Center of Abortion Debate as Unlicensed Clinic Supported by Mayor Pete Buttigieg Is Allowed to Open via Court Injunction," *Chicago Tribune*, August 6, 2019.

Angie Leventis Lourgos, "Memorials Held at Fetal Burial Sites amid Battle over Remains," *Chicago Tribune*, September 22, 2019, page 1.

Angie Leventis Lourgos, "Abortion Foes Tackle IVF, Frozen Embryos Concern: Fate of Discarded, Donated," *Chicago Tribune*, October 8, 2019, NEWS; ZONE C; page 1.

Angie Leventis Lourgos, "Missouri. Louisiana. Arizona. Patients Are Already Traveling Hundreds of Miles to Have Abortions in Illinois," *Chicago Tribune*, May 12, 2022.

Angie Leventis Lourgos, "Nonprofit Has Begun Offering Aid Providing Free Light Aircraft Flights for Patients Traveling to Get an Abortion," *Chicago Tribune*, June 26, 2022, page 1.

Angie Leventis Lourgos, "THE LIVES TOUCHED: Countless Women Have Been Tested by Abortion and Its Effects. Here Are 8 Stories," *Chicago Tribune*, June 26, 2022.

Angie Leventis Lourgos, "In Sign of a New Frontier, Online Clinic Offering Abortion Pills to Patients in Illinois and Elsewhere Who Aren't Pregnant for Future Use," *Chicago Tribune*, September 7, 2022.

Angie Leventis Lourgos, "South Bend Clinic Fought Hard for the Right to Provide Abortions, but Indiana's Ban Brings a New Reality—and More Patients to Illinois," *Chicago Tribune*, September 22, 2022.

Angie Leventis Lourgos, "50th Anniversary of *Roe v. Wade*: Some Pray for End to Abortion, while Others Mourn Loss of Reproductive Rights," *Chicago Tribune*, January 22, 2023.

Angie Leventis Lourgos, "Arson. Vandalism. Threats. Abortion Clinics, Abortion Opponents Face Violence after the Fall of *Roe*," *Chicago Tribune*, February 5, 2023.

Angie Leventis Lourgos, "As Court Battle over Abortion Drug Mifepristone Continues, Some Illinois Clinics Have a Backup Plan," *Chicago Tribune*, April 13, 2023.